Horsestory

Volume II:
Longhorns to Lady Wonder

by

Vicki Watson

Cover by Janet Griffin-Scott

Table of Contents

Introduction

Although our past is intertwined with horses, the stories of those strong and loyal helpers have mostly been forgotten. Many viewed the horse as simply a piece of equipment used to get a job done. For those people, writing an account of their horses would have been like someone today writing about the car they drive to work.

But horses are not lifeless machines. During the Great Epizootic of 1872, many came to realize how much they had taken these faithful animals for granted.

> *When we are born he fetches the doctor. He is the motive-power before the hearse that carries us to our last home. … He loves us all; he licks our hand; he kicks our enemies—sometimes ourselves. He propels street cars at five cents a ride, giving employment to large numbers of conductors and drivers. He eats oats, and hay, and corn, affording joy and sometimes profit to the farmer. … He runs races and runs away. He smashes buggies and gives wages to carriage-makers. He "sniffs the battle afar off," and gallops madly to death in the cavalry charge. He is a courageous creature, under the pressure of circumstances. … He is a luxury, a comfort, a convenience, a necessity, a docile patient slave, a creature capable of loving and of being loved, interesting and intelligent, competent to do most everything but stand on his head, climb up a ladder, talk, and vote …*
>
> *Chicago Tribune, November 5, 1872*

No one could ever feel that way about a hunk of metal, plastic, or silicon. Although "progress" was inevitable, we lost something valuable when we replaced horses with machines.

The Horsestory series highlights the diverse roles horses played over the years, and, when available, relates the stories of specific animals. As a lifelong horse lover, I was surprised to find so many ways horses collaborated with humans to accomplish amazing things.

A recurring theme in this second volume is change. At that time, equines were relied upon to power nearly everything that required power. But automobiles and other machines encroached on horses' territory until in the 1920s, automobiles outnumbered equines.

A book could be written about each of these chapters—and many have. If you're intrigued by a topic, dig in and do additional research.

1

Cowboys and Longhorns

Confederate money was worthless after the Civil War. However, the South was rich—in cattle. Texas Longhorns thrived on the open ranges. For forty years, ranchers made money driving herds of cattle north. The Longhorns provided a steady supply of meat for the beef-hungry Northerners after the Union Army soldiers had consumed most of their cattle.

With thousands of cows roaming the open ranges, cattlemen needed a way to show who owned which animals. They began hot branding cattle with a mark registered to each rancher. Brands were usually applied to the left hip but could be used elsewhere.

These guidelines applied to the design and reading of brands.

- The characters are read left to right, top to bottom, and outside to inside.

- Letters are always capitalized.

- A number or letter could be placed inside a box or circle.

- A leaning letter is "tumbling."

- A letter on its side is "lazy."

- An upside down letter is "crazy."

- A backwards letter is "reverse."

- Short "feet" at the bottom are "walking."

- A cursive letter or curved bottom lines means "running."

- Curved "wings" at the top mean "flying."

- A partial circle at the top means "swinging."

- A partial circle at the bottom means "rocking."

- — means "bar," __ means "rail," and / means "slash."

- Simple symbols such as a sun, cross, diamond, triangle, or heart could be used.

Sample Brands

Exact numbers are impossible to determine, but certainly millions of Longhorns traveled from Texas to northern rail centers. They followed four main trails, listed here from west to east.

Goodnight-Loving Trail

This trail began at Fort Belknap, Texas, traveled across the center of the state to Horsehead Crossing, turned north along the Pecos River into New Mexico to Fort Sumner. The trail continued north to Denver, Colorado and was later extended into Wyoming.

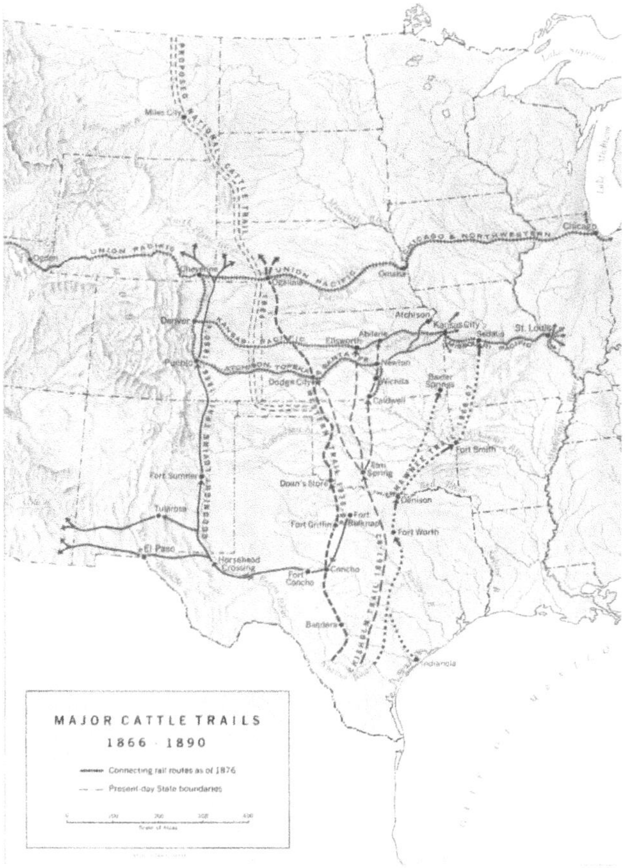

Western Trail

The Western Trail began at the Neuces River in South Texas and extended as far north as Nebraska

Chisholm Trail

This is the best-known trail, created by Jesse Chisholm. The trail started near San Antonio and ended in Abilene, Kansas.

Shawnee Trail

This trail was called the Texas Road, Sedalia Trail, or the Kansas Trail. It was based on old Indian paths and was the earliest trail used on the cattle drives, beginning in the 1850s. The trail began at the Neuces River in South Texas and extended north to Sedalia, Missouri. The Shawnee Trail lost popularity when the Chisholm Trail opened to the west of it, running through less populated areas.

The trails were necessary, because rail lines were nearly non-existent in the Southwest at that time; the Transcontinental Railroad wasn't completed until 1869. There were no semi-trucks, refrigerated cars, or interstate highways. There was simply no way, other than hoofing it, to get the cattle to areas where they could be transported to the Midwest.

An early destination for the drives was Abilene, Kansas, founded in 1867 along the Kansas Pacific Railroad. Dodge City, Kansas later became a popular destination. Once the cattle reached these rail stations, they were shipped to stockyards in Chicago, Illinois.

The towns that sprang up to service the cattle drivers were called "cow towns." Low moral standards were common as well as leniency in enforcing the law. Abilene, Kansas became known as "sin city." At one time, the town had thirty-two saloons, and its murder rate was ten times that of New York City.

The length of the trails combined with the slow pace of the cattle meant a drive took two to four months. Driving the cattle too fast would cause them to lose weight, and they would be no good for meat. Ten to twelve miles a day gave the animals time to graze and rest while maintaining their weight.

An average herd on one of these drives ranged from one to three thousand head. That required a crew of ten to twelve cowboys, with up to six horses per cowboy. The men weren't called cowboys at first. They were known as drovers, cowhands, cowpokes, or cowpunchers. The last two names came about because the men used a prod or pole to urge cattle into the rail cars.

The cowboys were young and small to medium in size. A heavy man was too hard for the horses to carry long distances. The cowboy "uniform" was functional, protecting them from the elements. Large, wide-brimmed hats kept the sun off their faces. Boots were best for riding and were a good defense against rattlesnakes. Chaps protected their legs from thorns and sharp brush. Cloth bandannas kept them from breathing too much of the dust kicked up by the massive herds.

The men's duties were to keep the herd moving in the right direction, protect them from predators, prevent cattle rustlers from stealing them, and keep the cattle calm to avoid stampedes.

> *About ten o'clock it began to thunder and lightning, which caused the herd to become unruly. Every time a keen clash of thunder would come the herd would stampede and run for a mile or two before we could get them to stop. It continued in that way all night so that we lost another night's rest...*
>
> 
> 
> 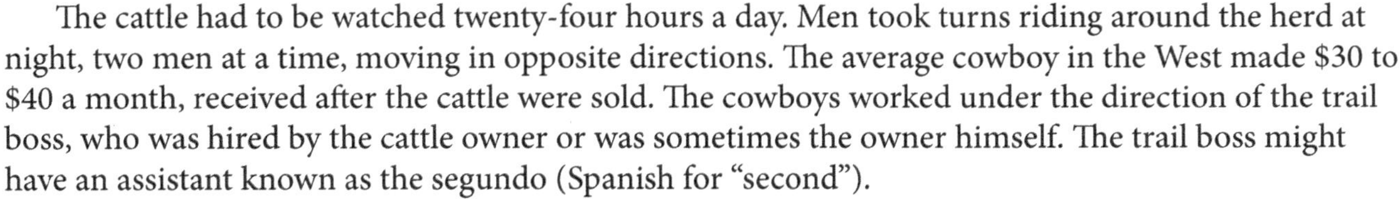
>
> — *Charles Siringo - A Texas Cowboy, 1885*

The cattle had to be watched twenty-four hours a day. Men took turns riding around the herd at night, two men at a time, moving in opposite directions. The average cowboy in the West made $30 to $40 a month, received after the cattle were sold. The cowboys worked under the direction of the trail boss, who was hired by the cattle owner or was sometimes the owner himself. The trail boss might have an assistant known as the segundo (Spanish for "second").

Next in importance on the drive was the cook, often known as Cookie. The cook drove the chuck wagon. Not only was he responsible for preparing meals, he was also in charge of medical procedures, barbering, and sometimes even dentistry.

Meals were basic—biscuits, cornbread, molasses, salted or dried meat, beans, and coffee. They were served twice a day—the first before dawn and another after dark.

One or more wranglers cared for the string of horses used by the cowboys. The wrangler might also be responsible for training and the treatment of any illnesses or injuries the horses experienced.

The cowboys came from diverse backgrounds, including settlers from the eastern United States, Europeans, African-Americans, Native Americans, and Mexicans.

Nat Love was a black cowboy known as "Deadwood Dick." Born into slavery in 1854 in Tennessee, Nat's father taught him how to read and write. At sixteen, Nat headed west, a free man. He was skilled at breaking horses. The trail boss of the Duval Ranch told Nat he would give him a job if he could ride a horse called Good Eye.

This proved the worst horse to ride I had ever mounted in my life, but I stayed with him and the cow boys were the most surprised outfit you ever saw, as they had taken me for a tenderfoot, pure and simple. After the horse got tired and I dismounted the boss said he would give me a job and pay me $30.00 per month and more later on.

— *The Life and Adventures of Nat Love, chapter 6*

During his years as a cowboy, Nat learned to speak Spanish, became a champion roper, and wrote his autobiography in 1907.

Co-founder of the Goodnight-Loving Trail (with Oliver Loving), Charles Goodnight was born in Illinois in 1836. Charles moved with his family to Waco, Texas when he was ten. By twenty, he was working as a cowboy and served with the local militia. Goodnight invented the chuck wagon or mobile kitchen used on the cattle drives.

He modified a Studebaker wagon, used by the army during the Civil War, by bolting a box onto the back and adding drawers and shelves to hold food and cooking utensils. A water barrel rode on the side and a canvas was hung underneath to carry firewood. For small outfits, the cowboys' supplies and horse feed were stored in the wagon's bed. Larger operations often had a second wagon to carry bedrolls, tents, spare saddles, and extra supplies. Mules or oxen pulled the chuck wagon. The Texas legislature designated the chuck wagon as its official state vehicle in 2005.

Although the vast majority of those on the cattle drives were men, a few women also rode the trails. Lizzie Johnson Williams, a schoolteacher, bookkeeper, and writer, realized there was money to be made in cattle. In 1871, she made her first cattle purchase and registered her brand (CY)[1]. Mrs. Williams, known as the "Cattle Queen of Texas," was the first woman to drive her own herds up the Chisholm Trail. When she died in 1924, Lizzie's wealth was valued at $250,000.

Mary Taylor Bunton "Mollie" rode the Chisholm Trail with her husband in 1886. Mollie described the journey, from a woman's perspective, in her book published in 1939, *A Bride on the Old Chisholm Trail, in 1886.*

Mollie fell in love with a full-blooded Spanish pony, cream-colored with a long, white mane and tail, and convinced her husband to buy him. Mollie rode sidesaddle in a dark-green, wool riding habit. Mrs. Bunton got along well with the pony, but he refused to allow any of the cowboys to ride or even saddle him.

> *When they attempted to saddle him for me to ride, he would paw, kick and fight every man that came near but the minute he heard my voice, he would neigh for me and as soon as I was in the saddle he was gentle and obeyed the slightest touch of my hand on the bridle. I had ridden him many times as much as thirty-five or forty miles on certain occasions and the going was so easy that I was not fatigued and my pony was none the worse for the trip.*
>
> *— A Bride on the Old Chisholm Trail, in 1886, p. 35*

When she wasn't riding her cream pony, Mrs. Bunton walked or drove a buggy pulled by a team of bay horses, Beauty and Darling. She described the cowboys' practice of pulling long hairs from the horses' and cows' tails to weave into hair ropes.

> *It was a generally accepted belief among the cowboys that if they stretched one of these hair ropes around their pallets at night, they would be protected from snakes and especially the poisonous rattlesnakes, as the snake's body was supposed to be entirely too sensitive to crawl over a hair rope.*
>
> *— A Bride on the Old Chisholm Trail, in 1886, p. 17*

Apparently, Mrs. Bunton didn't trust this rope technique as she feared sleeping on the ground at night.

> *Naturally, at first, it was a hardship for me to have to sleep on the ground. Oftentimes I was afraid to go to sleep as I remembered the harrowing tales I had heard of snakes, bugs and crawling and stinging things that infested the woods or prowled around hunting their prey at night. I am ashamed even now to tell how it frightened me when I first heard the snapping and snarling and fighting of the angry, hungry wolf packs as they came closer and closer to our camp at midnight, searching for food.*
>
> *— A Bride on the Old Chisholm Trail, in 1886, p. 37*

Mrs. Bunton often traveled near the front of the herd, avoiding the dust stirred up by the animals.

Riding ahead of the herd I would turn in my saddle and look back, and it would look as if the entire face of the earth was just a moving mass of heads and horns.

— *A Bride on the Old Chisholm Trail, in 1886, p. 38*

Here's an insight about the trail we'd likely have never gotten from a cowboy.

Wild flowers grew in the greatest profusion everywhere and there were many rare varieties that I had never seen before. I was fond of flowers and it afforded me the greatest pleasure and helped to while away the long, lonely hours to gather them in armfuls. Sometimes I would fill my buggy and decorate my horses' bridles and harness with the gorgeous blossoms.

— *A Bride on the Old Chisholm Trail, in 1886, p. 39*

There would have been no cattle drives without horses. Each cowboy on a drive needed three to six strong, sturdy horses. Many of these animals were early Quarter Horse types or Mustangs. Although the American Quarter Horse Association registry wasn't founded until 1940, the early horses from which the breed was formed trace back to Thoroughbreds and other types imported to colonial America in the 1600s.

The other main source of horses was the Mustangs who roamed free out West. Many were descendants of the Spanish Barbs brought to America by early explorers. Mustangs were crossed with the early Quarter Horse types to create animals well suited for the long cattle drives. Undoubtedly, other breeds were used on the drives, including Appaloosas and Morgans.

Cattle drives continued into the early 1900s, but decreased each year. A variety of factors contributed to this decline.

- The overproduction of cattle made beef prices drop, meaning little or no profit for the ranchers.

- The public desired a better grade of beef than the rangy Longhorns.

- Northern farmers and ranchers began raising their own cattle.

- When railroads reached Texas, ranchers could transport cattle to market more easily by train.

- With the invention of barbed wire, the open ranges were no longer open. Before barbed wire, the primary material for fences was wood. It was too expensive to enclose the ranges with wood fencing, but low-cost barbed wire made it possible. Ranchers and farmers erected fences, preventing free travel and restricting access to water.

- In the harsh winter of 1886-87, thousands of cows in the West froze to death.

- The Texas Longhorns carried a tick that did not harm them but could infect other cattle with "Texas Fever." Many areas established quarantines against the Texas Longhorns.

The cattle drive was a fixture of the American Old West, but this popular historical event was relatively short-lived.

---

1. *I'm curious why she chose the letters 'CY', but I could not find an answer anywhere.*

2

Speedy President

Many believe Ulysses S. Grant was a better general than president, but all agree he was an outstanding horseman—arguably the best of any U.S. president. A native of Ohio, born in 1822, Grant attended West Point Academy, graduating in 1843. At the Academy, Grant's skill with horses impressed the students and instructors alike.

In horsemanship, he was noted as the most proficient in the Academy. In fact, rider and horse held together like the fabled centaur.

— *James Longstreet (a classmate who went on to become a Confederate general)*

Later, his son Fredrick said his father, "preferred to ride the most unmanageable mount, the largest and most powerful one. Oftentimes I saw him ride a beast that none had approached."

Abraham Lincoln invited Grant to join him at Ford's Theater on the fateful evening of April 14, 1865, but the general declined. He and his wife planned to visit their children in New Jersey. When Grant heard of the assassination, he bitterly regretted not accepting the invitation. He called the president's death the "darkest day of my life." Grant was convinced that had he been there, he might have stopped John Wilkes Booth and saved Lincoln's life.

After the assassination, vice president Andrew Johnson served the remainder of Lincoln's term. Grant disagreed with Johnson's post-war policies which favored Southern whites. Although he wasn't a politician, Grant was well known and respected for his leadership during the war. When Grant decided to run for president, his nomination in 1868 was unopposed. He was unanimously named the Republican Party candidate. Grant defeated New York Democrat, Horatio Seymour, by a landslide—214 to 80 electoral votes.

The 18th U.S. president was inaugurated on March 4, 1869. Although the scandals of his subordinates plagued Grant's presidency, most believe Grant himself was not corrupt. President Grant pushed for fair treatment of Native Americans and former slaves.

In those days, the government was more frugal with their budget. The president was financially responsible for his own horses and their care.

A great many people think, that the expense of keeping the president's horses is borne by the government. Such is not the case. The government keeps up the office stable, of course, but all those horses on the north side are the president's own property, and their keeping is paid for by him. There are practically two distinct stables.

— *Washington Evening Star, "The President's Horses," April 5, 1884*

Reb and Billy Button, taking President Grant's children to school.
Harper's Weekly, April 17, 1869.

The president's horses were housed in larger box stalls at the White House Stable, while the additional government horses stayed in smaller ones. The president's carriages had no special security features. All the White House horses were on call around the clock, ready to be used as needed by messengers, secretaries, clerks, and the housekeeper.

In 1872, President Ulysses S. Grant had the last and grandest White House stable built. During his presidency, the U-shaped stable with a central courtyard was home to his beloved war horses—Cincinnati, Egypt, and Jeff Davis—as well as his harness racer, Butcher Boy, and other carriage horses.

The stable contained an apartment for the coachman and his family on the second floor. Albert Hawkins, an African-American, first served as the White House coachman under President Grant. He was well respected and continued as coachman until 1889 when his eyesight began to fail.

The White House stable was expanded in 1891 to accommodate twenty-five horses, twelve carriages, tack and harness rooms, as well as additional living quarters for the stable staff.

Grant's love of horses and fast driving accompanied him to the White House. He loved to drive his carriage at high speed down the streets of Washington, D.C. Once, he challenged a man driving a butcher's wagon to an impromptu race. Grant was amazed that the delivery horse proved to be faster than his own. He later sent a representative to the butcher shop to buy the horse. That's how the president acquired and named his speedy trotter, Butcher's Boy.

To modern minds, it seems amusing that speeding horses could be a problem, but there were laws regulating the speed of horse-drawn traffic—and Ulysses Grant was a serial offender.

After repeated warnings, African-American Metropolitan Police officer William West gained the notoriety of being the first, and only, police officer to arrest a president. Not long before Grant's arrest,

a woman and her six-year-old child were seriously injured by speeding horses near West's corner, so the officer was extra vigilant.

According to an article by J. LeCount Chestnut for The Washington Post, this is how West's encounter with the president went.

West shouted, the president's team was brought to a standstill, and West approached him. "Well, officer, what do you want with me?" Grant asked.

"Mr. President," was the reply, "I want to tell you that you were violating the law by driving at reckless speed. Your fast driving, sir, has set the example for a lot of other gentlemen. It is endangering the lives of the people who have to cross the street in this locality. Only this evening a lady was knocked down by one of the racing teams."

"I am very sorry," said President Grant, "and I'll promise that hereafter I will hold my team down to the regulation speed."

But the very next day, the good intentions were forgotten, and General Grant came racing down 13th St. fast as ever. When hailed, he turned into M St. and was almost at 14th before he could stop. As West approached, Grant said, "Do you think, officer, that I was violating the speed laws?"

"I certainly do, Mr. President," answered West, not a bit softened by the president's query. "I cautioned you yesterday, Mr. President, about fast driving, and you said, sir, that it would not occur again. I am very sorry, Mr. President, to have to do it, for you are the nation's chief executive, but my duty is plain, sir: I shall have to place you under arrest!"

At the request of the president, Officer West got into the executive's carriage, sat beside him and drove to the station house. Grant left $20 collateral, which was forfeited.

After this incident President Grant and Officer West grew very friendly and spent frequently hours at a time chatting. Their love of horses was the great bond of sympathy. Strange to relate, West himself was an inveterate fast driver. He confessed that he had been arrested at least 25 times for speeding.

Old timers around Washington yet remember West's remarkable horse, "Dan." This animal was so trained that when his master had cornered an offender, he would seize the culprit by the coat with his great front teeth. As a rule, the horse was careful not to catch a man's flesh, but if the

In 1879, the sultan of Turkey gave Grant two gray Arabian stallions, "Leopard" and "Linden" or "Linden Tree." The stallions were valued at $10,000 each. Grant stabled the Arabians at a farm, Ash Hill, owned by his friend, General Edward Fitzgerald Beale.

One morning, the two horses turned up missing. Beale sent for policeman West, giving him the only clue the thieves had left behind—a ragged cap. By interrogating farm employees, West determined that the cap belonged to a man named Ed Nolan, a former worker at the farm. West searched nearly the entire state of Maryland before tracking Nolan down. He and his two adult accomplices were each sentenced to ten years in prison. A boy who had worked with them was given a short jail sentence.

Apparently, the horses were recovered unharmed as Leopard became the earliest imported Arabian registered with The Arabian Horse Club of America. A book about the stallions was written by Randolph Huntington in 1885. Both Arabians lived into old age and were said to be "full of ginger to the last."

"LINDEN TREE"   "LEOPARD"

10

3

Blind Tom

The discovery of gold in California in 1848 resulted in an increasing number of settlers moving west. Without adequate waterways for a canal system, travel of any distance in the West had been primarily by stagecoach. When California became a state in 1850, Congress studied how to build a rail line to connect the new state to the East. Having the railroad pass through a small town would bring prosperity to that area, so representatives hotly debated the route for the transcontinental line. Should it follow a Northern route? A Southern one? Or perhaps it should be located more centrally, roughly along the Oregon Trail?

The beginning of the Civil War disrupted the plans for a time, but in 1862, the Union passed the Pacific Railway Act, funding the construction of a transcontinental railroad. After much wrangling, an 1800-mile variation of the central route was chosen. Two companies were selected to build the line. Payment was based on the miles of track laid, with higher rates paid when it was necessary to tunnel through mountains.

The Central Pacific began building in Sacramento, California on January 8, 1863 and worked eastward. Many Chinese immigrants were hired by the Central Pacific. The work at the western end of the line was difficult and dangerous as explosives had to be used to tunnel through the mountains.

At the opposite end, the Union Pacific worked westward. President Lincoln decided they would begin construction at Council Bluffs, Iowa. But that required building a railroad bridge across the Missouri River. To avoid a delay, in July 1865, they began laying rail west of the river in Omaha, Nebraska. It wasn't until 1872 that a bridge connecting the rail line to Council Bluffs was completed.

Native Americans weren't happy about the railroad crossing their land. They attacked workers and destroyed track. To retaliate, Union Pacific men killed bison, an important source of food for the Natives.

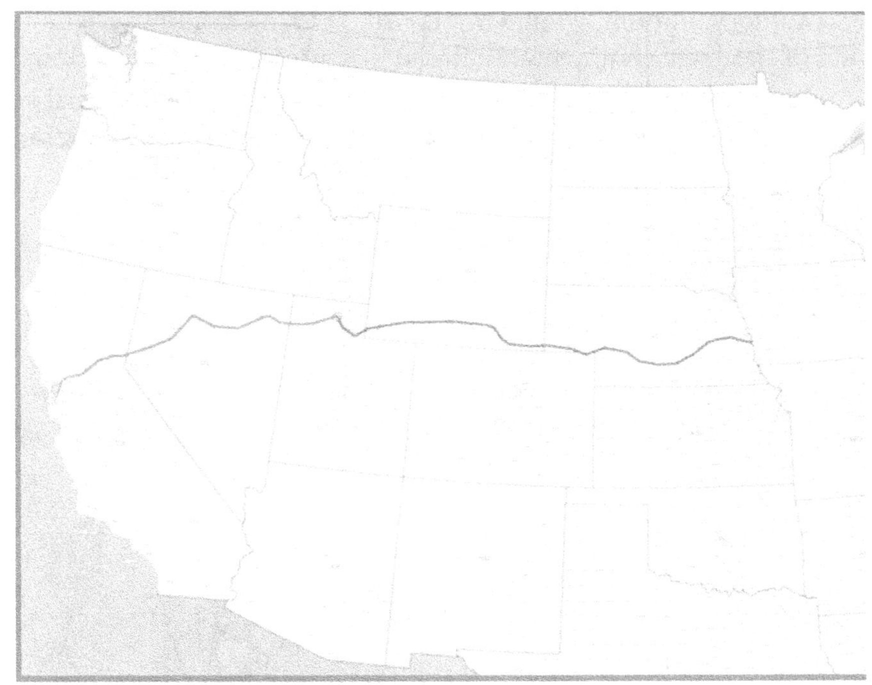

The Union and Central Pacific companies competed to see which could lay the most track. They needed many workers in addition to those who delivered and laid the rails. Manual laborers prepared and leveled the ground for the track. Surveyors, civil engineers, cooks, and delivery men were also required. As the railroad was built, telegraph lines were installed alongside the tracks to improve communication between the East and West.

Equines provided much of the power to complete this huge project. Horses and mules pulled supply wagons and flat cars that delivered the steel rails and wooden ties to the front of the tracks as they grew in one direction or the other.

Thomas O'Donnell, a track worker for the Union Pacific, remembered a special horse, Tom, that helped build the Transcontinental Railroad.

> *About every 20 miles they laid a side track, where we stored the material for the front, and our engine went back to bring material needed up to the front. Then it would back to the end of the track and throw off iron, ties, spikes, and bridge timbers on both sides of the track, and then it would pull back again. … We had two small flat cars built for the purpose of laying the rails. Each had two rollers on the top of the floor of the car, on both sides, and in the front part of the car. The rails were placed on these rollers when needed, and pulled ahead with little exertion by men laying the rails. This car was pulled ahead by old "Blind Tom" the horse. This horse was so well trained that I believe he never missed the proper length to go. As soon as he heard the rails flop down, he would start another rail length, and so on until finished.*

Blind Tom is said to have worked the entire route for the Union Pacific from Nebraska to Utah. No matter the weather, the faithful horse traveled back and forth, pulling the car that carried the wooden ties and steel rails that would be spiked into place to expand the track. Tom was only one of many equines who labored for the Central and Union Pacific companies, but it's amazing that he accomplished this while blind.

When the eastern and western rail lines neared each other, Congress decided they should meet at Promontory Summit, Utah. On May 10, 1869, a ceremony celebrated that meeting and the completion of the Transcontinental Railroad. It's rumored that Blind Tom was there for the party.

The last railroad tie was pre-drilled with holes so four special spikes could be driven into it—a gold spike, a second gold one of lesser quality, a silver spike, and one of blended iron, silver, and gold.

Neither of these photos may actually be Tom, but this is the type of work he did.

The laborers attending the ceremony had a good laugh when Leland Stanford, president of the Central Pacific, and former governor of California, attempted to hammer in the first gold spike. He missed it altogether and hit the rail.

After the four ceremonial spikes were in place, the two locomotives, Union Pacific No. 119 and Central Pacific No. 60, were moved forward until their cow catchers touched.

The gold and silver spikes were removed after the ceremony so they wouldn't be stolen. The first gold spike is on display at Stanford University in California.

A total of 1,777 miles of track were laid to complete the Transcontinental Railroad; the Union Pacific laying 1,087 and the Central Pacific 690. A trip from Omaha, Nebraska to San Francisco, California had previously taken six months by wagon or twenty-five days by stagecoach. Now, it could be traveled in a week by train.

Sadly, the Transcontinental Railroad contributed to the near extinction of bison. In 1867, the railroad hired "Buffalo" Bill Cody to hunt bison to provide food for the construction workers. He earned $500 a month for his work. In eighteen months, he killed 4,280 of the animals.

The pointed, iron wedge at the front of the locomotives, known as the cow catcher, was designed to push the large animals off the track. But, in pushing them, the bison were usually killed. Even worse were the later trains carrying passengers who shot bison for sport from the windows of the rail cars.

In the early 1800s, there were an estimated thirty to sixty million bison roaming freely across the Great Plains. By 1889, their numbers had dwindled to five hundred. Although it was never official government policy to kill bison, they did nothing to stop the hunts. In fact, some considered it a solution to the Native American "problem." Without the bison, they believed the Natives would leave the prairies.

> *Bison trample upon the plains upon which our settlers desire to herd their cattle and their sheep. They range over the very pastures where the settlers keep their herds of cattle. They destroy the pasture. They are as uncivilized as the Indian.*
>
> — *Congressman Omar Dwight Conger, 1874*

Some today don't think hunting was the only cause for the decimation of the bison population. According to Dr. Sam Fadala,

> *Sixty million free-ranging bison spread out over hundreds of thousands of square miles could have never been wiped out by hunters. The American buffalo (bison) was not shot off, because it could not be rendered extinct by bullets due to incredible numbers, vast and often unreachable habitat, primitive travel methods, and inferior firepower.*

Dr. Fadala believes it's more likely the bison died from diseases brought to the prairies by domestic cattle. In modern times, their number has increased, with estimates of over 500,000 bison on private and public land.

Replica of the Union Pacific No. 119

4

Fire Horses

In the late 1600s, homes in colonial towns were required to keep an item most people no longer have—a fire bucket.

The village cobbler (shoemaker) made the buckets from leather. Each bucket could hold two to three gallons of water. In the event of a fire, everyone was expected to join the bucket brigade. At the end near a water source, buckets were filled and passed down the line from one person to the next. When a bucket reached the other end, the water was thrown onto the fire. The leather buckets had the owner's name painted on them, so they could be returned after the fire was extinguished.

When volunteer fire departments formed in the mid 1700s, one surprising piece of equipment the men carried was a bed key. If the fire wasn't too advanced, the metal key was used to take a bed apart. Beds were valuable pieces of furniture, and if there was time to do so safely, they would be disassembled and removed from the burning building.

An improvement on the bucket brigade was the manual water pump. These pumps were carried on the first fire engines pulled by a team of men. Depending on the design, two to a dozen or more men pushed a bar up and down to power the pump which forced water through a hose and out the nozzle. Another type of pump was powered by firefighters stepping up and down on a treadle.

At this time, firefighters resisted the use of horses. They believed horses would put men out of work. They also considered the animals too dangerous because of their instinctive fear of fire. In 1832, the New York Mutual Hook and Ladder Company No. 1 was one of the first fire departments to purchase a horse to pull their equipment. One morning, soon after their horse arrived, the firefighters discovered someone had entered the stable overnight, shaved the horse's mane and tail, and painted a white stripe down his back.

In the mid 1800s, as steam-powered pumpers became popular, fire depart-

ments were forced to change. The heavy steam engines could pump water faster and longer, but they were too heavy for men to pull. Thus began the era of the fire horse.

It took a special animal to become a fire horse. He had to be strong but also fast, obedient, intelligent, and most of all—fearless. Weight requirements were established based on the type of equipment he would pull. The lightest horses, pulling hose wagons, weighed at least 1,100 pounds. To pull steam pumpers, the required weight was 1,400 pounds. Large draft horses pulled the big hook and ladder wagons used to access the increasingly taller buildings. The drafts might weigh as much as 1,700 pounds.

Fire horses needed to be ready for action as soon as an alarm sounded. They had to be sure-footed and able to gallop away from the station in any kind of weather. Horses naturally fear fire, so it took a brave horse to pull the equipment close to a burning building.

Because of their size, strength, willingness to work, and gentle temperament, a favorite for fire departments was the Percheron. This draft breed originated in France in the 1600s as war horses. Black or dapple gray Percherons were also used in agriculture and for transporting heavy loads.

Fire horses often worked in pairs or three to a hitch. Three horses driven abreast is known as a "troika" from the Russian word for "triplet" or "trio." A fire horse prospect was tested by pairing him with an experienced horse to pull one of the wagons. This helped the firemen determine whether the horse had the strength and stamina to continue with further training. It took a year or two to fully train a horse for fire work. Many companies trained their own animals, but there was also a fire horse college in Detroit, Michigan. The college was set up to simulate a fire department. Their graduates were used in fire stations across the country.

Active-duty horses were stabled at the fire station, usually behind the parked equipment. The firefighters were housed on the second floor. When the alarm rang, the fireman on watch used a battery-powered device called the Horton Trip to unlock the stall doors. The horses were trained to hurry from their stalls and stand at a specific spot in front of the wagon they pulled. During the training phase, they were rewarded with treats each time they went to the correct position and stood still.

When responding to a fire, speed is of the essence, but harnessing a horse can be a slow process. A quick-hitch system was developed that could be fastened on with just a few snaps. The harnesses were suspended from the ceiling by rods called spiders, hanging directly over the place where each horse stood. As soon as the horses were in position, the harnesses dropped down over the animals' backs, and the snaps were fastened. James Kennedy of Chicago invented one version of this harness. His system was known as Kennedy's Automatic Harness Holder and Hanger.

Bits were usually kept in the horses' mouths except when they were fed grain. That way, all that needed to be done to complete the harnessing was to hook the reins onto the bit rings.

Once fully trained, the horses ran to their positions by themselves when an alarm rang. With the quick-hitch harnesses, firefighters were out the station door in thirty seconds, often faster. The horses were so eager to take off, they sometimes left before the driver was in the wagon! In at least one case, the driver was on board, but no one had been able to attach the reins to the horses' bits. The driver couldn't steer his team, but the horses made it to the fire without his guidance.

Fire departments kept lists of the horses they owned. Each horse was assigned a number, and its color, height, weight, and age were recorded. The horses were more than numbers to the firefighters, though. The men knew their lives often depended on their equine partners.

In addition to the firefighters, each station employed one or more hostlers whose duty was to care for the horses and their equipment. Hostlers were up early in the morning to feed the horses and clean stalls. The hostler often drove the first team out of the station, pulling the hose wagon, with the Fire Captain riding beside and directing him. When they arrived at a fire, the hostler unhooked the horses and moved them to safety. After the fire was out, the hostler hooked the teams up again. Once they were back at the station, he would sponge down, water, and feed the horses, and clean the harness and bridles.

One of the most destructive fires in America was the Boston Fire that occurred on November 9th and 10th, 1872. By the time the alarm sounded, a six-story building in Boston's business district was engulfed in flames. Because most of the buildings were constructed of wood, the fire rapidly grew out of control.

Making things even worse, horses across America suffered that year from equine influenza, what was known as The Great Epizootic. Boston was past the worst of the disease outbreak, but they were short of horses, and the ones they had were not back to full strength. Men had to pull some of the fire

fighting equipment. A sixty-acre area within the city was destroyed, including 776 buildings. Thirty people were killed. If not for the Epizootic, perhaps the fire could have been stopped sooner with less damage to buildings and fewer lost lives.

The work of a fire horse was strenuous. They typically worked for only four or five years, however, one of the last fire horses in the U.S., Firehorse Fred, pulled a hose wagon for the Atlantic Company in New Bern, North Carolina for seventeen years (1908 to 1925). New Bern had six fire alarms or bells, representing different locations in the town. Fred recognized the distinct tones and knew what direction to head when an alarm sounded. When Fred wasn't busy fighting fires, the horse worked his second job, pulling a trash pickup wagon through town. Firehorse Fred died at twenty-five while responding to what turned out to be a false alarm. The horse's stuffed head is on display at the New Bern Firemen's Museum.

Not only did the fire horses serve a vital role in saving lives, people in their communities loved them. Visitors went to the firehouse to admire the beautiful horses and feed them sugar cubes and other treats. If they hadn't responded to a fire in a while, the horses were hooked to a wagon for exercise. On those days, neighborhood children often went along for the ride.

Dogs also played an important role in the early days of firefighting. The dogs stayed near the horses' stalls at the station and became their companions. When an alarm sounded, the dog's job was to run ahead of the horses to clear the way. Sometimes two dogs were used—one on each side to keep other dogs or animals from spooking or attacking the horses.

After the horses were unhitched from the wagon at the site of the fire, the dogs stood guard to prevent the theft of the animals or equipment. Dalmatians were commonly used because of their larger size. Dalmatians had enough energy to keep up with the fire engines, and they got along well with horses.

Although thousands of fire horses served faithfully over the fifty or more years of horse-drawn firefighting, little is known about most of them.

Jim

Jim, a seven-year-old, dapple gray, served at the Toledo, Ohio fire department in the center position of a three-horse hitch, pulling a large steamer. Although he had only served two years, he was known as one of the most intelligent fire horses. One day, the strong horse responded to eight alarms. When the ninth sounded, Jim dutifully moved to his position, waiting to be harnessed. His driver was horrified when he noticed Jim standing on three legs. The finest veterinary surgeons in the city were called, but the injury the big gray had suffered earlier in the day was too severe. Jim could not be saved.

Goliath

When the alarm sounded at 10:48 AM, on Sunday, February 7, 1904 in Baltimore, Maryland, Goliath was the lead horse of a three-horse team at Engine House 15. His partners were two other Percherons, Decoration and Electioneer. Goliath had begun work at Baltimore's fire service in 1899 at the age of six.

The three powerful horses were harnessed and in twenty seconds were out the station's doors, pulling a sixty-five foot, five-ton water tower. Within minutes, the team had the tower positioned in front of the Hurst building, a six-story, brick warehouse. The captain believed it was just a small fire in the basement that would quickly be put out. Soon, they'd be back at the fire house.

But then, an explosion shot flames out the front door and sprayed brick and stone everywhere. Still hitched to the heavy water tower, Goliath stood at the curb in front of the flaming building. Decoration and Electioneer were already unhitched and had been moved further away.

Goliath was burned on one side from his neck to his flank. The big horse strained, trying to move the tower that was now blocked by the fallen rubble. Unable to go forward, he managed to turn the bulky equipment around in the narrow street. Goliath pulled it through the flames, away from the building. As soon as he had the equipment safely around the corner, the Hurst building collapsed.

Goliath saved the lives of driver Eugene Short and the five firemen on the tower. The explosion and flames injured Mr. Short and all three horses, but Goliath received the worst of it. They rushed the big Percheron to a veterinary hospital, where he spent six months recovering.

The Great Baltimore Fire burned for two days before 1,200 firefighters finally got it under control. The fire destroyed 1,500 buildings over an area of 140 acres.

On September 13, 1906, after the downtown area was rebuilt, a parade honored the firefighters. Goliath pranced proudly alongside them. The scars from his burns were visible for the rest of his life, but Goliath returned to work, serving the fire department a total of fourteen years. The twenty-year-old horse died after a brief illness, in 1913, at the Fire Department's Horse Hospital.

Frank and Fox

When fire horses became too old or were injured and could no longer work for the department, they were sold or retired. Two such horses in Hannibal, Missouri, were the Percherons, Frank and Fox. The horses were purchased by competing dairy companies to be used for milk deliveries.

Frank took quickly to the milk business, which was surely much easier than his previous career as a fire horse. There was no need for a driver to guide him. Frank soon knew the route and stopped at each customer's house. He even backed himself between the wagon shafts when it was time to be hitched.

H. A. Herman and his father worked separate sides of the street, walking back and forth to the wagon while Frank kept pace with them, pulling the driver-less vehicle. One summer morning in 1914, the fire alarm sounded in the middle of their deliveries. Neither father nor son was close enough to the wagon to stop the old fire horse. They could only stare as Frank took off for the station at a mad gallop. His former teammate, Fox, a few blocks away, recognized the alarm as well and joined Frank in a mad dash for the fire house.

With milk cans, bottles, and milk flying everywhere, Fox caught up with Frank. The two ran so close together, their wagons locked wheels, and then flipped onto their sides. That didn't bother either of the horses—they had a fire to put out! The pair reached the station, dragging the wrecked wagons behind them. By then, the fire engines were gone and the station doors closed, leaving the poor, confused horses standing outside, breathing heavily.

After that episode, Frank and Fox were trained to ignore the fire alarms. (That must have been a difficult job.) Both went on to pull their milk wagons another seven or eight years. Frank was retired from deliveries at twenty and lived to be twenty-five.

Fire horses began to be replaced by motorized vehicles in the 1920s. In Chicago, a driver, William Moir, wept as his horses were retired in 1922. "I feel like I've lost my best friends." Moir had joined the department because of his love for horses. He announced he would quit the day his two "black beauties" were sent out to pasture.

As stated in the January 5, 1908 issue of The Baltimore Sun,

> *There is no engine house in the city that cannot produce at least one thrilling tale about one of its horses. The firemen regard an animal that has been their comrade for many years with as great affection and trust as they do a long-tried human brother.*

It's unfortunate that so few of those "thrilling tales" survive.

5

Wonder Horses

Legends from Oregon's past mention a wild stallion with long, flowing hair. Men, eager to capture the beautiful stallion, caught an occasional glimpse of him and his herd, known as the Oregon Wonder Horses.

> *In the early history of Oregon traditions of a herd of magnificent wild horses that roamed at will over her mountains and valleys were told the settlers, and, like many other tales of like character, seemed beyond belief. It was said this herd was led by an enormous chestnut stallion, whose mane and tail were so abundant and of such length as to almost envelop the entire animal in a wealth of flowing hair. For years this "Wild King of Oregon Wonder Horses" roamed over the country, ever alert to stampede his followers and flee with almost the rapidity of the wind at the approach of a human being. So subtle was this wild leader of his race that it was only at rare intervals that the best hunters were able to even secure at a distance a glimpse of these marvelous equines. Frequent hunts were inaugurated by those who had heard of the surpassing beauty of these horses for the purpose of capturing them to be placed in subjection and used for improving the breeding of the settlers' horses; but, though all the advantage that the intelligent hunter could command was brought to bear, added to which were large rewards for the capture of the magnificent leader, or some representative member of the herd, for years the intuitive cunning of this remarkably intelligent horse rendered his capture, or that of his followers, impossible.*
>
> — *Philadelphia Times, October 27, 1895*

The story goes that as the stallion aged and finally passed away, his band was left without the wise horse's protection, and one of his offspring, the "Oregon Queen," was captured. Her captors hoped the mare would pass on the genetics responsible for the herd's flowing manes and tails.

While the legend makes a good story, it's uncertain whether there's any truth to it. The horse may have been a draft crossed with another breed, perhaps an Andalusian. In 1870, Oregon Queen had a filly, Oregon Beauty, the first long-haired Oregon horse born in captivity. Beauty, in turn, had a colt named Linus. Born in Marion, Oregon, on May 20, 1883, Linus was owned by the Rutherford brothers. People flocked to see the beautiful horses.

Oregon Beauty met an unfortunate end when lightning struck and killed her at Coney Island in New York.

> *During the storm of Friday night, lightning struck the stable of H. C. Morse, at Brighton place, Coney Island, and killed the valuable show mare, Oregon Beauty. She was owned by M. D. Reed of San Francisco. She was a chestnut sorrel, 16 hands high, and had a white mane 9 feet 8 inches long. Her tail, which swept the ground, was also perfectly white. She was 8 years old, and had made the circuit of the principal towns of California. She was shown to Mrs. Cleveland, who*

The Rutherfords sold Linus to Charles H. and Herbert W. Eaton for $30,000 in 1890. The Eaton Brothers had stock farms in Calais, Maine and Lexington, Massachusetts. Linus appeared to have been part Clydesdale or Percheron. His weight was advertised as 1,435 pounds. The Eatons exhibited Linus until his death in 1894.

An extraordinary horse has recently been brought to Boston. He is a beautiful golden Chestnut, with light mane and tail, white hind feet, and white face. He is 7 years old, weighs 1435 lbs., stands 16 hands high, and is 3/4 Clyde, 1/8 French, and 1/8 Printer. Linus – that is his name- was born in Marion Oregon on May 28th, 1883 and is considered a perfect and beautiful animal. The fact that at the present time his foretop is 8 ft, mane 8 feet 8 in, and tail 12 ft 3 inches in length, is certainly wonderful and makes him an extraordinary attraction.

— Breeders Magazine, February 7, 1891

Linus II, one of two sons of Linus (the other was Aurelius), was born in 1890. His tail was nineteen feet long, with a thirteen-foot mane, and a forelock five feet six inches long. Some surviving photos of Linus II may be his brother, Aurelius. The dam of both colts was a Morgan mare, Jennie Morgan. Linus II was sold to Frank Bostock, who exhibited him in England and Australia.

The Oregon Wonder Horses, many of whom were a rich chestnut color, were known not only for their long, thick hair but also for their intelligence and endurance. It's hard to imagine the incredible length of these horses' manes and tails being maintained in the wild. Their hair was allowed to stream down while being exhibited. But when not on display, their manes, tails, and forelocks were braided and looped up into bags so they wouldn't be stepped on.

No descendants of these horses appear to exist today. But Oregon wasn't the only source of long-haired horses. In 1869, Prince Imperial, a Percheron stallion, was purchased from Napoleon III in France by Jacob Howser of Marion, Ohio. He brought Prince Imperial to America and exhibited the horse at fairs and horse shows. Imperial was billed as having the longest hair of any horse at that time. His forelock was seven feet long, and his mane measured nine feet and ten inches.

Prince Imperial died in 1888, but the show went on. Howser had Prince stuffed and continued to tour with him. When not traveling, Howser kept the stuffed horse in his living room. After Howser died, his sons, grandsons, and even a great grandson, Jake Howser, exhibited the stuffed Prince Imperial.

Jake requested that, after his death, his sons burn the horse. Instead, they sold Prince Imperial to a local family, who mounted him on wheels and exhibited him in local parades. Eventually, Prince was donated to the Marion County Historical Society and put on display in their museum.

Long-haired Pony

Chief, born in 1889, was a 42" jet-black Shetland pony who also had unusually long hair. The pony's tail was fifteen feet long. He was described as being "gentle as a lamb and playful as a kitten." Chief was owned and managed by J. W. Skelly in Connecticut and was exhibited across the U.S., Canada, and Europe.

During one of his journeys, Chief survived a train accident in which fifty horses, twelve men, and many wild animals died. The pony's survival was attributed to him being lodged between a camel and a water buffalo, with an elephant behind him.

A Marvelous Pony to Be Seen in Kansas City This Week "The greatest equine curiousity in the world," a tiny pony with a tail fifteen feet long, will be seen in Kansas City this week. The pony is a Shetland, is only 3 1/2 feet high and weighs only 300 pounds. "Chief" will indeed be a sight worth seeing. It is not stated what hair invigorator the equine Paderewski applied to his "narrative," in fact: it is not positively known that he used any; but the hirsute development is marvelous nevertheless.

— Kansas City, Missouri October 13, 1895

6

Ten-Foot Cops

Today, we take the existence of police officers for granted, but prior to the mid 1700s, law enforcement was usually handled by private citizens, often as volunteer community watchmen. In the 1800s, paid police departments appeared in major cities such as Boston, Philadelphia, New York City, and San Francisco.

Officers quickly realized they could patrol more effectively on horseback than on foot. They organized mounted units following the pattern set by the Bow Street Horse Patrol, formed in 1763 to work the streets of London, England. New York City created the first mounted police force in the United States in 1871. That first year, they had twelve officers and fifteen horses. At its peak, the New York Police Department (NYPD) had eight hundred horses.

Over the years, thousands of horses have served in law enforcement around the world, but most of their names and stories are unknown. Teddy represents the type of horse who served faithfully as a police officer's mount. He worked in Buffalo, New York in the early 1900s, with his partner, Patrolman Meyer.

Perhaps the most astonishing feat that Teddy ever accomplished was the capture, unassisted, of a burglar on Grider street. Patrolman Meyer was riding along Grider street late one rainy night when he alighted to try the door of a vacant house, leaving Teddy standing in the street. After examining the rear of the house, the patrolman returned to the street and was astounded to find his faithful steed had disappeared. The night was dark, but, after some time, he discovered the horse standing near a tree in a lot about 100 yards away. When the policeman went to the horse he found him holding a man by his coat with his teeth. The fellow had been sleeping in the house

From the 1920s on, as motorized vehicles became popular, the use of horses declined in all areas, including police work. By the 1950s, many cities had reduced the number of police horses or disbanded their mounted units altogether.

In recent years, police departments have again realized there are advantages to using horses, resulting in a resurgence of mounted units. They can purchase a horse for less than the cost of a new police car. Some animals are even donated for police use. Daily food and bedding costs are lower than the gas required to fuel a car and the repairs and maintenance to keep it running.

Beyond the financial factors, the horses function as ambassadors to their communities. The mounted units develop positive relationships with community members. Most people won't approach a police officer in a car just to chat, but it's common for them to walk up to a mounted officer.

"May I pet your horse?" is the most frequent question.

The police department in Ontario, Canada has capitalized on the popularity of their mounted patrols by creating trading cards for each horse. They pass the cards out to community residents to collect. Besides a photo of the horse, the back of the card contains his age, breed, and height.

There isn't a breed best suited to police work, although draft horses or draft crosses are favored because of their height. Many departments want their horses to look similar, preferring dark, solid-colored horses. But more important than a horse's breed or appearance is his age and temperament. Geldings are used more often than mares, as they tend to be steadier and more predictable. Five or six is considered a good starting age for a horse recruit. By that time, the animal is full grown and more emotionally mature. The playful energy of his youth has faded, yet he still has years of service ahead of him.

Not every horse has the temperament to become a police horse. As prey animals, horses are always on the alert, watching for the slightest sign of danger. And, to some horses, a plastic bag blowing in the wind may seem as threatening as a mountain lion preparing to pounce. A horse's first response to danger is to run. If that fails, their second option is to fight by biting, striking, or kicking. None of those are appropriate reactions for a police horse.

Police horse prospects go through a rigorous training program before being accepted into a mounted unit. Since the horses often work in noisy, chaotic cities, they must be able to accept fearful sights and sounds. They encounter bright, flashing lights, large buses and trucks, honking horns, wailing sirens, firecrackers, gunshots, smoke, and more. It's usually obvious within a few weeks or months of training whether a horse is too nervous to be suitable for police work.

The training used with the horses is called desensitization. A horse is introduced to a scary object, such as a large flag waving from a pole—at a great distance. Once the horse becomes accustomed to the faraway flag, it's brought closer—until the horse just begins to feel uncomfortable. The person carrying the flag stops to give the horse time to adjust and realize he is safe. This is repeated until the horse accepts the item close to or even touching him.

It's important that desensitization training proceed gradually. The idea isn't to scare the horse but to teach him he doesn't need to be afraid. The training should build the horse's confidence that his rider will look out for their safety. Taking advantage of their strong herd instinct, young animals are worked alongside veteran police horses. The younger horse will grow to trust and accept the more experienced horse's judgment. Once the horse completes his training and is assigned to an officer, he will gradually transfer that trust to his human partner. This type of training may take up to two years, depending on the horse's temperament and intelligence.

A few stables specialize in preparing horses for sale to the police while some police departments prefer to train the horses themselves. The Louisiana State Penitentiary in Angola has a large horse-training program. Inmates work up to eight hours a day with the horses. The prison holds an annual rodeo and horse auction to showcase their work. Police departments purchase many of the Angola horses. Maddie, a 17 hand, bay Percheron cross, born in 2005, was trained at Angola and later used by the U.S. Park Police in Washington D.C.

Horses aren't the only ones who go through training. In order to apply to most mounted programs, officers are required to have several years of law enforcement experience. If accepted, they take part in a training program with the horses for five to six hours a day over several months before beginning to patrol. A new mounted officer is paired with an experienced horse.

Police departments have different ways of selecting names for their horses. Some have a contest, getting the public involved in choosing the name for a new animal. Others use the names of former officers. Sometimes, as a cost-saving measure, the stall nameplates from deceased or retired horses are recycled to be used as names for new horses. England's Manchester Mounted Police department has a unique approach. They name their horses after characters in Charles Dickens' novels, such as Pip from *Great Expectations*, Bumble and Crackit from *Oliver Twist*, and Pickwick from *The Pickwick Papers*.

Once an officer is paired with a horse, they often remain as teammates for many years. Spending so much time together develops a strong bond between the two. They learn to trust and look out for each other just as two human officers would.

A typical police horse's day begins early with breakfast and grooming at about six. Horses are tacked and ready to go by eight o'clock. If the stable is near the patrol area, officers ride the horses there. For stables at a distance, the animals are loaded into trailers and driven to their patrol area.

A police officer on horseback is often referred to as a "ten-foot cop." Given the officer's height when mounted, he can see farther than a person on the ground. The officer and horse are also more visible to potential criminals which serves as a deterrent to crime. Horses are often used to patrol parks and activities where a crowd gathers, such as parades and sporting events. The horses are given several breaks during their shift to drink fresh water and eat.

Mounted units are especially effective for crowd control during riots. In those situations, the horses wear special gear such as face shields to protect them. Just as their human counterparts, a police horse sometimes finds himself in dangerous situations where he may be injured or killed on the job. But usually, a police horse serves many years and retires at about twenty. After leaving the department, they spend their well-earned retirement grazing in a pasture.

The horses in the mounted unit in Manhattan, New York are stabled in the ground floor of the Mercedes House, a 1.2-million-square-foot, thirty-two-story luxury apartment building. The stable contains twenty-seven stalls and includes a farrier center, heated riding arena, two horse showers, and a leather shop where the unit's custom saddles, bridles, and halters are made and repaired.

Here are a few glimpses of modern police horses.

AAA Andy—San Francisco, California

Dogs are one danger police horses face. In 2003, AAA Andy had an unfortunate encounter with a vicious one. When a woman unleashed her Pit Bull in Golden Gate Park, a mounted officer requested she put the leash back on the animal. The Pit Bull's attention was drawn to the horse. He raced toward Andy and bit him on the abdomen and back legs. In the ensuing chaos, Andy kicked the dog's owner and the officer was thrown.

Andy, now riderless, took off. The dog chased him for half a mile. In order to stop the attack, another officer shot the dog. The Pit Bull ran into the bushes where it was found by animal control authorities, still alive. A park visitor caught the horse.

Andy was off work for several months. When fully recovered, the horse returned to duty and was soon in the news again for assisting in the apprehension of the "Spider Man Burglar"—a thief known for his ability to climb through skylights and ventilation shafts.

Brigadier—Toronto, Canada

After seven months of intensive training, Brigadier, a Belgian cross, joined the Toronto police department in 2000. His first partner was officer Ted Gallipeau. Initially, Brigadier and Ted were paired with a more experienced police horse and officer, but despite his youth, Brigadier was fearless.

The big horse became a favorite with the officers and was exceptionally good at his job. He won the North American Mounted Police Competition in 2003 and placed highly at the event two other years. The people in the community loved Brigadier. Children, especially, were attracted to the horse because of his sweet, gentle nature.

Due to officer transfers, Brigadier had three human partners. One afternoon in February, 2006, Brigadier and officer Kevin Bradfield rode to their patrol on the east side of Toronto with another officer, Ron Gilbert, and his horse, Blue Moon. That evening, someone notified the officers of a commotion at a nearby bank. A man in a van was acting aggressively toward another driver at the ATM.

Officer Bradfield asked the man to pull aside, but he started to drive away. Then, the unthinkable happened. The man made a u-turn and sped back toward them, striking Brigadier and Officer Bradfield. Brigadier was injured so badly he was put down immediately. Bradfield was transported to the hospital with injuries to his ribs, back, and neck.

That night, police arrested Dirk Sankersingh, the forty-two-year-old driver of the van. He was sentenced to two years of house arrest. After the memorial service for Brigadier, Toronto Councilwoman Gloria Lindsay-Luby wrote a letter seeking stricter penalties for anyone intentionally harming service animals.

> *I am asking the Government of Canada to update and strengthen the Criminal Code to include the protection of law enforcement service animals against intentional harm. These animals should be recognized for the dangers and risks they face to serve and protect the public. The legislation is very dated and needs to change. If we can do this, then perhaps Brigadier's death will not have been in vain.*

To date, the law, commonly referred to as Brigadier's Law, has not been passed.

Nine months after Brigadier's death, a replacement horse was selected. A community contest was held to suggest names for the new horse. Commodore was chosen, a rank in the navy equivalent to the Army's brigadier.

Yoder—Lexington, Kentucky

One evening in 2018, officer Shawn Davis rode his horse Yoder, a Quarter Horse and Belgian cross, down the street on their way to a Christmas parade. Suddenly, the horse went down. One of Yoder's back legs had fallen into a utility access hole in the middle of the street. Davis was unharmed, but Yoder's leg was trapped.

The gelding's calm disposition helped him survive the ordeal. A veterinarian, Dr. Julie Suarez, arrived within ten minutes to sedate the horse while rescue workers pondered how to free him.

They placed Yoder in a sling to keep the weight off his legs. Then, the firefighters went to work, chipping away at the street. When they had a hole large enough, they discovered a corner of Yoder's metal shoe was stuck on a pipe. After an hour's work, they were able to free him. Yoder was transported by ambulance to an equine hospital.

The horse had no broken bones, and within a half hour of arriving at the hospital, Yoder was back on his feet. Veterinarians predicted the horse would begin feeling like himself again within a week or two.

Relieved that his partner was going to be all right, Officer Davis said, "He's going to get a little time off and we'll train him back up to it. Don't know that we'll go down Sixth Street anytime soon, but yes, we're looking forward to getting back out there."

By January, Yoder and officer Davis were back on patrol.

Smash—Houston, Texas

Deafness in horses is rare, but an injury or a congenital defect can cause it. Deafness at birth occurs most frequently in Paint horses, particularly those with blue eyes. This connection to a horse's color may be related to the high frequency of deafness in blue-eyed, white cats.

Deafness in a horse rarely affects his performance, and for a police horse is likely an advantage. The horse will not spook at loud sounds it cannot hear—firecrackers, fireworks, honking horns, etc.

Smash, a nine-year-old Paint gelding who is totally deaf, was donated to the Houston Police Department in 2013. He has one blue and one brown eye. His registered name is A Box Office Smash!

Officer Jeff Harris, Smash's partner, considers his horse's deafness a strength. Smash has also been an inspiration to young horse lovers. A group of girls with learning disabilities met Smash and fell in love with him. The "Smash Girls" visit the horse often and organize events to raise money for his care. Smash even has his own Facebook page.

7

The Great Epizootic

I magine the impact today on our economy and daily life if we experienced a massive failure of motorized vehicles. Deliveries of food and other merchandise would be nearly impossible. Most people would be unable to travel to where they needed to go. This would have a disastrous impact on our lives and our economy.

People experienced that type of upheaval in 1872. In those days, equines provided the horsepower for transportation and deliveries. The horses didn't organize and go on strike. It was much worse; many of them became so ill they couldn't work.

In September 1872, a mysterious illness began affecting horses in Toronto, Canada. Within days, the disease reached nearly all the city's livery stables, infecting the horses who pulled Toronto's street-cars. By October, the disease had made it to the northeast coast of the United States. From there, the illness, thought to be equine influenza, spread west across the U.S. It became known as "The Great Epizootic of 1872." (An epizootic is a disease outbreak in an animal population analogous to an epidemic in humans.)

The disease reached the west coast by March 1873. From there it moved north, returning to Canada that summer. The Great Epizootic temporarily debilitated most horses. Densely populated areas were hit the hardest. Although trains were in use at that time, horses delivered the coal that powered them. Horses were also responsible for the local transport of cargo to and from the rail stations. Without healthy horses, transportation screeched to a halt, food prices soared, and merchandise piled up at canals, train stations, and piers.

This sketch, from Harper's Weekly, November 1872, shows city life during the Great Epizootic. "Temporary expedients" included the use of man-powered carts, or oxen, who were unaffected by the illness.

The Great Boston Fire, the city's largest, started on November 9, 1872. By the time the alarm sounded, flames engulfed a six-story building in

THE HORSE PLAGUE—SKETCHES ABOUT TOWN DURING THE EPIDEMIC.—BY THEO. R. DAVIS.—[SEE PAGE 899.]

Boston's business district. The fire leaped rapidly from one building to the next. A lack of building codes and wooden buildings built too close together contributed to the rapid spread of the fire, but the epizootic played a role as well.

The Great Epizootic of 1872 was the largest recorded outbreak of its kind in history. It's estimated that 75 to 90% of the horses in the United States became ill before the outbreak subsided in 1873. The equine death rate ranged from two to ten percent of infected horses with the highest rates in large cities where horses were kept in crowded stables.

In an 1873 report for the American Public Health Association, Dr. Adoniram Judson collected quotes from newspapers around the country.

> *At least seven eighths of the entire number of animals in this city were suffering from the disease.* —Boston, Mass.
>
> *The horses not affected by it are the exceptions.* —New Bedford, Mass.
>
> *The epizootic has attacked nearly every horse in this city.* —St. Joseph, Mo.
>
> *Every one of the sixty horses in the barn was affected, and such a coughing, wheezing, and blowing of noses no horseman ever heard before.* -Springfield, Mass.
>
> *On account of the epizootic the street cars will cease running regularly until further notice.* —Salt Lake City, Utah Terr.
>
> *The horse has almost entirely disappeared from the street, the ox becoming more and more the chief reliance for transportation.* —Cincinnati, O.
>
> *The stage has come in for the last two or three days drawn by oxen.* —Vermillion, Dak. Terr.
>
> *Our grocery men, provision dealers, etc., are delivering their goods by means of hand-carts, wheelbarrows, and wagons drawn by man-power.* —Pottsville, Penn.

Some horse owners, desperate to keep working, used their horses even when they were sick. This exertion often resulted in the animal's death. Angered by such cruelty, Henry Bergh patrolled the streets of New York City, stopping vehicles he suspected were pulled by sick horses. Bergh, founder of the American Society for the Prevention of Cruelty to Animals (ASPCA, 1866), reported drivers of horses he believed were suffering from influenza.

An attack of the illness was very sudden. The horse might be well in the evening but sick the next morning. Initial chills and shivering were followed by profuse perspiration. Symptoms experienced by the horses were outlined by Professor Liautard, of the New York College of Veterinary Surgeons. "Rigors (cold with shivering), febrile action (fever), loss of appetite, sneezing, cough, abundant discharge from one or both nostrils, accelerated respiration, listlessness, weak and compressible pulse."

> *In the barns they are all coughing. If they coughed simultaneously all over the city [Chicago] they would be heard in New York, and might bring the houses down like the walls of Jericho...*
>
> — *Chicago Tribune, November 5, 1872*

If no one knew what caused the illness, they knew even less about how to treat or cure it. That didn't stop some from offering their advice or attempting to make a profit by selling their patented medicines. Stables were disinfected and fumigated with caustic chemicals. Horses were subjected to harsh treatments such as turpentine rubbed on their gums. The practice of bleeding or blood-letting was diminishing, but even that was sometimes tried as a cure.

The simple truth was that the horses who recovered did so by being blanketed, kept warm in a well-ventilated stall, and allowed to rest. Since loss of appetite was common, more appealing feed such as a warm bran mash, encouraged them to eat.

Over the course of the nearly year-long epizootic, it's estimated 160,000 horses died in the United States. Some feared the horse influenza would be transmitted to humans, but that never happened. Most sick horses that survived were back to full health within a month.

One long-term result of the Epizootic was an increased push for research into veterinary medicine and the development of health-care practices and procedures for horses and other animals.

The epizootic made some people realize how much they had taken for granted the contribution of horses to their own lives as well as to their communities and country. Several newspapers included articles in which the authors expressed appreciation for the service of so many unrecognized horses.

It is only when we are threatened with the loss of his services that we appreciate the extent of our reliance upon the horse. Without him we would gradually go back to the condition of Troglodytes. The transient suspension of his uses, next to scarcity of bread or an earthquake, is one of the most serious disasters which can befall a community. The present malady, so mysterious in its origin, and so incredibly rapid in its spread and progress, does not seem to imperil the lives of the animals which it attacks, if ordinary precautions are taken; …

At present it seems as if the horse doctors were delirious, and know not what to do. Each one prescribes a different remedy. There is immense unwisdom in this multitude of counselors, and the horses stand in more peril from their curative endeavors than from the malady.

— Springville Journal, Springville, New York, November 16, 1872

Horses, it need hardly be observed, are very useful. Woman has the honor of being "God's last best gift to man," and horses might well put in a claim for the second place. We never fully appreciate the worth of a friend until the friend is taken away, leaving an aching void that cannot be filled. …

So it is when disease threatens to deprive us of the horse. We mourn him sincerely, not himself exactly, but his services, and feel disposed to remember and enumerate his virtues. He certainly contributes largely to our comfort. When we are born he fetches the doctor. He is the motive-power before the hearse that carries us to our last home. …

He loves us all; he licks our hand; he kicks our enemies—sometimes ourselves. He propels street cars at five cents a ride, giving employment to large numbers of conductors and drivers. He eats oats, and hay, and corn, affording joy and sometimes profit to the farmer. …

He runs races and runs away. He smashes buggies and gives wages to carriage-makers. He "sniffs the battle afar off," and gallops madly to death in the cavalry charge. He is a courageous creature, under the pressure of circumstances. …

He is one of the pioneers of civilization on the frontier beyond the city limits. He helps to rebuild the city, conveying the material to the buildings and elevating it to the topmost story. He is a luxury, a comfort, a convenience, a necessity, a docile patient slave, a creature capable of loving and of being loved, interesting and intelligent, competent to do most everything but stand on his head, climb up a ladder, talk, and vote, and in these days of universal suffrage he ought to have the ballot, considering that he knows nearly as much as many that have.

We appreciate the horse now, if we never did before; we pity him in his suffering; we are kind to him, we nurse him, we pour physic down him, we wrap him in flannel, give him dainty food, restrain the hand raised to strike him; for the time being we become voluntary members of the Humane Society, and are gentle and considerate in proportion to the value of our animals.

— Chicago Tribune, November 5, 1872

8

Williamsburg Warnings

Several men received medals for their heroic actions on Saturday, May 16, 1874. The men passed on a warning more immediately urgent than the one carried by the patriot Paul Revere. Undoubtedly, there were many unrecognized heroes that day, including several faithful horses.

The men warned villagers of the collapse of the Williamsburg Dam, high on the east branch of the Mill River in Western Massachusetts. Some hearers heeded the warnings, hurrying to safety on higher ground. Tragically, not everyone received the message in time. Some who did, didn't take the warning seriously.

In two hours, flood waters ripped an eight-mile path through the villages in the narrow valley along the banks of the Mill River—Williamsburg, Skinnerville, Haydenville, Leeds, and Florence. It was the first man-made dam disaster in America and would be the worst until the Johnstown, Pennsylvania flood fifteen years later. More than two thousand lives were lost in the Johnstown flood.

As the Civil War came to an end, owners of the mills and factories on the banks of the Mill River wanted a dam to control the water power they harnessed to run their equipment. The businesses produced a variety of items, including buttons, brass works, baskets, brushes, sewing machines, rifles, hoes, rakes, paper, silk, cotton, and wool.

The mill owners were tired of being at the mercy of nature. In the early spring, too much water rushed down the river. Then, the flow slowed to a trickle during the hot, summer months. A dam and reservoir would allow them to store the early rains and release the water as needed throughout the year.

In 1865, the state legislature granted a charter to the Williamsburg Reservoir Company to create a dam. The Company consisted of representatives from the village mills. The first order of business was to receive designs for the project. Two engineering firms presented proposals which were rejected because of the Company's limited budget of $30,000.

Lucius Fenn, a railroad surveyor and friend of one of the mill owners, also presented a design. Fenn had never built a dam before, and his initial concept was not strong enough. It was even less so after the mill owners convinced him to lower his standards. Nevertheless, the Company approved Fenn's design, and then selected a construction company. The builders, Emory Wells and Joel Bassett, cut corners even further.

Construction was completed on January 11, 1866. The Williamsburg Dam stood forty-three feet high and six hundred feet wide. The dam would hold back the water of a one-hundred-acre reservoir capable of holding six hundred million gallons. That amount of water weighed two and a half million tons. Once completed, the dam developed a slow leak almost immediately.

Joel Hayden, Sr., supervisor of the reservoir for seven years, kept the water low at first, not confident the dam would hold at higher levels. On rainy nights, Hayden, in his late sixties and early seventies at the time, sometimes lay awake unable to sleep because of his anxiety about the dam's safety. He often saddled his horse and rode up to check the condition of the dam. When Joel Hayden died in 1873, the villagers lost the oversight of its most concerned mill owner.

Onslow Spelman, owner of a button factory in Williamsburg, became the unofficial overseer in Hayden's place. However, next to Joel Hayden, the man most concerned about the dam was its tender or gatekeeper, George Cheney. Cheney, twenty-nine, had held his position since 1871. He lived with his wife, five children, and his parents in a cabin near the west end of the dam. George was a conscientious man and had repeatedly warned the mill owners of seepage through the dam's embankment.

Besides monitoring the status of the dam and reservoir, Cheney's other duty was to open and close the gate pipe. When the river level dropped, he opened the pipe, allowing water to flow from the reservoir into the river. When the river reached the height needed for the mills and factories, Cheney shut the gate pipe to stop the flow.

In April 1874, heavy storms dumped large amounts of snow in the area. When the snow began to melt in May, Cheney was instructed to close the gate pipe so the reservoir could fill. On Friday, May 15, Onslow Spelman accompanied Cheney for an official inspection of the dam. By this time, the reservoir was full and spilling over into a designated overflow area. Finding no new leaks, the two concluded the dam was in its "normal" condition.

At six the following morning, George went out in the rain to perform his early check. Finding nothing out of the ordinary, he returned to the cabin for breakfast. After the family finished eating, George's father, Elias, looked out a window and saw a huge slab of earth, forty feet wide and twenty-five feet high, slide off the east side of the dam's bank.

With no thought of the danger to himself, George rushed to the dam and opened the gate pipe. He hoped draining water from the reservoir might relieve enough pressure on the walls to prevent a collapse.

Cheney then rushed to the barn to bridle his horse, a thin, twelve-year-old, chestnut mare he'd purchased for $75.[1] She was described as "a sharp-boned animal, poor in flesh, and not a pleasant animal to ride."

Cheney didn't waste time saddling her, but galloped bareback three miles down the hill toward the first village of Williamsburg. Within minutes, Cheney reached Onslow Spelman's home, the largest and fanciest in the village. Newspapers at the time erroneously reported Cheney's horse dropped dead in the street after the hard ride. She did not.

When informed the dam was about to give, Spelman refused to believe it, arguing with Cheney that it wasn't possible. Later, some claimed the two argued as long as fifteen minutes—precious time that could have been used to warn more people.

Convinced at last, Spelman ordered Cheney to ride on to warn people in the next village. After the mad gallop down from the dam, Cheney's mare was exhausted. He hurried to Belcher's Livery nearby for a fresh mount.

Milkman, Collins Graves, in the middle of his normal delivery route, observed Cheney's frenzied pace and caught up with him at Belcher's. Cheney explained about the dam giving way. Collins' only question was, "Do you mean it?"

"Yes. I do," Cheney responded.

George Cheney and his mare

"Well, if that's so, somebody's got to let them know it; you, George, alarm the folks here, and I'll drive down the river." Graves jumped back into his milk wagon to head toward Skinnerville, leaving Cheney to warn the people in Williamsburg.

Cheney started off on a fresh livery horse and warned a few more people before high water prevented any further advance. Concerned for his own family, he turned around and started back for the cabin, taking an alternate route on higher ground. His mare, left hot and exhausted in the livery stable, stood for hours in flood water up to her back, but she survived the ordeal.

In George's absence, his wife, Elizabeth, watched the dam. Twenty minutes after the initial slide, she saw the eastern half of the dam explode from the bottom upward "as though someone had inserted a giant shovel under the base and thrown the dirt skyward."

The gaping hole in the embankment allowed the water to rush out of the reservoir, making "an awful noise, like an earthquake." An hour later, all six hundred million gallons of water had drained out of the reservoir.

Collins Graves galloped his black mare through Williamsburg, a half dozen milk cans clattering in the wagon. As he drove, he shouted, "The reservoir is right here! Run, 'tis all you can do!" But with the noise of the rain and the machines in the factories, few heard his warning.

At seven-thirty, a twenty-foot-high wall of flood water hit Williamsburg, taking houses and factories with it, including the skeptical Onslow Spelman's button factory.

Collins Graves and his mare

Just five minutes ahead of the flood, Graves drove to Skinnerville which had thirty-five buildings and a population of two hundred. From there, he continued another mile to Haydenville, stopping first at the large brass works factory where he spoke to the superintendent, Samuel Wentworth. Wentworth ridiculed Graves, claiming that if there was a flood, it wouldn't reach his factory for days.

Since Graves hadn't seen the flood himself, he began to doubt. If Cheney was wrong and there was no flood, everyone would think Graves was foolish. He turned around and headed back to Williamsburg. Graves hadn't gone far when he met the third hero of the day, Jerome Hillman, rushing toward him on horseback, shouting, "Go back! A flood is coming!"

Now, Graves saw the flood for himself, in the distance behind Hillman. Graves and Hillman went different directions in Haydenville, with just two minutes to warn as many as they could.

Hillman asked a man at the church to ring the bell. When the man refused to believe him, Hillman climbed the tower and rang the bell a few times. By then, the river was rising into the village streets.

Graves' last stop was a hotel where the proprietor, Luther Loomis, let the horses out of his stable so they could run to safety. Then, Graves had no choice but to move to higher ground himself to avoid the approaching flood.

Twelve-year-old Jimmy Ryan also took heroic action that day. Upon hearing of the flood, Jimmy helped his mother and five younger brothers to safety, then drove his family's farm wagon from Williamsburg to the brass works at Haydenville to warn the workers, including his father and a brother. It's unclear whether Graves or Ryan arrived at the brass works first.

At seven-forty-five, the flood arrived in Haydenville with a deafening roar. But now, it wasn't just water. Houses, barns, factories, bridges, and trees tumbled along in the massive flood wall that swept through the village.

Another hero, farmer Myron Day, had heard Hillman's warning in Haydenville. He raced his horse and wagon toward Leeds, yelling, "Fire!" Day figured that might get a better response than a flood warning.

A few minutes after eight o'clock, the flood reached the village of Leeds. From Leeds, it was another mile to Florence. The flatter land in Florence allowed the water to spread out and subside. The flood lost its force, leaving behind mud and gravel two to three feet deep with a layer of debris above that reaching another six to ten feet high.

38

Cheney (l) and Graves (r), Cheney starts his ride

Although the actions of George Cheney, Collins Graves, Jerome Hillman, Myron Day, and Jimmy Ryan saved the lives of many, one hundred and thirty-nine people died in the Mill River flood. The first four men received specially designed gold medals in an award ceremony in November 1874. Jimmy Ryan's role was not recognized until years later.

Jerome Hillman's medal was small consolation. Hillman lost his wife and house in the flood. His seven-year-old daughter, Clara, survived.

Poems were written about Cheney and Graves.

> *Ride! Cheney, ride! For close beside,*
> *On a ghostly galloping steed,*
> *Is a grizzly shade, in a shroud arrayed;*
> *Death rides behind thee! Speed!*

And the beginning of one written of Graves:

> *His hat is gone—his hair in the wind*
> *Streams back from his earnest face,*
> *And turning his head he glances behind,*
> *Yet never relaxes his pace.*

George Cheney's family survived. Contemporary newspaper reports indicate a man, S. J. Hobbs, purchased Cheney's mare. His intent was to exhibit her around the country with Cheney, who would speak about his ride and the collapse of the dam. It doesn't seem this tour ever took place. The cabin the Cheneys lived in burned in 1880, destroying his medal.

Collins Graves' mare became lame after her race from Williamsburg to Haydenville. She never recovered and had to be put down less than a year later. A few criticized Collins Graves, claiming he abandoned the people of his own village, Williamsburg, to warn the people of Skinnerville and Haydenville. This criticism wounded him. Graves had done his best and only left Williamsburg because he believed Cheney was warning the people there.

William Worthen, a member of ASCE, the American Society of Civil Engineers, inspected the dam site after the collapse.

> *Men were employed who were ignorant of the work to be done, and there was nothing like an inspection, although money and life depended upon it. I do not believe, however much we are an evolved species, that we are derived from beavers; a man cannot make a dam by instinct or intuition.*

After the flood, testimony at a five-day inquest was heard from forty-two witnesses. The blame for the collapse of the dam was determined to rest on:

- The state legislature, because there were no laws regarding the construction or inspection of the dam
- The dam owners, who cut corners on the design and construction of the dam to save money
- Lucius Fenn, whose design was not strong enough to hold the reservoir's water
- Wells and Bassett the builders, for poor construction practices
- The County commissioners, who didn't perform adequate inspections and repairs of the dam

Despite identifying the parties responsible for the catastrophe, no criminal charges or civil lawsuits were filed. No one was held financially responsible for the loss of lives and property.

The horses of the five heroes provided a vital service by transporting the men as they spread their warnings that day. Horses also provided the power to clean up the devastation left behind by the flood. Later, horses hauled the materials to rebuild the mills, factories, and homes in the valley. The dam was never rebuilt.

The Mill River catastrophe prompted the passage of stricter regulations for the design and construction of dams and provided for more rigorous inspections.

---

1. An average horse at the time sold for $150. Based on the photo of Cheney on the horse, the mare is not very tall and may actually have been a pony.

9

Aristides

The Kentucky Derby, known today as the Run for the Roses, is the oldest continuously held sporting event in the United States. The Derby has been run every year since 1875. The race was the idea of Meriwether Lewis Clark, grandson of William Clark of the Lewis and Clark Expedition. After watching popular races in England, such as the Epsom Derby, Clark wanted to create a similar event in the United States. He founded the Louisville Jockey Club in Kentucky and leased eighty acres of land for the racetrack from his uncles, John and Henry Churchill.

The May 17, 1875 race was held on a beautiful, sunny day at the new Louisville Jockey Club track (later renamed Churchill Downs). The Kentucky Derby was open to three-year-old Thoroughbreds. Fifteen horses entered the mile and a half long race—thirteen colts and two fillies. Ten thousand spectators were in attendance.

Henry Price (H. P.) McGrath had two horses in the race. Aristides, a chestnut with a star and two hind stockings, was a small horse, standing about 15 hands. McGrath favored his second horse, a large bay named Chesapeake, considering him the better prospect to win the race.

Chesapeake was Aristides' half-brother. Both horses were born on the McGrathiana Farm in Fayette County, Kentucky, near Lexington. Ansel Williamson was their trainer. Ansel, a former slave, born in 1806, had worked as a racehorse trainer for his owners before the Civil War.

McGrath explained his game plan to Aristides' jockey, nineteen-year-old African-American Oliver Lewis. Lewis was to take Aristides out front early while Chesapeake's jockey, William Henry, held the favored horse back. Once Aristides' fast pace tired the field, Aristides would fade, allowing Chesapeake to come from behind for the win.

The only problem was they forgot to inform Aristides of the plan.

McCreery got off to a quick lead with Aristides second and Volcano third. But McCreery hadn't fully recovered from an illness and didn't have the stamina to continue the fast pace. Although Volcano and Verdigris challenged Aristides, they couldn't match the small chestnut's speed that day. Knowing his horse wasn't

supposed to win, Oliver Lewis glanced back, looking for Chesapeake. But the other horse wasn't close enough to make up the difference.

H. P. McGrath waved the jockey on, and Aristides crossed the finish line ahead of Volcano by two lengths. McGrath's favorite, Chesapeake, finished a distant eighth. Not only did Aristides win by a good margin, he set a new American record for the mile and a half distance—2:37.75. The winner received $2,850 and the second-place finisher $200.

The field for the first Kentucky Derby finished in this order.

<table>
<tr><td>1. Aristides</td><td>9. Searcher</td></tr>
<tr><td>2. Volcano</td><td>10. Ascension (filly)</td></tr>
<tr><td>3. Verdigris</td><td>11. Enlister</td></tr>
<tr><td>4. Bob Woolley</td><td>12. McCreery</td></tr>
<tr><td>5. Ten Broeck</td><td>13. Warsaw</td></tr>
<tr><td>6. Grenoble</td><td>14. Vagabond</td></tr>
<tr><td>7. Bill Bruce</td><td>15. Gold Mine (filly)</td></tr>
<tr><td>8. Chesapeake</td><td></td></tr>
</table>

The following month, Oliver Lewis rode Aristides to a second-place finish in the Belmont Stakes. The winner of the Belmont was another McGrath horse named Calvin, also trained by Ansel Williamson. Aristides raced twenty-one times with nine wins. He died on June 21, 1893 at twenty-one. The Aristides Stakes race at Churchill Downs was named in honor of the horse. A life-sized, bronze statue of him stands in the Clubhouse Gardens.

African-Americans dominated horse racing in the 1800s. Not only was Oliver Lewis black, so were thirteen of the fifteen jockeys in that first race. Black jockeys won fifteen of the first twenty-eight Kentucky Derbies, and black men trained six of the first seventeen Derby winners.

Oliver Lewis never rode in the Kentucky Derby again and may never have raced after 1875. It seems he switched to the gambling side of racing, becoming a bookmaker, a legal profession at the time. Lewis died in 1924 in Lexington, Kentucky.

In 1896, the Derby was shortened from a mile and a half to a mile and a quarter. That same year, the tradition of placing roses on the winning horse began. Today, a garland of 554 roses is draped over the winner's neck.

In 1915, general manager, Matt Winn, convinced Harry Payne Whitney to enter his filly, Regret, in the race. Regret became the first filly to win the Derby. The resulting national publicity helped increase the prestige and popularity of the race, especially with women. Two other fillies have won the Kentucky Derby—Genuine Risk (1980) and Winning Colors (1988). Out of eleven starts in her four seasons of racing (1914–1917), Regret won nine times and placed second once.

Since 1932, the Derby has been held on the first Saturday in May. Sometimes called "The Most Exciting Two Minutes in Sports," the Derby is the first leg of the Triple Crown. The other two Triple Crown races are the Preakness Stakes in Baltimore, Maryland, and the Belmont Stakes in Elmont, New York.

On May 16, 1925, the first live broadcast of the Kentucky Derby aired on radio stations in Chicago. And on May 7, 1949, the race was first televised.

10

Sleepy Tom

An English Thoroughbred, Messenger, foaled in 1780 and later exported to the United States, was the great-grandsire of Hambletonian 10. Every Standardbred horse traces his lineage back to Hambletonian.

In the early days, trotters dominated harness racing, but the first harness horse to break the two-minute mile was a pacer. On August 28, 1897, Star Pointer raced a mile in 1:59 1/4.

At the pace, a horse's legs move laterally, the right front and right hind hit the ground together and then the left front and left hind. The trot is a diagonal gait. The right front and left hind move together, then the left front and right hind.

Before Star Pointer, there was Sleepy Tom. Although he never beat the two-minute mark, Tom was arguably a more amazing record setter. Sleepy Tom set his mile pacing record in 1879. That record stood for two years until another pacer named Little Brown Jug beat it.

Over the years, racing records are continually set and beaten. What made Sleepy Tom's special? The Boonville Enquirer stated it rather bluntly.

> *The fact that Sleepy Tom was stone blind and ugly only tended to increase the public interest in him. He was about the toughest looking piece of horseflesh ever seen on a speed ring and was generally the laughing stock of spectators who were not familiar with his marvelous powers of speed.*
>
> *— The Boonville Enquirer, Boonville, Indiana, September 3, 1887*

A totally blind horse setting speed records? It sounds unbelievable, but many contemporary newspaper articles confirm Tom's racing career.

Sleepy Tom was foaled in the village of Bellbrook, Ohio on June 22, 1868. His name was chosen because of his laziness as a colt. Tom was a chestnut with bold white markings. At three, Charley Dingler trained Tom. He first raced in Columbus, Ohio with a time of 2:40 1/2. During his years with Dingler, Tom was often driven hard. Some reports say a hot, lathered Tom was once driven into a river to cool off, and the abrupt change in temperature damaged his health. Others believe Tom developed a severe cold which settled in his eyes. Whatever the cause, Tom gradually lost his sight and was completely blind by the age of seven.

Considering Tom's racing days over, Mr. Dingler sold him in 1875. The blind horse was ill-treated and passed between several owners before being purchased by a harness racing trainer, Stephen C. Phillips.

Phillips was aware of Tom's early racing days and had kept an eye on the horse. The price for Tom was $7.50 and a jug of whiskey. Other accounts say a pint of whiskey and $5. Either way, Phillips wouldn't be out much if he couldn't turn Tom around.

With compassionate care and careful training, Phillips restarted the blind horse's career. The new team started racing in 1878 and began to win—often. In fact, Sleepy Tom became one-fourth of a famous quartet of pacers who attracted great crowds in their day. The others included Mattie Hunter, Lucy, and Rowdy Boy. The four competed against each other in a series of races known as the Grand Circuit.

Phillips considered an August 1879 race against those three to be his horse's best performance. He was the eventual winner of the race that went to six heats with Tom winning the second (2:16 1/2), fifth (2:13 1/2), and sixth (2:14).

But it was the month before, on July 27, 1879, in Chicago Illinois, that Sleepy Tom set his world record for the mile pace. Tom won two of the first four heats on the 26th, but darkness prevented the race from being completed. The next heat was postponed until the following day. In the fifth and final heat, Tom set a pacing record of 2:12 1/4.

A reporter for The Star Tribune described the blind horse's amazing performance, referring to Tom as "Sleepy Tom, the blind whirlwind of the Buckeye state."

> *To a blind horse there is necessarily more in the human voice than one with sight. It is sound and not object that claims his attention. For a blind horse to be a successful racer he most have absolute confidence in his driver. Let once a serious mishap befall him; let him once feel that he is liable at any moment to rush upon an accident, and his usefulness is gone. With the sense of sight closed, those of feeling and hearing are necessarily quickened, and, as it is by these he must be guided, it is needless to say that they should never be deceived or abused.*

At the peak of Tom's success, Phillips sold the horse to Joe Udell of Wisconsin for $6,000. Phillips used the money from the sale to purchase a farm in Ohio where he raised, trained, and sold Standardbreds. Sleepy Tom continued racing, winning a few more races from 1880 to 1882, but his age and early neglect caught up with him, and the horse slowed down.

Later, Phillips returned to search for Tom. He wanted to buy him back so the horse could spend his last days on Phillip's Ohio farm. But Sleepy Tom had been sold one last time to a man in Indiana. He died there in a barn fire in 1886.

In 1939, Dwight Akers wrote a fictional account of the horse titled, *Sleepy Tom*.

The blind pacing wonder was inducted as an "immortal" into the Harness Racing Museum and Hall of Fame in 1992.

A nephew of Stephen C. Phillips, Stephen G. Phillips, developed the first successful mobile starting gate for harness racers. Before starting gates were used, races began with a rolling start. Horses were driven in circles until they formed into a straight line. If stewards determined a competitor wasn't fairly in line with the others, a false start was called, and the race would be started over again. Several false starts might occur before the race got off to a fair start.

Little Brown Jug, the horse that broke Sleepy Tom's record, didn't have an easy life either. As a thin yearling, covered with lice, he was sold for less than $50. At two, a sharecropper purchased him to plow fields. At three, he was sold again and began racing. After enormous success, Little Brown Jug continued to be sold for lower and lower prices, into more difficult situations, until Captain Campbell of Cleburne Stock Farm in Spring Hill, Tennessee, rescued him. Little Brown Jug lived out his last days at Campbell's farm, dying in 1899 at twenty-four.

Edward "Pop" Geers never drove Little Brown Jug in a race but had driven him in workouts. He said of the horse,

> *What he was as a racehorse we know, but what he might have been had he received the care and attention in his early career bestowed upon promising racehorses in modern times is a matter of conjecture.*

The horse has a race named after him. The Little Brown Jug, held in Ohio at the Delaware County Fairgrounds on the third Thursday after Labor Day, is one of the most prestigious races for three-year-old pacers, dating back to 1946. A horse must win two heats to be declared the winner of the "Jug."

11

Comanche

Slavery and the treatment of Native Americans are two of the biggest stains on the United States. Time after time, the U.S. Government broke treaties with Native American tribes and pushed them off of land white settlers decided they wanted.

First, they were pushed from the East to west of the Mississippi River by the Indian Removal Act of 1830 signed by President Andrew Jackson. The Trail of Tears occurred in 1838, and the last Cherokees were forced to travel 1,200 miles on foot. Thousands died along the way.

In 1851, the Indian Appropriations Act created a reservation system and provided funds to move Native Americans onto reservations where the government hoped they could control them. The goal was for the Natives to abandon their nomadic lifestyle and begin farming.

The U.S. signed the first and second Treaties of Fort Laramie in 1851 and 1868 with Natives in the areas of Montana, Wyoming, Nebraska, and the Dakotas. Promises were made to provide protection for the tribes and not to claim land in those areas.

George Armstrong Custer was appointed lieutenant colonel of the Army's 7th Cavalry Regiment. In 1874, men on an expedition he led found small amounts of gold in South Dakota's Black Hills. This discovery triggered the Black Hills Gold Rush.

According to the Treaty of Laramie, that area belonged to the Sioux, however that didn't stop thousands of gold prospectors from flocking into the Black Hills. Some miners made fortunes with gold found along the creeks in the Black Hills.

The government offered to buy the land. When the Natives refused, Custer was sent to force the Lakota Sioux out of the area.

As he approached, Custer discovered an Indian encampment along the Little Bighorn River in Montana Territory. Crow scouts working for Custer warned him it was the largest village they'd ever seen. But Custer insisted it was best to attack immediately. If they lost the element of surprise, he believed the Natives would scatter. Custer's regiment of seven hundred men was no match for two thousand Native warriors—the combined tribes of the Lakota, Cheyenne, and Arapaho.

On the morning of June 25, 1876, Custer divided his companies into three groups. One, under the command of Major Marcus Reno, would attack from the south. Captain Frederick Benteen's force would scout out the area further south to prevent anyone from escaping and then report back to Custer. The largest group of 210 men was under Custer's command and would approach the village from the north. Custer hoped to capture women and children as hostages, forcing the Natives to surrender and then relocate.

Major Reno's force crossed the Little Bighorn first, attempting an attack from south of the village. Custer's Arikara scout, Bloody Knife, was killed in this attack. Most of the other scouts escaped. Surprised by the number of warriors opposing him, Reno ordered his men back across the river in a disastrous retreat. When the supply wagons reached them, it's said Reno drank a bottle of whiskey and was so intoxicated he couldn't command his troops.

Captain Benteen wasn't much better. Custer sent a message to Benteen to join him and bring additional ammunition packs. Instead, Benteen remained with Reno's forces who had regrouped along steep bluffs east of the village. Both officers were later accused of cowardice for abandoning Custer and his men.

Custer's men approached the village from the north and were met by the warriors who had forced Reno's retreat. Custer and every man in his force were killed in less than half an hour. Custer's two younger brothers, Thomas Ward Custer (31) and Boston Custer (27), were killed in the battle as was his nephew, Henry Armstrong Reed (18), and a brother-in-law, James Calhoun (30).

From atop the bluff, Reno and Benteen's forces held off the remaining Natives until late in the afternoon of the 26th, when the Indians broke up their village and moved south.

> *Reno proved incompetent and Benteen showed his indifference—I will not use the uglier words that have often been in my mind. Both failed Custer and he had to fight it out alone.*
>
> *— Private William Taylor, M Troop 7th US cavalry, veteran of Little Bighorn*

Ulysses Grant blamed the horrific losses at the Little Bighorn on Custer's determination to attack the Native village early to catch them by surprise. Additional forces led by General Alfred Terry and Colonel John Gibbon would have reached them the following day, making it a more even battle. Others claim Custer's chances would have been better if he hadn't split the men into three groups.

The Battle of the Little Bighorn, also known as Custer's Last Stand, was the worst U.S. Army defeat in the Indian Wars. It increased the government's efforts to subdue the tribes. Within five years, nearly all the Sioux and Cheyenne were confined to reservations.

If there is any bright spot to that horrible event, it's the story of the one living thing found on the gruesome battlefield. When men arrived two days later to bury the fallen soldiers, Sergeant Milton J. DeLacey discovered the horse, Comanche.

Comanche lay in a ravine, barely alive. He had suffered multiple wounds and injuries to his neck, shoulder, and hindquarters. A steamer, Far West, transported the horse to Fort Lincoln, 950 miles away, where he spent the next year recuperating.

Farrier John Rivers of Keogh's Company I described Comanche's care.

> *He was raised up and tenderly cared for. His wounds were serious, but not necessarily fatal if properly looked after … He carries seven scars from as many bullet wounds. There are four back of the foreshoulder, one through a hoof, and one on either hind leg. On the Custer battlefield three of the balls were extracted from his body and the last one was not taken out until April 1877.*

Comanche was not Custer's horse. Custer had two horses at the time—a sorrel Thoroughbred, a former racehorse, Vic (for Victory). His second was a Morgan mix, a bay named Dandy. He rode Vic into this last battle. Some reports claim Vic was captured and became the mount of a Native, Walks-Under-the-Ground. Others insist the horse's remains were identified on the battle field. Dandy survived since he had been left with the supply train. He was later returned to the Custer family.

Comanche was the mount of Myles Walter Keogh. During this campaign, Keogh had a second horse, Paddy. Natives reported that Keogh fought bravely to the very end, dying with Comanche's reins still gripped in his hand.

Born in Ireland, Myles Keogh served in the cavalry of the Union Army during the Civil War. Keogh's horse during much of the war was Tom. In a letter to his sister, Keogh claimed the horse saved his life when they'd been surprised by Confederates. The horse jumped sideways over a fence and run off into the woods. In 1864, while trying to free Union soldiers from the Andersonville prison in Georgia, Confederate soldiers shot and killed Tom. Keogh mourned the horse's loss and was certain he would never have another animal as good as Tom.

After the war, Keogh was selected to command Company I in George Custer's 7th Cavalry Regiment. In need of additional horses, Thomas Custer, George's younger brother, purchased a group of forty-one Mustangs in Fort Leavenworth, Kansas. The horses received the "US" brand on their left shoulder and "C" on their left thigh, for U.S. Cavalry. They were loaded into rail cars and transported to the cavalry encampment.

Comanche was six years old when he was purchased by the Cavalry for $90. He may have been part Morgan. Although some call him a bay, his body was a lighter reddish color with a dark red mane, tail, and lower legs, probably a dun. He stood 15 hands and weighed about 925 pounds. His only markings were a small star on his forehead and a coronet on his left hind leg.

It's unclear how Comanche and Keogh connected. Keogh may have purchased him as his personal horse rather than just using him as a cavalry mount. The horse wasn't called Comanche at first. Various theories exist as to how he acquired his name. Some claim that when shot by an arrow, the horse let out a yell like a Comanche war cry.

Many tributes were paid to the brave horse. This one is from John Hay, who served as Abraham Lincoln's private secretary.

> *… of all that stood at noonday in that fiery scorpion ring,*
> *Miles Keogh's horse at evening was the only living thing.*
> *Alone from that field of slaughter, where lay the three hundred slain,*
> *The horse Comanche wandered, with Keogh's blood on his mane …*

In April 1878, U.S. Army Colonel Samuel D. Sturgis, whose son died at the Little Bighorn, issued United States Cavalry Order No. 7.

1. The horse known as "Comanche," being the only living representative of the bloody tragedy of the Little Big Horn, June 25th, 1876, his kind treatment and comfort shall be a matter of special pride and solicitude on the part of every member of the Seventh Cavalry to the end that his life be preserved to the utmost limit. Wounded and scarred as he is, his very existence speaks in terms more eloquent than words, of the desperate struggle against overwhelming numbers of the hopeless conflict and the heroic manner in which all went down on that fatal day.

Miles Keogh

2. The commanding officer of Company I will see that a special and comfortable stable is fitted up for him, and he will not be ridden by any person whatsoever, under any circumstances, nor will he be put to any kind of work.

3. Hereafter, upon all occasions of ceremony of mounted regimental formation, "Comanche," saddled, bridled, and draped in mourning, and led by a mounted trooper of Company I, will be paraded with the regiment.

For years, Comanche remained at Fort Meade, South Dakota, where he was named Second Commanding Officer of the 7th Cavalry. Excused from all duties, he roamed the grounds, occasionally appearing in parades, saddled but always riderless, in memory of the soldiers who lost their lives at the Little Bighorn.

Comanche bonded with Gustave Korn, the farrier of the 7th Cavalry. The two had something in common—surviving the Little Bighorn. Korn, a German, immigrated to the U.S. from Prussia in 1873. Upon joining the Army, he was assigned to Keogh's Cavalry Company I.

Korn's unruly horse saved his life on that fateful day. Several members of the surviving companies confirmed the story of Gustave's horse running off with him.

Comanche followed Korn around the fort like a faithful dog. It's said he even tracked Korn to his girlfriend's home in town if the man remained there too long. The animal neighed and pawed at the door until Gustave came out and led him back to the post.

Gustave and Comanche were together for fifteen years until Korn was killed at the Wounded Knee Massacre on December 29, 1890, in South Dakota. Due to the loss of his friend and his advancing age, Comanche's health declined the following year. Another farrier, Samuel Winchester, cared for Comanche after Korn's passing.

In November 1891, Comanche suffered a bad attack of colic. Winchester held the horse's head in his lap on the night of November 7th as the great horse passed away at the age of twenty-nine.

Although Comanche was the only surviving horse found on the battlefield, there may have been more than one hundred Cavalry horses taken alive as the spoils of battle by the victorious Native Americans.

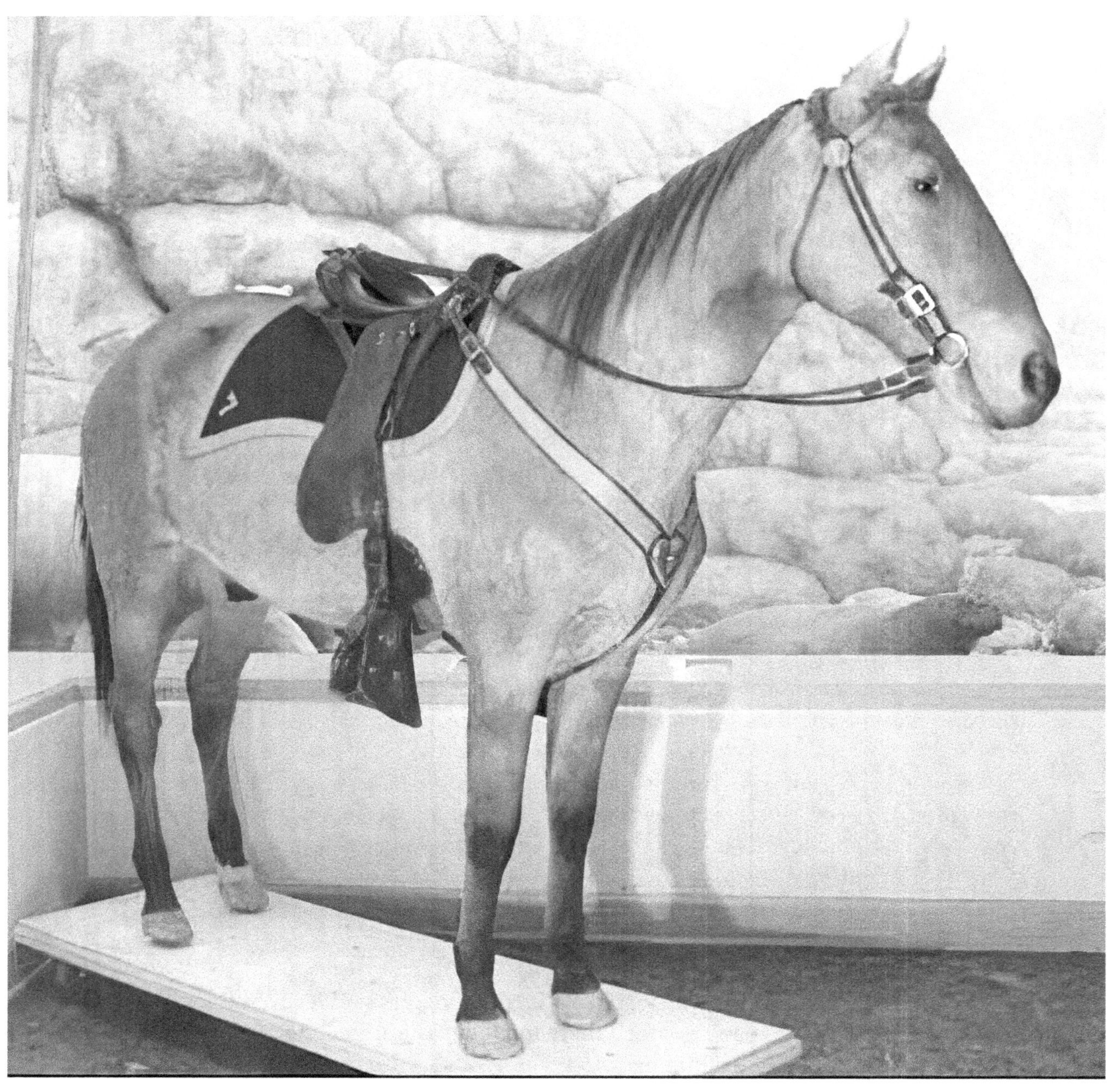

Taxidermist Lewis Dyche preserved Comanche who is now on display in a humidity controlled glass case at the University of Kansas Museum of Natural History in Lawrence, Kanasas.

12

Black Beauty

When Abraham Lincoln met Harriet Beecher Stowe, author of *Uncle Tom's Cabin*, he greeted her with, "So you're the little woman who wrote the book that made this great war!"

As Stowe's book helped raise awareness about the evils of slavery, Anna Sewell's *Black Beauty* had a similar impact for the humane treatment of horses.

Although Black Beauty was a fictional character, he represented the living horses used for work and transportation in the days when city streets were crowded with horse-drawn vehicles. The impact of this fictional character on the future treatment of horses was incalculable.

Black Beauty is narrated from the imaginative point of view of the horse himself, covering his life and treatment from birth to retirement. Black Beauty had several owners, some kind, others ignorant, and a few downright mean. Her aim was to help the reader see that horses weren't unfeeling machines to be cruelly worked to death on the streets of England.

Sewell opposed overwork and any inhumane treatment. One of her biggest objections was to the use of the bearing or check rein. This leather strap fastened from the horse's bridle to the harness near his withers to hold the animal's head up. When not too tight, it can be a useful part of the harness. But it was considered stylish, at the time, to have horses' heads pulled high—the higher, the better. This unnatural position was tiring, painful, and didn't allow the horse to use his strength effectively. Black Beauty describes his experience with the bearing rein.

WITH BEARING REIN.

Day by day, hole by hole, our bearing reins were shortened, and instead of looking forward with pleasure to having my harness put on, as I used to do, I began to dread it. …

What I suffered with that rein for four long months in my lady's carriage it would be hard to describe; but I am quite sure that, had it lasted much longer, either my health or my temper would have given way. Before that, I never knew what it was to foam at the mouth, but now the action of the sharp bit on my tongue and jaw, and the constrained position of my head and throat, always caused me to froth at the mouth more or less. Some people think it very fine to see this, and say, "What fine spirited creatures!" But it is just as unnatural for horses as for men to foam at the mouth; it is a sure sign of some discomfort, and should be attended to. Besides this, there was a pressure on my windpipe, which often made my breathing very uncomfortable; when I returned from my work my neck and chest were strained and painful, my mouth and tongue tender, and I felt worn and depressed.

— Black Beauty, chapter 22, 23

Sometimes sympathy and compassion are most pronounced in those who have known suffering themselves. Such was the case with Anna Sewell. Her struggles with illness and injury gave her a unique insight into the poor treatment of the horses she loved.

Anna was born to Quaker parents, Mary and Isaac Sewell, on March 30, 1820 in Great Yarmouth, England. Their mother initially educated Anna and her younger brother, Philip, at home.

Anna and Philip often visited their maternal grandparents' farm where Anna learned to drive horses and ride (sidesaddle).

In 1832, when Anna was twelve, the family moved from their cramped home near London to Palatine Cottage, part of a former stable and coach house. The children were delighted with the meadow and gardens and the opportunity to raise their own animals. Anna attended a day school about a mile from their home.

Two years later, Anna fell while returning home from school. She injured her ankle and was lame, to some degree, for the rest of her life. Anna spent six months with her grandparents as she convalesced, and while there, grew well enough to ride horses again.

At nineteen, Anna's health worsened. She experienced chest and back pains, fatigue, inability to concentrate, and depression. Various cures were sought and tried, but the medical practices of the day were not advanced enough to determine the illness or provide a cure. Once she was bled so severely that the "cure" proved worse than the disease.

Despite these difficulties, Anna could see God working in her life through the lameness and ill health.

I have felt it very sweet to receive this improvement in my feet (which continues) from the Hand of Jesus. I would not be without this dispensation, and pray Thee, Lord, to do with me what Thou seest best. I thank Thee, for my lameness. I am sure it is sent in love, though it be a trial. I should without it have too much pleasure in the flesh, and have forgotten Thee.

In 1871, Anna's health took another turn for the worse. Just before her fifty-first birthday, her doctor predicted she had only eighteen months to live. In November of that year, Anna was inspired to write a story about the life of a horse. Even conversation and reading were tiring for her, but she worked on the book as her strength permitted, writing parts of the story in pencil or dictating sections to her mother.

In late 1876, Anna's health improved enough that she could complete most of her book. In addition to her crusade against animal abuse, she wove other themes she felt strongly about into the story, including the use of alcohol, smoking, fox hunting, war, and the Sabbath as a day of rest. She drew ideas from people and horses she'd known to create the characters in the book. In particular, Black Beauty was patterned after her brother Philip's horse, Bessie.

In December 1876, Anna wrote in her journal.

> *I have for six years been confined to the house and to my sofa, and have from time to time, as I was able, been writing what I think will turn out a little book, its special aim being to induce kindness, sympathy, and an understanding treatment of horses.*

When Anna completed her first draft, her mother edited the story. Once revised, Mary took the final version of the manuscript to Jarrold and Sons. They purchased the work outright for forty pounds (some sources say thirty), with no provision for royalties to the Sewells. Although it turned out to be a terrible deal financially, it was a common arrangement, especially for an author's first book. *Black Beauty* was published just in time for Christmas, 1877.

Anna's health deteriorated rapidly after the book's publication. Her doctor diagnosed her with tuberculosis and hepatitis. On April 25, 1878, in her last moments, Anna said, "Pray."

Her brother, Philip, prayed, thanking God for Anna's salvation and giving her into God's hands.

Anna responded with "Amen; it is all quite, quite true," and "I am ready."

Mary said of Anna's passing, "The angel had gone out of the house, and left a void never to be filled till we meet again."

Anna never knew the amazing success her book experienced. By 1878, it was already in a fifth printing, and by 1890, it had sold over 100,000 copies in England.

In 1890, George Angell, founder of the American Humane Education Society, was introduced to *Black Beauty* and saw the novel as a way to promote the humane treatment of animals in America. Ignoring any British copyrights, within three months Angell had printed and given away 70,000 copies to American stable hands and drivers. He added the subtitle "The Uncle Tom's Cabin of the

Horse World." By 1910, the AHES had
distributed three million copies of Sewell's
book in America.

Although now considered a children's
book, that was never Sewell's intention.
Black Beauty is one of the best-selling
books of all time. As of 2008, fifty million
copies had been sold.

> *…there is no religion without love,
> and people may talk as much as
> they like about their religion, but if
> it does not teach them to be good
> and kind to man and beast, it is all
> a sham…*
>
> *— Black Beauty, chapter 13*

56

13

Animal Welfare

Many early animal welfare organizers had Christian backgrounds. They believed there was a Biblical foundation for the kind treatment of animals. The early Puritans thought cruelty to animals was caused by Adam and Eve's sin and the resulting curse on creation.

People who wanted to protect animals often shared concerns with those working on other social issues such as the abolition of slavery and the temperance movements opposing the use of alcohol.

Although it wasn't until the 1800s that animal welfare groups formed, the earliest record in America of regulations for animal protection came from two sections of the Puritan Body of Liberties in 1641.

No man shall exercise any Tirranny or Crueltie towards any bruite Creature which are usuallie kept for mans use.

If any man shall have occasion to leade or drive Cattel from place to place that is far of, So that they be weary, or hungry, or fall sick, or lambe, It shall be lawful to rest or refresh them, for a competent time, in any open place that is not Corne, meadow, or inclosed for some peculiar use.

A brief time line of the formation of animal welfare agencies:

1824: Society for the Prevention of Cruelty to Animals (SPCA) England

1840: The SPCA becomes the RSPCA Royal Society for the Prevention of Cruelty to Animals

1866: American Society for the Prevention of Cruelty to Animals (ASPCA), Henry Bergh

1868: Massachusetts Society for the Prevention of Cruelty to Animals (MSPCA), George Angell

1869: Canadian Society for the Prevention of Cruelty to Animals

1877: American Humane Association (AHA)

1886: The Home of Rest for Horses, England

1889: American Humane Education Society, George Angell

1897: National Humane Alliance, Hermon Lee Ensign

1897: Our Dumb Friends League (ODFL) England

1912: Blue Cross Fund established by the ODFL to provide care for animals used in war

1916: American Red Star Animal Relief, created by the AHA, to rescue wounded horses, mules, and donkeys on the battlefields of World War I

1954: The Humane Society of the United States (HSUS), based in Washington, D.C.

SPCA - William Wilberforce

Wilberforce, one founder of the Society for the Prevention of Cruelty to Animals (SPCA), was a British politician. As a leading abolitionist, he's remembered most for his work in Parliament to pass legislation against slavery. The Slavery Abolition Act of 1833 abolishing slavery in England was passed shortly after Wilberforce's death.

The RSPCA provided support for the Army Veterinary Corps in treating animals such as donkeys, horses, dogs, and birds that served on the battlefields of World War I.

Horses are expensive animals to care for, and despite the best of intentions, the animal welfare agencies can't always save all of them. In 2014, the RSPCA euthanized 205 healthy horses.

> *Sadly the RSPCA sometimes has to put some animals to sleep simply because there are not enough people willing to give them a home. The country is currently in the grip of a horse crisis with the RSPCA and other horse welfare charities struggling to cope with the numbers of abandoned, neglected and abused horses. We are stretched to breaking point with about 125 places at our equine centres but more than 800 horses in our care.*

ASPCA - Henry Bergh

President Abraham Lincoln appointed Henry Bergh as a diplomat to Russia. In 1863, Bergh stopped a Russian carriage driver who was beating a horse. Deeply troubled by the cruel treatment of animals, he resigned his post and returned to New York.

In 1866, he founded the American Society for the Prevention of Cruelty to Animals, the first humane society in America. The ASPCA's original seal depicted an angel protecting a fallen cart horse from an abuser.

In addition to the treatment of overworked horses, the society worked to stop dog and cock fighting and to eliminate the use of live pigeons in shooting matches.

In 1867, the ASPCA operated the first horse ambulance—two years before New York City had an ambulance for people. The ASPCA opened a horse veterinary hospital in Manhattan in 1912. Bergh invented a canvas sling to hold injured horses that was used extensively on World War I battlefields.

Mary Ellen Wilson

In 1874, a Methodist mission worker, Etta Angell Wheeler, learned that a ten-year-old child, Mary Ellen Wilson, was being horribly abused by her foster mother, Mary Connolly.

While New York had basic laws regarding the abuse and neglect of children, authorities were reluctant to intervene when Mrs. Wheeler requested their help. In frustration, she turned to Henry Bergh of the ASPCA.

Bergh's response—"No time is to be lost — instruct me how to proceed."

An animal cruelty investigator was sent to the dirty tenement home, posing as a census worker to gain entrance. Once he verified the abuse allegations, ASPCA attorney, Elbridge Thomas Gerry, prepared the legal paperwork to remove Mary Ellen from the home. On Thursday, April 9, 1874, the girl was rescued. Mr. Bergh had accomplished this within forty-eight hours of hearing of Mary Ellen's situation.

This was the first recorded case of child abuse in the United States. On April 21, 1874, Mary Connolly was found guilty of felonious assault and sentenced to a year of hard labor in the penitentiary. When leaving the Court House after Connolly's trial, Mrs. Wheeler thanked Henry Bergh for his help and asked if there could now be a Society for the Prevention of Cruelty to Children.

"He took my hand and said very emphatically: 'There shall be one.'"

After her removal from the foster home, Mary Ellen lived with the Wheeler family. She married at twenty-four and had two daughters. She named the first Etta after the missionary who had rescued her. The second was Florence. As adults, both became teachers.

Bergh followed through with his promise. In 1875, he formed the New York Society for the Prevention of Cruelty to Children (NYSPCC), the first child protection agency in the world.

MSPCA George Thorndike Angell

Angell, the son of a Baptist minister, overcame early poverty to become a successful lawyer and abolitionist. In 1868, Angell saw two horses die during a forty-mile harness race. His letter protesting the cruelty of the race was printed in a Boston newspaper. The article caught the attention of Emily Appleton. Within a month, she and Angell had formed the Massachusetts Society for the Prevention of Cruelty to Animals (MSPCA).

A few months later, Massachusetts passed the state's first anti-cruelty laws. The MSPCA began printing a monthly magazine, *Our Dumb Animals*—its mission: "To speak for those who cannot speak for themselves." Two hundred thousand copies of the first issue were distributed, enough for every family in the state.

In 1881, Angell started the "Bands of Mercy" clubs to educate boys and girls about the humane treatment of animals. Within a few years, Bands of Mercy groups across the country totaled 250,000 members. In 1889, the idea expanded to become the American Humane Education Society, which offered instruction to adults as well.

Angell learned of the book *Black Beauty* in 1890. Recognizing its power to advance the humane movement, he published the first American edition and distributed two million copies through the Bands of Mercy clubs.

When George Angell died in 1909, the work of the MSPCA continued with its second president, Dr. Francis Rowley. The MSPCA purchased its first motorized horse ambulance in 1910. In 1917, the organization opened Nevins Farm for retired police horses.

AHA - The American Humane Association

In 1877, delegates from humane organizations across the U.S. met in Cleveland, Ohio to form the American Humane Association (now American Humane). They hoped to more effectively achieve their goals by uniting efforts in a national organization. The mission was to prevent cruelty, abuse, neglect, and exploitation of children and animals.

An early focus of the American Humane Association was to advocate for public water troughs for working horses.

During filming of the 1939 movie *Jesse James*, a horse died after being forced to run off a seventy-foot cliff. The AHA stepped in to monitor the production of movies and television programs to ensure the humane treatment of animals on the sets.

The regulations that protected animals on film were made voluntary in 1966, allowing directors to keep AHA representatives from monitoring animal safety.

In 1980, four horses died during the filming of *Heaven's Gate*. Now, the AHA provides its trademarked certification "No Animals Were Harmed" in the credits of movies where they have monitored the care of the animal actors. Even with AHA monitoring, two horses died during the 2006 filming of *Flicka*. In the 2011 movie, *War Horse*, an animatronic horse was used for the most dangerous scenes.

The AHA was appointed to the Federal Wild Horse and Burros Advisory Board in 1986 to help manage and protect Mustangs and burros on public lands. One idea they came up with was the Colorado Wild Horse Inmate Program, the first prison program in which inmates train wild horses that are then offered for adoption.

The Home of Rest for Horses - The Horse Trust

After reading *Black Beauty*, Ann Lindo of North London was inspired to provide a place where sick and exhausted horses could rest. While they recovered, healthy horses were loaned out to replace them, so the owners could still earn a living.

In 1886, Lindo's idea became the Home of Rest for Horses. Horses were purchased or donated to be used as loaners. The home was a great success, but Miss Lindo died five years later, at fifty-two.

During WW1, the charity provided a motorized horse ambulance to transport wounded horses in France. In two years, the ambulance carried more than 1,000 injured horses to safety. By the end of the war, fourteen similar ambulances were in operation, saving thousands of horses' lives. At war's end, the Home of Rest for Horses provided a retirement home to some of the horses who returned from the war.

ODFL Our Dumb Friends League

In 1897, a group of animal lovers in England founded Our Dumb Friends League (ODFL), "A Society For The Encouragement Of Kindness To Animals." Initially, it was formed to ensure humane care for working horses.

The ODFL opened their first animal hospital in London in 1906 to provide veterinary care for the animals of poor people. The hospital is still in operation.

The Blue Cross Fund was started in 1912 to collect public donations to help care for horses during the Balkan War.

A Blue Cross Horse Ambulance

Two years later, when World War I broke out, the ODFL wanted to help. The British Army, who had their own veterinary corps, turned down the organization's offer of assistance. But ODFL was able to assist the French.

Believing animals have no nationality, the ODFL treated horses from any country. They sent one ambulance as far as Egypt. By the end of 1914, there were four Blue Cross horse hospitals in France. Veterinary supplies were also donated.

In 1915, the Blue Cross produced a booklet titled, *The Drivers' and Gunners' Handbook to Management and Care of Horses and Harness*. This proved helpful, as many young soldiers came from the cities and had never worked with horses.

> *Every type and breed of horse in Western Europe passed through our hands; also horses from North Africa were brought by the French Colonial troops, such as Barbs and Arabs - beautiful small horses. I saw many Percheron mares and geldings, and Nivernais, Ardennais, and Boulannais. Occasionally we got a shire or a Clydesdale gelding - some horses that had escaped from the British and got into the French lines. Many thoroughbreds were seen that had been requisitioned from racing stables. We also had a few wounded mules, and once in a while we got a German horse. But horses have no nationality; a horse is a horse and equal care and attention are lavished on all.*
>
> — *The Blue Cross at War, p. 12*

Flags with a blue cross flew above the animal hospitals to distinguish them from the Red Cross tents that treated wounded soldiers. Veterinary surgeons sent by the ODFL treated injured horses and other animals on the battlefields. One horse who had been wounded and treated at a Blue Cross hospital in 1916 was injured again in 1917. As they approached the hospital, the horse escaped from his handler and ran to the stall he had occupied the previous year. Over the course of the war, more than 50,000 horses and 18,000 dogs were treated in the Blue Cross hospitals.

At the end of the war, the ODFL rescued 4,000 mistreated war horses who had been sold as work animals. They also helped soldiers with the cost of bringing back dogs they had served with on the battlefields. In the 1950s, the name of the ODFL was changed to The Blue Cross.

In modern times, overworked horses are not a big problem, however neglect still occurs, often by people who experience difficult financial times and are no longer able to feed and care for their horses.

Cases of abuse today are more sinister in nature. Various cruel techniques, known as soring, are used to produce animated gaits for the show ring. This is practiced primarily by some owners or breeders of Tennessee Walking Horses or related breeds where the extreme action wins at the shows.

The Horse Protection Act, a federal law passed in 1970, prohibits sored horses from participating in shows, exhibitions, sales, or auctions. The act also prohibits the transportation of sored horses to or from events. As funding permits, inspectors attend Walking Horse shows to check the horses.

According to the Horse Protection Act, soring includes:

> *an irritating or blistering agent applied internally or externally, a burn, cut, or laceration inflicted on any limb, a tack, nail, screw, or chemical agent injected into or used on any limb, any other substance or device which causes a horse to suffer, physical pain or distress, inflammation, or lameness when walking.*

Despite this law, soring continues. In 2011, an undercover investigator filmed horses being beaten, and the use of electric cattle prods and chemical soring at the farm of grand champion Walking Horse trainer Jackie McConnell. The trainer was sentenced to one year of house arrest, fined, and banned from showing at or attending Walking Horse events for life. But in 2021, McConnell was photographed at the National Celebration event in Shelbyville, Tennessee.

At the 2013 National Celebration, USDA testing showed 67% of the show horses were positive for substances used to hide soring.

In 2019, the U.S. House passed H.R. 693, the PAST Act, Prevent All Soring Tactics. This law would eliminate the use of stacked shoes and ankle chains on horses and would increase penalties for abusers. As of 2022, the bill is still languishing. It's never been presented for a vote in the Senate. Even if passed, the lack of funding for adequate enforcement is the main issue.

14

Equine Movie Star

When you think of horses in movies, the beautiful black ones in the *Black Stallion* or *Black Beauty* might come to mind. But few know the first movie star horse was a plain Thoroughbred mare—Sallie Gardner. Although Sallie was unaware of it, her owner, Leland Stanford, was in the midst of a heated debate about whether a horse ever had all four feet off the ground while trotting or galloping. Stanford was of the opinion they did, but he couldn't prove it.

Some old images of galloping horses showed all four legs in the air with the front two extended forward and the backs stretched out behind, in rocking horse style, a position no horse ever assumes. But a horse's leg motion is too fast to see with the unaided eye.

Why this was so important to Stanford isn't clear. He owned a horse farm of over 17,000 acres in Santa Clara, California where he raised Standardbred trotters and Thoroughbreds. Perhaps he thought he might somehow improve the performance of his racing horses if he fully understood their gaits.

Having that much land and a stable full of horses requires a lot of money, and Stanford had that. He'd become a lawyer in 1848. In 1852, he migrated to California with his wife and five brothers. They opened a general store to provide supplies for gold miners. Stanford became wealthy as a merchant and later in the railroad business.

Leland Stanford was elected governor of California in 1861, serving two years. He was president of the Central Pacific Railroad Company, one of the two companies that built the Transcontinental Railroad. In fact, Stanford drove the golden spike at the completion ceremony in Utah. Stanford also served eight years as a United States Senator from 1885 until his death in 1893.

But in the 1870s, Stanford's interest was horse racing. Photographer Eadweard Muybridge photographed Stanford's Standardbred Occident at a trot in 1873, but the images were blurry. For several years, Muybridge experimented with faster shutter speeds and more sensitive film emulsions. During this time, the photographer was tried for murder but was acquitted on the grounds of justifiable homicide.

In 1877, he re-photographed Occident with better results. However, the image was still fuzzy and required retouching by an artist to improve its quality.

This may be another Stanford mare, Annie G.

It wasn't until 1878 that Muybridge had cameras with fast enough film and shutter speeds to freeze the motion of a galloping horse. That horse was Stanford's Kentucky Thoroughbred, Sallie Gardner.

To capture the galloping mare's movement, Muybridge set up twenty-four cameras, twenty-seven inches apart, with chest-high trip wires rigged across the track. Each time the Thoroughbred hit a wire, an exposure was made in the connected camera.

The resulting twenty-four images were placed on a disc to be viewed in a machine Muybridge had invented—a zoopraxiscope. Cycling rapidly through the stop-action photographs produced a movie-like effect.

The photographic study proved that at a gallop, the horse does, at one point, have all four feet off the ground. That airborne moment occurs when the horse's legs are up under her abdomen, not when extended. Additional photographs taken of Stanford's trotting horse, Abe Edgington, proved that there is a moment of suspension at the trot as well, when the horse switches from one pair of diagonal legs to the other.

Not only did Muybridge's photos settle the question about the horse's gaits, his zoopraxiscope is regarded as an early version of a movie projector. The process he used to photograph and display the images was a step toward the development of motion pictures.

Stanford and a friend, J.D.B. Stillman, used drawings of the photos in a book, *The Horse in Motion*, but didn't credit the photographer. Muybridge was highly offended and sued Stanford, but a judge dismissed the lawsuit. Needless to say, the collaboration between Muybridge and Stanford was over, but Muybridge continued photographing other animals and people in motion. He published a book of his own in 1887, *Animal Locomotion: an Electro-Photographic Investigation of Connective Phases of Animal Movements*. His work influenced Thomas Edison, who would invent another early movie projector, the kinetoscope, in 1893.

Nothing more is known about Sallie Gardner, the star of the prototype moving picture, however, the future turned bleak for the Stanford family.

In 1884, Leland Stanford and his wife, Jane, lost their only child, fifteen-year-old Leland, Jr., to typhoid fever. As a memorial to their son, the Stanfords founded Stanford University, using 8,000 acres of their Palo Alto farm for the college campus. The school opened in 1891. Its legal name is still the Leland Stanford Junior University.

After her husband's death in 1893, Jane Stanford took over leadership of the college. On January 14, 1905, Mrs. Stanford became violently ill after drinking from a bottle of mineral water. Vomiting was induced, and she recovered. Analysis determined that the water contained the poison strychnine.

Stanford University hired the Morse Detective Agency to investigate. They concluded that a servant added the poison to Mrs. Stanford's water, but no further action was taken.

Stanford was shaken by the knowledge that someone had attempted to kill her. She left California and sailed to Hawaii, checking into the Moana Hotel in Honolulu.

At 11:00 PM on February 26th, Jane woke, feeling ill. Fearing she'd been poisoned again, she cried out for help.

Two doctors quickly arrived, but by 11:30, Jane Stanford was dead.

After a three-day investigation, the coroner's jury stated,

> *Jane Lathrop Stanford came to her death from strychnine poisoning, said strychnine having been introduced into a bottle of bicarbonate of soda with felonious intent by some person or persons to this jury unknown.*

The case remains unsolved.

MRS. LELAND STANFORD IS POISONED

WIDOW OF CALIFORNIA'S FORMER SENATOR A VICTIM OF HATE.

SHE HAD FLED TO HONOLULU

Fate Pursued Her and Dose of Bicarbonate of Soda Quickly Ended Her Life in Great Agony.

By Associated Press.

Honolulu, March 1.—Mrs. Jane Lathrop Stanford of San Francisco, widow of United States Senator Leland Stanford, died at 11:40 o'clock last night at the Moana hotel here. Suspicious circumstances surround the death of Mrs. Stanford. She was taken ill at 11 o'clock, and said: "I have been poisoned."

Her last words were: "This is a horrible death to die."

Austin American-Statesman,
March 2, 1905

15

Tom Bass

Tom Bass, who some consider the most talented black American horseman, was born into slavery on January 5, 1859. His mother, Cornelia Gray, was a slave on Eli Bass' plantation near Columbia, Missouri. Eli's oldest son, William Bass, was Tom's father. When the plantation's slaves were freed after the Civil War, Cornelia moved away to find work. Six-year-old Tom was left in the care of Cornelia's parents, Presley and Eliza Gray, who stayed to work as sharecroppers on the plantation.

Tom was able to ride alone at four. By six, he was jumping fences fearlessly. During those early years, Tom learned to treat horses with kindness and respect.

> *My interest in saddle horses was by breeding and environment. I slept in the stables when I was so tiny I got covered up in the straw, and I rode the old mares when I was no bigger than a horsefly.*
>
> — *Tom Bass*

Tom's training experience began with the transformation of a cantankerous mule named Mr. Potts. William Bass' white sons, Tom's half brothers, mocked him when he appeared on Mr. Potts to demonstrate what the mule had learned. The brothers weren't laughing after they saw what the nine-year-old trainer had accomplished. Mr. Potts circled the ring in a collected canter and even racked like a fine saddle horse.

Tom's first official job was to drive customers from the local train station to the Ringo Hotel, but word of his ability with horses spread. People brought animals to him that no one else was able to ride or train. He came to be known as the black horse whisperer.

At twenty, Tom was hired by Joseph Potts to work as a trainer at the Mexico Horse Sales Company in Mexico, Missouri. The stable, owned by Potts and his brother-in-law, Cyrus Clark, raised and sold the "Cadillacs" of the horse world. Some of their horses were foundational to the American Saddle Horse or Saddlebred breed. (The American Saddlebred Horse Association was formed in 1891.)

Cyrus Clark expressed the thought of many at the time that training show horses was no business for a black man. But Potts defended Tom, saying he'd never met a man with a better eye for horseflesh than Tom Bass.

It was around this time that Bass invented a milder version of a bit. His experience with problem horses had convinced him that ill-fitting, harsh bits, used more for punishment than communication, were a major source of horses' problems. Horses who fought the pain caused by cruel bits were whipped and punished which only compounded their behavioral issues.

When presented with Tom's new bit, Joseph Potts urged him to have it patented. Tom didn't want any money for his invention. He just wanted to ease the suffering of horses. The bit was widely copied with few realizing whose idea it had originally been.

While still with Pott's stable, Tom received his most challenging training project, a horse known as The Blazing Black. The mare was considered a man-killer. Whether she was actually guilty of that is unclear, but it was certain that Tom was the mare's last chance. If he couldn't train her, she would be destroyed.

The beautiful but vicious mare screamed at anyone who approached her. If that wasn't enough to scare them away, she tried to kick or bite them. In the past, a group of men armed with pitchforks worked together to get her into or out of her stall.

After weeks of Tom's firm but gentle handling, The Blazing Black began to trust him. To everyone's amazement, he was not only able to ride her; he brought her up to the level of a top show horse. But The Blazing Black never allowed anyone else to ride her.

Several months later, Potts and Clark didn't have a horse to compete in the four-year-old and under mare category of a big horse show. The Blazing Black would be perfect for the class. A win by the flashy mare would improve their stable's reputation and bring in more sales.

But no black man had ever competed against whites at a show of that caliber. Disregarding tradition, Joseph Potts entered Tom Bass on The Blazing Black. It's difficult to determine whether the spectators were more shocked by Tom's appearance or the man-killing mare's.

Tom and The Blazing Black performed well and received a red ribbon for second place. Tom was pleased with the results, but Potts believed they had deserved first. Color barriers were beginning to break down in the horse show world. Other contestants recognized Tom's ability, and it became an honor to beat him.

In 1883, when the Mexico Horse Sales Company was sold, Joe Potts urged Tom to start his own training stable. It wasn't long before Tom's new business was booming. But he felt something was missing. He told his wife, Angie, he needed a "brag" horse—a horse he could train to a polished degree that would bring fame and publicity to his stable.

One day, Tom found just the horse he'd been looking for—a long-legged, gray colt he named Columbus.

> *Found him in a field full of cows and bought him for $100. He's got the fastest moves I ever saw on a colt. Columbus discovered America and I discovered Columbus.*

Over the next few years, in between training his client's horses, Tom worked with Columbus. The horse was fearless and followed Tom everywhere. He learned to obey voice commands and could open gates with his teeth.

When the gelding was ready, Tom decided their debut would be in St. Louis, one of the largest shows in the Midwest. The pair pranced and racked their way to an amazing performance which culminated with Columbus standing on his hind legs and turning in a circle, then bowing to the judges. Columbus' fame spread across the country.

One day, Tom's wife urged him to hurry home as they had an unexpected guest. Buffalo Bill Cody wanted to buy Columbus for his Wild West show. Tom agreed to sell the horse. It wasn't about the money; he knew through Buffalo Bill's show, more people would see Columbus perform.

In 1902, Bill Cody brought Columbus to Missouri for Tom Bass to ride in a show. During the performance, Columbus reared up on command, but the horse lost his balance and fell over backward, crushing Tom beneath him. Columbus scrambled to his feet unharmed. When he saw his rider on the ground, the horse pawed and tried to lift Tom with his teeth. With a crushed pelvis, Bass was lucky to be alive. Doctors informed him he would never ride again. But, after a long year of recovery, Tom returned to riding and training horses.

In 1910, Tom's opinion of Buffalo Bill Cody soured. Columbus had become a legend throughout America for his Wild West performances. The horse's picture was featured on posters, showing Cody on him racing after buffalo, saving damsels in distress, or leading the Wild West parade.

But Bass learned Cody had sold the prize horse to the 101 Wild West Show. Later, the 101 leased Columbus to a carnival. Tom's beloved horse died there in a barn fire in Augusta, Georgia.

Not long after that, the Miller brothers, owners of the 101 Show, came to Bass to buy another of his horses to replace Columbus. The Millers wanted to purchase Tom's most recent marvel, a gelding named Louis A. who was similar in size and color to Columbus.

Because of their callous treatment of Columbus, Tom insisted none of his horses were for sale to the 101 Show—not for any amount of money. Bass later sold Louis A. to a doctor for thousands less than what the Millers had offered.

Buffalo Bill Cody wasn't the only famous acquaintance of Tom Bass. Others included several Missouri governors, William Jennings Bryan, P. T. Barnum, Will Rogers, and Presidents William McKinley, Theodore Roosevelt, Grover Cleveland, and Calvin Coolidge. In 1897, Queen Victoria invited Bass to attend London's Diamond Jubilee. He declined, insisting that neither he nor his horses were good sailors.

Bass rode his most famous mare, Belle Beach, until 1928, when he retired the twenty-four-year-old horse. In 1931, at the age of seventy-two, Tom Bass suffered a heart attack in the show ring. He never fully recovered and didn't ride again. Belle Beach died the following year, and Tom Bass passed away a year later.

Upon Bass' death, Will Rogers devoted his entire newspaper column to the great trainer.

> *He trained thousands that others were applauded on. A remarkable man, a remarkable character. If old St. Peter is as wise as we give him credit for being, Tom, he will let you go in on horseback and give those folks up there a great show and you'll get the blue ribbon yourself.*

Tom never considered a man's color, just how he treated horses. He founded the American Royal Horse Show in Kansas City, Missouri. For his contributions to the state, Bass was inducted into the Hall of Famous Missourians in 1999.

16

Buffalo Bill

Buffalo Bill is a more catchy name than William Frederick. It was later in life that William, or Bill, earned his memorable nickname. Bill was born to Isaac and Mary Ann Cody on February 26, 1846 in Iowa Territory. Iowa became a state later that year.

In the 1850s, Kansas was not yet a state either. The question of whether Kansas should be accepted as a slave or free state was hotly debated. People supporting both positions flooded into the area to influence the outcome. At least fifty-six deaths, perhaps as many as two hundred, were attributed to conflicts over this question, causing the area to be known as "Bleeding Kansas."

Isaac Cody was strongly opposed to slavery and its expansion. He sold their Iowa farm and moved his family to Kansas in 1853. A pro-slavery man was so angered by an antislavery speech Isaac gave that the man stabbed him. Isaac never fully recovered from his wounds and died three years later.

Young Bill had to work to help support his mother and sisters. At eleven, he delivered messages on horseback for the freighting firm of Majors and Russell. In his autobiography, Cody makes claims that likely stretch the truth to the point of breaking. At fourteen, he was struck with gold fever and started west for California. On his way, he met an agent for the Pony Express and began working for them. On one of his routes, the men who were supposed to relieve him were either missing or killed, forcing Cody to ride a total of 322 miles. That account may be pure fiction. Cody would have been relatively young, fourteen and fifteen, during the time the Pony Express operated. His name doesn't appear in the official Pony Express records, but some believe he may have served as a rider for a time.

When the Civil War started in 1861, Bill was fifteen, too young for the Union Army. He joined an anti-slavery militia in Kansas and later enlisted as an official Union soldier.

After the war, he worked as a meat contractor for the Kansas Pacific Railroad. Bill's job was to kill buffalo (bison) to provide meat for the railroad crews. That's how he acquired the name "Buffalo Bill." He considered Brigham, a horse he bought from a Ute Indian, to be the best horse for chasing buffalo.

Later, he served as an Army scout during the Indian Wars. His primary mount then was a military horse, Buckskin Joe. Although not much to look at, Joe had exceptional endurance and was considered one of the best long-distance horses of that time. After going blind, the government sold Buckskin Joe in 1877. The man who bought him donated the horse back to Cody. Joe remained at Cody's ranch until he died of old age in 1882.

Other horses Cody rode during this time were Tall Bull, Powder Face, Stranger, and Charlie. He considered Tall Bull "the fastest running horse west of the Mississippi."

When things calmed down in the West, Bill decided to preserve the memories of frontier life by creating a traveling show—Buffalo Bill's Wild West. Charlie was Cody's star horse in those early shows. Cody said of the horse,

Charlie was an animal of almost human intelligence, extraordinary speed, endurance and fidelity. When he was quite young, I rode him on a hunt for wild horses, which he ran down after a chase of fifteen miles. At another time, on a wager of $500 that I could ride him over the prairies 100 miles in ten hours, he went the distance in nine hours and forty-five minutes.

Charlie died on board ship as the Wild West returned from a European tour.

Ah, Charlie, old fellow, I have had many friends, but few of whom I could say that I love you as you loved me. Men tell me you have no soul; but if there is a heaven and scouts can enter there, I'll wait at the gate for you, old friend.

Each Wild West show began with a horseback parade through the town, consisting of U.S. soldiers, cowboys, Native Americans, and colorfully costumed performers from all over the world. Two two-hour shows featured historic western figures performing a variety of acts—Geronimo (Apache), Sitting Bull and his Lakota braves, and Annie Oakley (female sharpshooter Phoebe Butler).

The Wild West featured live buffalo, the Deadwood stagecoach, roping, trick riding, bronc riding, and re-enactments of events like a Pony Express ride, Indian attacks on wagon trains, stagecoach robberies, and Custer's Last Stand at the Little Bighorn.

During the 1899 season, Buffalo Bill's Wild West performed 341 shows in 132 cities, traveling 11,000 miles. That year, when the show was performing in Paris, world-famous artist Rosa Bonheur painted a portrait of Cody on a white horse. Some say this horse was Tucker; others claim its name was McKinley. In the early 1900s, Cody's mount was a magnificent chestnut named Duke.

At its height, the show included five hundred cast and crew members. Transporting that many people, animals, and equipment was challenging. James Bailey, of Barnum & Bailey Circus helped Buffalo Bill streamline their travel. Two trains, each containing fifty cars, transported hundreds of horses, up to thirty buffalo, grandstand seating for twenty thousand spectators, and acres of canvas to cover the seating in the event of bad weather.

The show was wildly successful in America and toured Europe eight times, although it was not without problems and tragedies. The show almost ended before it had gotten established.

In 1884, a steamboat, W. P. Thompson, carrying the show's performers and equipment down the Mississippi River toward New Orleans, collided with a U.S. Mail steamer, Miller, near Rodney, Mississippi. The Thompson's hull was crushed and she sank on a sand bar. No lives were lost on either ship.

— *The Daily Bulletin, December 10, 1884*

In 1888, Antonio Esquivel, a Mexican rough rider, was accidentally shot in the face at the conclusion of a performance and lost the sight in his right eye. At least two Native Americans were killed in riding accidents during the European tours. Paul Eagle Star, of the Brulé Lakota band, died of complications from injuries caused when his horse fell on him. White Star Ghost Dog (female), of the Oglala Lakota band, also died after a horse-riding accident.

On October 29, 1901, Buffalo Bill's train was traveling through North Carolina to Norfolk, Virginia for their last show of the season. Frank Lynch, the engineer of a freight train in the vicinity, was instructed to pull onto a side track to let the Wild West trains pass. Lynch pulled his train over, but he missed the detail that two trains carried the show. After the first Wild West train passed, Lynch's freight train resumed its journey.

When they saw each other, the engineers of both trains hit their emergency brakes, but they were traveling too fast to stop. The trains collided head-on near Linwood, North Carolina.

Over one hundred horses, including Cody's personal mounts, Old Pap and Old Eagle, were killed. Duke, Cody's favorite, was one of only two horses to survive the crash. The other was Shoo Fly.

Rosa Bonheur painting

Annie Oakley, who had been asleep in her train car, suffered severe injuries which caused temporary paralysis. Early newspaper accounts reported she had died in the accident. Doctors thought she would never walk again, but after multiple spinal surgeries, Oakley recovered. She left Buffalo Bill's show, but later continued performing in less-demanding stage plays.

Some of the freight-train crew leaped from their train before impact. When Cody, who had traveled on the earlier train, arrived at the scene of the accident, he chased the crew members with his gun drawn. The engineer, Frank Lynch, fled the accident scene, jumped onto another train at the next station, and was never heard from again.

Unlike Lynch, people from all over the area came to help, housing the surviving show animals in their barns and pastures. Buffalo Bill purchased the entire food stock from a local store for his performers who were camping near the accident. A nearby resident, Wesley Young, his wife, and two daughters cooked for the show people and sheltered some of them in their barn. To show his appreciation for the Young family's help, Cody gave Wesley the horse Shoo Fly.

Cody described the train accident as a "calamity that forever changed his life."

The show struggled after the accident. Despite dwindling attendance, the Wild West continued until 1913 when the show went bankrupt. Its animals were auctioned off. Colonel C. J. Bills from Lincoln, Nebraska purchased the white horse, Isham, for $150 and had him shipped to Cody's Wyoming ranch.

Buffalo Bill Cody helped to found the town of Cody, Wyoming in 1895, and a local newspaper, The Cody Enterprise, in 1899. He owned the TE Ranch near Cody, where he raised cattle. The ranch, at its height, consisted of eight thousand acres. Cody died on January 10, 1917.

17

Twenty Mule Teams

While many have written about the 1849 Gold Rush in California, much less is known about the "White Gold of the Desert" also known as the "magic crystal." Many have never heard of it.

It's borax, a naturally occurring salt containing boron—not as glamorous as gold or silver but tremendously useful. Borax was used in ceramics, gold mining, and soaps of all kinds. In the 1800s, it was touted as a cure-all for every illness known to man.

Discovered in California in the 1860s, it would be twenty years before Borax was mined on a large scale. Aaron Winters and his wife, Rose, discovered borax in Death Valley in 1881. The couple sold their mineral holdings for $20,000 to William Coleman. Coleman set up the Harmony Borax Works to process the cottonball borax his forty workers scraped from the surface of Death Valley.

The Harmony Borax Works, in operation from 1883 to 1888, produced three tons of borax daily, except for the months of June to September when temperatures reached as high as 136 degrees in Death Valley. This wasn't out of consideration for the working conditions of the men or animals but simply because the borax wouldn't crystallize in such heat.

Coleman's workforce consisted primarily of poorly paid Chinese men who performed the harsh labor of collecting the raw borax under the brutal desert sun. The laborers loaded the cottonball borax into one-horse carts, then hauled it back to the Harmony Works plant where it was crystallized in large vats before being sent to market.

Transportation had been the major factor preventing the mining of borax in the past. The closest rail line was in Mojave, California, a grueling 165 miles away. How could they transport the partially refined mineral from these hot, dry, remote areas to market?

As in the past, the transportation solution was horsepower, more precisely in this case—mule-power. Wouldn't you love to know the names and stories of some of those animals? Not only do we not know their stories, even the names of the men who drove and cared for them have been lost to time.

> *All the old Death Valley teamsters are gone. And not one of them who handled the teams during the epic Death Valley-Mojave years of 1884-1888 seems to have left his story behind. Even the names of the muleskinners of those halcyon days of the twenty mule teams are unknown or uncertain.*
>
> *— 20 Mule Team Days in Death Valley, chapter 5*

But, here is what we do know.

Two massive wagons carried the borax. A third vehicle, a 1,200-gallon tanker, held drinking water for the men and animals as they crossed the desert. Mule teams pulled the three-vehicle caravan from the Harmony Borax Works near Furnace Creek to the railhead at Mojave, California.

It took ten days to cover the 165 mile one-way trip, averaging seventeen miles a day. Then, they turned around and took another ten days to return for the next load. When the wagons were emptied, feed and supplies were hauled on the return trip and dropped off periodically along the route for use by the next mule train heading to Mojave. They had constructed cabins for the men's use at these nightly stops.

Five teams freighted Coleman's borax. A team loaded up and left the Harmony Works every four days. Between 1883 and 1888, the mule teams hauled over twenty million tons of borax out of Death Valley. During those years, it's said no wagons broke down and not one animal was lost.

The solid oak wagon beds were sixteen feet long, six feet deep, and four feet wide. First was the "trailer." Behind it was the "tender." An empty wagon weighed 7,800 pounds. The rear wheels were seven feet tall, each wheel weighing 1,000 pounds. It took five or six men to change a wheel. The front wheels were shorter at five feet. The two wagons, when loaded, along with the water tank, weighed over 73,000 pounds.

It wasn't just any team that could haul that much weight. William Coleman wasn't the first to use such teams, but the name Twenty-Mule-Team, soon became synonymous with borax. Although called twenty-mule teams, they usually consisted of eighteen mules and two horses.

Why didn't a twenty-mule team contain twenty mules?

Wheelers were the animals at the rear of the team, the two closest to the wagon. It was vital that these two animals be exceptionally strong as they provided the muscle to get the massive load moving. Rather than mules, wheelers were large horses, sometimes up to 1,800 pounds. The two wheelers had a wooden shaft, the wagon tongue, between them. The main driver, known as the muleskinner or teamster, often rode the left wheeler.

After the wheelers, eighteen mules made up the rest of the team. They were all connected in pairs to either side of an eighty-foot chain. From the nose of the lead mules to the back of the water wagon, the caravan stretched out to 180 feet. Mules were used because some considered them smarter than horses. Some even said, "A dumb mule—if there is such a thing—is smarter than a smart horse."
— *20 Mule Team Days in Death Valley, chapter 4*

Their level of intelligence might be debatable, but mules were more hardy than horses. They could go longer without water and were better suited to working in desert conditions.

> *Mules were usually matched up for size and color and sold by the span, frequently full brother and sister or brothers, at $350 to $500 a span. … Mules shouldn't do heavy freighting until five years old. Even then they'll be pretty well stove up at 12 or 14. But I think a mule will last ten years longer than a horse. He doesn't waste energy pawing and running off here and there.*
>
> — *20 Mule Team Days in Death Valley, chapter 4*

Jumping from the back of the team to the front, the first pair of mules were the leaders. These were the two smartest mules in the team. They wore harness bells to warn any oncoming traffic of their presence. The rhythmic ringing of the bells also helped set the pace for the mules behind them.

The left leader, the line mule, was the only animal in the team to have a rein connected to her bit, and that was on the left side only. That 120-foot rein, known as the jerk line, wove back through the rings at the sides of each left-hand mule's harness, all the way to the muleskinner seated on the left wheeler.

The teamster communicated both left and right turns through the jerk line. The left leader, often a mare, was trained to interpret a steady pull on the line to mean a left turn while several quick jerks meant to turn right.

The line mule was connected to her partner by a wooden rod an inch in diameter and four or five feet long. This "jockey stick" connected to the harness on the right side of the line mule, then fastened to the bit ring on the left side of the right leader. When the line mule started a right turn, the jockey stick pushed her partner's head to the right. In a left turn, the stick pulled her to the left. The animals behind them had no choice but to follow wherever the leaders went.

Each of the wagons had manual brakes controlled by levers. These were essential when traversing a steep downgrade. There was no way the wheel horses, or even the entire twenty-animal team, could hold back a load that weighed over twice their combined weight.

The teamster controlled the brake of the first wagon. Instead of riding the wheeler, the teamster sometimes drove from the seat of the first wagon. In either case, he held the jerk line in one hand and the brake lever in the other. The team was stopped by a verbal command.

A second man, the swamper, rode on the side of the second wagon and controlled its brake.

Both men were responsible for the entire team—inspecting each animal and their tack, harnessing and unharnessing, feeding and watering at a midday stop and at each overnight stay, caring for sick or injured animals, gathering firewood, cooking meals, and making any necessary wagon repairs.

> *In freighting over the desert with a twenty animal team, every driver has an assistant called a swamper. On the down grade, he climbs to a perch on the rear wagon and puts on the brake; on the upgrade he reasons with and throws rocks at the indolent and obstreperous mules. As mealtime approaches, he kicks dead branches from a grease-bush along the route and pulls up sage-brush roots for fuel. When the outfit stops, he cooks the food while the driver feeds the animals, and when the meal is over, washes the dishes which, with the food, are carried in a convenient box in the wagon.*
>
> *The mules get their grain from boxes which are arranged to be secured to the wagon tongue and between the wheels, when feeding. They eat their hay from the ground. Beyond feeding and watering they get no care—they curry themselves by rolling on the ground with cyclonic vigor. The cloud of dust raised is suggestive of a Death Valley sandstorm.*
>
> *— John R. Spears, reporter for the New York Sun, 1891 from 20 Mule Team Days in Death Valley p. 49*

As for the rest of the team, the ten mules behind the leaders made up the swing team. They served as a power source and required no special training beyond responding to the commands to pull and stop.

The three pairs between the swing team and the wheelers were known as pointers. Pointers had an important role. They were crucial for steering the wagons safely around curves.

Assume the narrow road had a tall mountain to the right and a steep cliff on the left. When navigating a sharp curve to the right, given the length of the team and the chain's tendency to maintain a straight line, the wagons would be pulled sharply right—directly into the side of the mountain. Or vice versa. On that same road, a sharp left turn, without the pointers, would send them over the cliff.

The pointers prevented such a catastrophe. The teamster directed commands to the pointers individually by name. Each mule was trained to leap right or left over the central chain as needed to pull the chain outward, forcing it to conform to the shape of the turn. This alteration in the mule's position allowed the wagons to follow a curved path.

Some mules learned when their jump was required and did it without being commanded. Once the turn was completed and the team needed to return to a straight line, any pointer mules who had jumped the chain needed to jump back into their normal positions.

> *When you made it around the curve and began to straighten out, they would gradually come in to the chain and bounce right back over where they belonged. Going up a steep hill the leaders might be a dozen feet above you. That would bring the chain up high. But I've seen Sadie - one of the pointers on that exhibition twenty mule team - jump the chain when it was three feet off the ground, and land pulling.*
>
> *— 20 Mule Team Days in Death Valley, chapter 4*

As William Coleman purchased additional properties, borax was overproduced, resulting in a drop in its price. The Harmony Works, which at one time had an income of $14 million per year, eventually collapsed. He sold out at a loss to Francis Marion Smith in 1890. Coleman died in 1893.

Smith, who was known as "Borax Smith," focused on his Pacific Coast Borax Company, located closer to the railheads. He closed the Harmony operation, and it fell into ruin.

Smith believed mules were an inefficient means of transportation and reduced his reliance on them. Instead, he turned to steam-powered tractors and trains. However, in 1891, an employee Stephen Mather persuaded Smith to add the name "20 Mule Team Borax" along with the sketch of a mule team to their product boxes. They later registered a trademark for the name.

People loved the mules, and the Pacific Coast Borax Company used live teams to promote its products. A mule team appeared at the 1904 St. Louis World's Fair and the 1917 World's Fair in New York City.

The company, then known as Borax Consolidated, sponsored the Death Valley Days radio program in the mid-1930s and later, the television show of the same name from 1952 to 1975.

The modern production facility in the Mojave Desert, now known as Rio Tinto Borax, supplies more than half of the world's borax. What remains of the Harmony Borax Works is a National Park Service historical site in Death Valley National Park. The 20 Mule Team Borax cleaner is now manufactured by The Dial Corporation.

Borax is still used in soaps, cosmetics, and medicines, but it is also used in a surprising number of other products such as fiberglass, Pyrex glassware, optical lenses, porcelain enamel, ceramic glazes, antifreeze, brake fluid, fireproofing and protection of lumber and other building materials, and as a soil micro-nutrient.

18

Riding For Ladies

In past years, some females rode astride, but that style of riding was considered immodest or even immoral. Horse books in the 1800s often used men to illustrate the correct positioning of the legs when riding sidesaddle, as it was considered inappropriate to see a woman's legs, even in a pencil sketch. Not all women rode sidesaddle, though. Marie Antoinette had a portrait painted of her riding astride.

Anne of Bohemia made the sidesaddle popular for women in the Middle Ages. This "saddle" was a cushioned chair in which the rider sat completely sideways with her feet on a dangling footrest or planchette. A man or boy would then lead the horse.

In the 1500s, Catherine de' Medici of Italy modified the saddle, adding a horn or pommel in the front so the rider could face forward with her right leg wrapped over the horn. An iron stirrup replaced the old footrest.

The 1800s introduced the two-pommel design, the one still in use today. Prior to this, sidesaddles had a single pommel, known as the fixed head or top pommel, located near the center, top of the saddle. The rider's right leg wraps around it and rests along the horse's left side.

The second pommel, known as the leaping head or lower pommel, is located below the top one. The rider's left leg fits under the downward curve of the second pommel. This helps keep the leg in position, making for a more secure ride. A balance strap runs diagonally from the left front to the right rear of the saddle, under the horse's abdomen, to keep the saddle from shifting side to side.

During the 1800s, female equestrians wore specially designed garments known as riding habits. The habit was longer than a typical skirt, so that when seated on a horse, the rider's lower body remained covered. To keep the skirt from flying up while riding, some habits had weighted hems. Others had a loop near the bottom to slip over the rider's boot. Since it was difficult to walk in the bulky garments, there was an attached loop that allowed woman to hold the skirt up. Lady riders wore a wide-brimmed hat to keep their pale complexion from being darkened by the sun.

An 1877 book, *Riding For Ladies*, by Mrs. Power O'Donoghue of London gives insight into women's riding during this time period.

Mrs. O'Donoghue was an accomplished horsewoman who loved to follow the hunt (sidesaddle, of course). Mrs. O'Donoghue thought it unwise to allow young children, especially girls, to ride.

Few persons will be found to dispute the fact that a child on horseback, especially a girl, runs at least as many risks as a grown person. She may at any moment be jerked off, run away with, overpowered by the strength or temper of her mount, cannoned against by awkward or reckless riders, or subjected to the unpleasantness of discovering that the animal she herself is riding is given to slipping, stumbling, falling completely under her, or behaving in some unseemly manner that is entirely beyond her powers to check or control. To these dangers and discomforts—as well as to many others with which equestrians, old and young, are uncomfortably familiar—she is at all times liable to be exposed, and, this being an admitted truth, I ask whether it can for a moment be asserted that a child is as capable as an adult of coping with such risks? The answer must be "No." …

I have seen children over and over again subjected to the most fearful risks through riding horses that were too much for them. It is so easy for a girl to be overpowered,—and, once she is so, good-bye for ever to all or any pleasure in riding the animal who has been her conqueror. He will always remember his victory, and presume upon it.

— *Riding For Ladies, Chapter 1, Ought Children to Ride?*

Mrs. O'Donoghue thought girls, since they were forced to ride sidesaddle, would grow up crooked and deformed because they couldn't sit straight on horseback.

There are other reasons, also, on which I ground my objections to children riding. Little girls are exceedingly apt to grow crooked. … One child out of five hundred may, perhaps, be an habitual straight-sitter, but to counterbalance her perfection in this particular, the remaining 499 will be either hanging to one side or the other (usually the near, or left side), or sitting square enough, it may be, yet with the right shoulder thrust forward and upward, thus sowing the seeds of a deformity which in ten years' time, when the little one of eight shall have grown into a belle of eighteen, will have become an incurable disfigurement…

— *Riding For Ladies, Chapter 1*

Although she believed women could become accomplished equestrians, O'Donoghue recommended they wait until they were between fifteen and twenty before beginning to ride. For those who went against her advice and allowed their girls to ride, she has this recommendation for riding attire.

> *Little girls learning to ride should be dressed in neat skirts, just long enough to cover the feet; loose-fitting jackets—(jerseys are excellent)—hair left flowing, never fastened up; and soft hats or caps, well secured under the chin, in such a manner as to prevent the possibility of their coming off. Nothing should be left undone to inspire confidence in the breast of a child-rider. Her mount should be the gentlest, her teacher the kindest, all her appliances (saddle, &c.) new, comfortable, and reliable.*

> — *Riding For Ladies, Chapter 2*

Riding sidesaddle meant women couldn't apply both legs for the common commands such as turns or changes in gait. Ladies' riding horses responded to verbal commands and to taps with a whip.

Nearly all sidesaddle riders rode with their legs on the near, or left, side. But there were a few who wanted to alternate sides. A new saddle was designed to allow a rider to place her legs on the right side. The horse had to be trained to accept mounting and riding from the right, or off, side.

O'Donoghue warns against overly exuberant male assistants who would boost a female rider up—and right on over the other side of the horse.

> *A lady may saddle and bridle her own horse, may give him the finishing touches herself, and canter away, independently, when once she is on his back—but to get there she must, as a rule, seek for assistance from some source or another…*

If no experienced and capable mounting assistant was available, this was her advice.

> *lead your horse to a low wall, should such a thing be near enough, or take him, at all events, out of sight of the crowd, and utilise any sort of stepping-stone to reach his back…*

> *It is, of course, in some cases, quite possible for a lady to let down her stirrup and mount by it, unassisted—drawing it up again to the required length when seated on her saddle.*

> — *Riding For Ladies, Chapter 9*

The bulky material of the riding habit presented a danger women faced more than men—getting caught up on the saddle if a fall occurred. To avoid having the skirt of one's riding habit catch on the pommel of the saddle, O'Donoghue recommended using only a single layer of cloth in the hem, making it weaker so it would tear if caught on the saddle.

Many would find riding sidesaddle enough of a challenge, but in the past, women not only rode, they participated in fox hunts and high jump competitions.

Esther Martha Stace, an Australian equestrian, set a sidesaddle high jump record of six feet six inches in 1915 at the Sydney Royal Show on her twelve-year-old gelding, Emu Plains, who stood over 16 hands tall. Their record stood for ninety-eight years. Mrs. Stace always rode sidesaddle and competed in a plush, scarlet outfit. She continued to compete until within a few years of her death of an illness at forty-six in 1918.

Mrs. Stace's record wasn't beaten until 2013, when Susan Oakes jumped six feet eight inches on her seventeen-year-old gray stallion, Siec Atlas, in Dublin, Ireland. Oakes currently holds the Guinness World Record for the highest jump by a horse ridden sidesaddle.

Oakes said, "The horse threw his heart over, followed by his body and all I had to do was give him encouragement and hang on."

Because of her skill in training and riding horses, Emma Peek, from Mendon, Michigan, joined with D. H. Harris to tour the country as an equestrian performer. The two later married, and she became known as "Madame Marantette—Queen of the Saddle."

It wasn't only horses Peek trained. The couple traveled with an ostrich named Gaucho, who pulled a carriage, either alone or teamed with a horse. Gaucho was said to be the fastest trotting ostrich in the world, although whether any other trotting ostriches existed to race against is doubtful.

Emma claimed she never rode astride, even as a child, always preferring to ride sidesaddle. Marantette described a horse named Filemaker as the best horse she ever owned. It's claimed the pair jumped seven feet three and a half inches during an exhibition in Massachusetts in 1891.

Esther Stace

After Filemaker passed away in 1896, she jumped another horse, St. Patrick, a 16 hand Irish hunter. St. Patrick surpassed Filemaker's record with a seven-foot ten-inch jump in Michigan in 1904. None of Marantette's jumps were witnessed by any equestrian organization, so they were never officially recognized as records. In 1918, a grass fire in St. Patrick's pasture burned his back legs, and the great jumper had to be put down.

After World War I, it became more acceptable for women to wear split skirts or pants, making riding astride possible. By 1930, astride was the preferred method of riding for women. In recent years, there has been renewed interest in sidesaddle riding, particularly in show events.

19

Bucking Horses

Nearly all riders consider bucking an undesirable and dangerous behavior, often a reason to get rid of a horse. This type of animal has been known as a "bronco" from the Spanish word, meaning "rough."

Today, that type of unridable horse might find his way to a starring role in a rodeo. Some ranches intentionally breed for horses that buck—the harder the better. Rodeo stock providers call this the "Born to Buck" program. The United States has the Bucking Horse Breeders Association (BHBA), a breed registry for bucking horses. The Calgary Stampede, the largest rodeo in Canada, has its own ranch, established in 1961, to breed bucking horses for their event.

It's difficult to pinpoint the first rodeo in America. The concept originated back in the days when cowboys tried to "break" wild colts out West by riding them until they no longer bucked. It didn't take long for that to turn into a competition with one cowboy trying to outdo another by riding the toughest horse. In the late 1800s, bronc riding became a form of public entertainment at shows like Buffalo Bill's Wild West.

Some of the earliest formal rodeos were:

- Prescott, Arizona, on July 4, 1888

- Cheyenne Frontier Days, Wyoming, 1897

- Pendleton Round-Up, Oregon, 1910

- Calgary Stampede, Alberta, Canada, 1912

The Rodeo Association of America (RAA) was formed in 1929 to standardize the events. The association created a set of rules for competing and established world champions for bronc riding, bareback riding, bull riding, steer roping, calf roping, bulldogging, and team roping. This organization protected the managers and organizers of the rodeos not the contestants.

Rodeo cowboys didn't unite until 1936 when many of them walked out of a show at Boston Garden to protest the low pay. Although the rodeo was projected to take in $80,000, total prize money for the cowboys was only $7,000.

The organizers soon realized that, without cowboys, it was hard to have a rodeo. They scrambled to round up grooms, stable boys, and anyone else willing to fill in. The substitute cowboys' performances were abysmal, and the spectators' money was refunded.

Boston Garden Cowboys

The cowboys chose a surprising name for their first organization—the Cowboys' Turtle Association (CTA). The name reflected the fact that they'd been slow to unite but eventually "stuck their necks out." In 1945, the name was changed to the Rodeo Cowboys Association. And in 1975, it became the Professional Rodeo Cowboys Association, PRCA.

Two of the most popular rodeo events are bronc riding and bareback riding. Both involve bucking horses, although the bronc horses are saddled. Saddle broncs are larger, stockier horses, sometimes draft crosses.

Riders in both events use spurs. However, a rider may be disqualified if his spurs are too sharp or they injure the horse. The horses wear a flank strap, which some claim is cruel and hurts the animal. The straps are lined with fleece or another soft material and are not fastened tightly. They feature a quick-release mechanism that allows the pickup riders to remove the strap once a rider is off. Some horses find the flank strap annoying, but for most it's merely a signal that it's time to buck.

The Professional Rodeo Cowboys Association looks out for the safety of the rodeo livestock. One or more veterinarians are on site during the events. Bucking horses are valuable animals. It's in their owners' best interests to keep them safe and healthy.

Early rodeos are remembered for their legendary bucking horses. There's some disagreement over which was the greatest bucking horse of those days. Some claim it was Steamboat. Others insist Midnight was the greatest.

Steamboat was foaled on the Foss Ranch in Wyoming in 1894. Although Frank Foss' six-year-old son sometimes led the big, black colt, no one could saddle or ride him. When Foss realized he couldn't train the four-year-old horse, he sold him to the Two Bar Ranch.

A cowboy at the ranch was so angry when Steamboat (shown above) bucked furiously with him, he struck the horse across the nose with a whip, injuring his nasal cavity. The injury caused the horse to make a whistling sound when he breathed. That's how he acquired his name, "Steamboat—the whistlin' hoss." At least, that's one explanation for the horse's breathing abnormality. Other accounts claim no one knows how he received the injury.

It quickly became obvious to the Two Bar foreman that the 1,100 pound Steamboat was not suited for ranch work. He sold him to another Wyoming man, John Coble. Coble recognized Steamboat's potential as a bronc horse. He entered him in the Cheyenne Frontier Days rodeo, and Steamboat's career as a rodeo bronc began.

In the early days, there were no chutes for the broncs. Steamboat was blindfolded, then a rider mounted, and he was released. Eight seconds didn't constitute a successful ride. The battle continued until either the rider was thrown or the horse gave up. At the height of his career, from 1900 to 1908, only two cowboys stayed on the horse for more than a few seconds. Steamboat had a violent style of bucking. Some described him as part tornado, part horse. World champion, Guy Holt, claimed his back never recovered from a ride on Steamboat.

Although Frank Stone rode Steamboat in 1904 for ten seconds, he grabbed the saddle, a disqualification. Stone suffered a possible concussion and his throat was so damaged he couldn't speak above a whisper for weeks.

In a muddy arena, in Cheyenne, in 1908, Dick Stanley rode Steamboat until the exhausted horse stopped bucking. The deep mud made the bronc's job much more difficult. Steamboat's owner challenged Stanley to ride the horse again the following year in a dry arena, but the rematch never occurred.

In 1914, the twenty-year-old Steamboat got tangled up in barbed wire and had to be euthanized. Steamboat was inducted into the National Cowboy Hall of Fame in 1975 and the Pro Rodeo Hall of Fame in 1979. The logo of the University of Wyoming is based on a photo of a bucking Steamboat with the rider possibly being Guy Holt. The image is also on Wyoming license plates and the state's quarter.

The other contender for world's greatest bucking horse is Midnight (1916-1936), born two years after Steamboat's death.

Originally owned by Jim McNab, Midnight was foaled in Alberta, Canada. The 15.1 hand, black horse weighed 1,300 pounds. He had Thoroughbred blood on his dam's side, but his strong build came from the Percheron/Morgan lines of his sire.

Some say McNab was unable to train Midnight. Others say he used him as a ranch horse for a few years. But Midnight always tended to buck and was never reliable.

In 1924, McNab entered Midnight in the Calgary Stampede rodeo. Like Steamboat, the horse had found his niche. During the 1920s, as he toured the rodeo circuit, Midnight was considered unridable. By then, a successful ride was ten seconds, but most who attempted to ride Midnight were thrown off in two or three. Champion cowboy, Pete Knight, rode Midnight four or five times and holds the record for the longest ride on the horse at seven seconds. No one is on record as ever having officially ridden him.

Midnight was later sold to Verne Elliot. The two traveled to England where the horse participated in a few exhibition rides. (Maybe they should be called "non-rides.") When they returned home, Midnight was retired to pasture. He died on November 5, 1936.

Midnight's remains were later moved and reburied on the grounds of the National Cowboy and Western Heritage Museum in Oklahoma City, Oklahoma. He was inducted into the Pro Rodeo Hall of Fame in 1979.

Stallions and geldings aren't the only bucking horses. Mares are used nearly as often as geldings. A bucking horse's career typically begins around the age of five and often continues into their twenties. Since today's bucking horses travel around the country to various rodeos, they're taught basic manners, including how to load into a trailer, to stand in the bucking chute, and to move to the out gate once a rider is removed. Some "broncos" can be quite gentle when they're not being ridden.

Midnight's gravestone reads:

Underneath this sod
lies a great bucking hoss.
There never lived a cowboy
he couldn't toss.
His name was Midnight,
his coat as black as coal.
If there is a hoss-heaven,
God please, rest his soul.

The bay mare, Medicine Woman, was born in 2003 in Oklahoma, a product of a breeding program by the Frontier Rodeo Company to produce bucking horses as rodeo stock.

Medicine Woman (shown below) first reached the National Finals Rodeo in 2009 as a bareback horse, but the following year was switched to saddle bronc. She reached the National Finals twelve times and was named Saddle Bronc Horse of the Year four times (2011, 2014-16).

Bronc riding is scored based on a possibility of 100 total points, 50 for the rider and 50 for the animal. The score for the ride is the total of those two scores. Scores in the 80s are considered very good. The 90s are exceptional. The harder and more spectacularly a horse bucks means the potential for higher scores for the ride. Medicine Woman helped many cowboys achieve 90+ point rides.

The great bucking mare retired from rodeo in 2020. She had her first and only foal, a colt, on Mother's Day, 2021. Medicine Woman passed away in December of that same year.

Classic Velvet is an example of a horse who, because of being untrainable, found a career in the rodeo. Velvet was a registered Quarter Horse from California, a grandson of a racing horse named Three Bars. Originally intended to be a team roping horse, he proved to be an incurable bucker. Velvet was sold to Calvin Milhous, a rancher, horse trainer, and cousin of President Richard Nixon. Milhous attempted to train Velvet as a driving horse, but that didn't work out either.

The gelding was then purchased by Cotton Rosser, a California stock contractor who recognized the horse's rodeo potential. Velvet was named the Bareback Bucking Horse of the Year in 1981. Classic Velvet did what he did best—buck—for seventeen years, until he retired to pasture at twenty-four.

20

Beautiful Jim Key

In the late 1800s and early 1900s, there were several horses whose abilities seemed to indicate they possessed near-human levels of intelligence. These horses were exhibited in various areas and performed feats that went beyond the usual trick-trained horses. For example, many of the horses could paw a number of times to show answers to math problems.

Why there was this surge in "educated" horses during this time period is unclear, but they became the subjects of psychological and behavioral studies. The consensus was that horses do not possess intelligence on the level of humans, but they are far more intelligent than people had given them credit for. The first of this group was Beautiful Jim Key.

Jim Key wasn't always beautiful. In fact, when the bay colt was born in the spring of 1889, his owner, William Key, said the foal was "the most spingled, shank-legged animal I ever did see!" He'd planned to give the colt a fine name from the Bible, but William was so disappointed in him he named the foal, Jim, after a drunken man who lived nearby.

Born a slave in Winchester, Tennessee in 1833, William was given the last name of his owner, Captain John Key. Upon John Key's death, five-year-old William was bought by the captain's nephew, also named John Key. The animals on the Key farm seemed to sense young William was a friend. They greeted the boy affectionately each time he entered the barnyard. Because of his skill with animals, as William grew older, he was sent to neighboring farms to train horses or mules. Usually within a week's time, he had the animal tamed and ready to ride or drive.

It was uncommon in the South to teach slaves to read, but William learned alongside John Key's children. When the Civil War began, William joined the Confederate army with the Key sons in order to protect them.

After the war, William Key was a free man, and his ability with animals served him well. Considered a veterinarian, despite a lack of formal training, William was called Doc Key. One of Doc's dreams was to raise a successful racehorse.

Lauretta, Jim Key's mother, was a full-blooded Arabian, formerly owned by a Persian sheikh. The beautiful gray mare was stolen from the sheikh and sold to P. T. Barnum's circus while it toured Europe. Lauretta came to America, and for years, was exhibited as the Queen of Arabian Horses.

It's uncertain whether the part about the sheikh is true, but years later, William Key found Lauretta abused and neglected at a ramshackle circus in Mississippi. He purchased the mare, and over the next year, using the Keystone liniment he'd developed, Lauretta was restored to health.

Many horsemen traveled to races at the track on Doc Key's farm. When Doc spotted the horse, Tennessee Volunteer at one of those races, he knew right away that was the horse who should sire Lauretta's foal. Volunteer, a Standardbred, was a descendant of the famed racer Hambletonian. Lauretta was the smartest horse Doc Key had ever known, and Tennessee Volunteer was the fastest. How could those two produce anything but a champion racehorse?

The night the foal arrived, Doc's hopes were dashed. As he surveyed the scraggly colt, Doc wasn't sure the weak, wobbly thing would be able to walk, let alone race.

As if the little colt hadn't gotten off to a bad enough start in life, Lauretta died when Jim Key was young. His beloved mare's death was devastating. As he grieved, Doc kept to himself—except for the presence of Jim Key. The colt seemed to sense Doc's sadness and wouldn't leave the man's side.

A few days later, Doc was standing in the yard when he felt something nudge his arm. When he turned around, there was Jim Key, holding a stick in his mouth. The colt pushed it toward Doc as if he wanted him to throw it. Doc did. The colt raced after it and brought it back. It was as if Jim had seen Doc play fetch with the family dog, and he wanted to play the game, too. Perhaps he thought playing fetch might make his master smile again. For the first time, Doc realized there was something special about Jim.

That night, the colt refused to be led to his stall. Instead, he followed Doc into the house. Apparently, Jim now considered himself a member of the family. His bed was a deep pile of straw, covered with blankets. The colt was house-trained and always went out behind the house for his bathroom needs. Doc began to teach the colt to identify and retrieve household items. Jim Key even taught himself a trick. He learned to open the gate, so he could wander down the road.

By the time he was a yearling, in 1890, Jim Key's legs had straightened. He truly was a beautiful horse now—a big one—too big to remain in the house. Jim was not happy about returning to the barn. He threw such a fit that Doc set up a cot outside his stall and slept near him. What Doc intended as a temporary arrangement, to help Jim Key adjust to living in the stable, ended up lasting the rest of Doc's life. He even moved his desk to the barn to create an office.

The next revelation of Jim's intelligence came when Doc stored a supply of apples in his desk drawer. For the next few days, each time he returned to the barn, Doc found the drawer closed and its contents missing. He questioned his wife and the stable help, but none of them knew what had become of the apples.

Doc refilled the drawer, exited the barn, and watched through a window. Sure enough, Jim Key strolled inside, grabbed the drawer handle, and pulled it open. The horse ate every apple, closed the drawer, and moseyed back outside.

One day, Doc's wife, Lucinda, was in the barn eating Jim's favorite fruit. She asked him if he wanted an apple, and the horse nodded his head. Stunned, she ran to tell Doc. From that point on, Doc began working with Jim more earnestly. In addition to answering questions by nodding "yes," he learned to move his head side to side for "no."

When Jim Key was a year and a half old, Doc brought him along as he traveled the countryside selling his Keystone Liniment. The colt's ability to fetch and several other tricks drew crowds. Doc trained the horse to act as if he were sick— kicking at his stomach, staggering, then dropping to the ground to roll and kick violently, as if he were in pain. When Doc gave Jim Key a dose of the

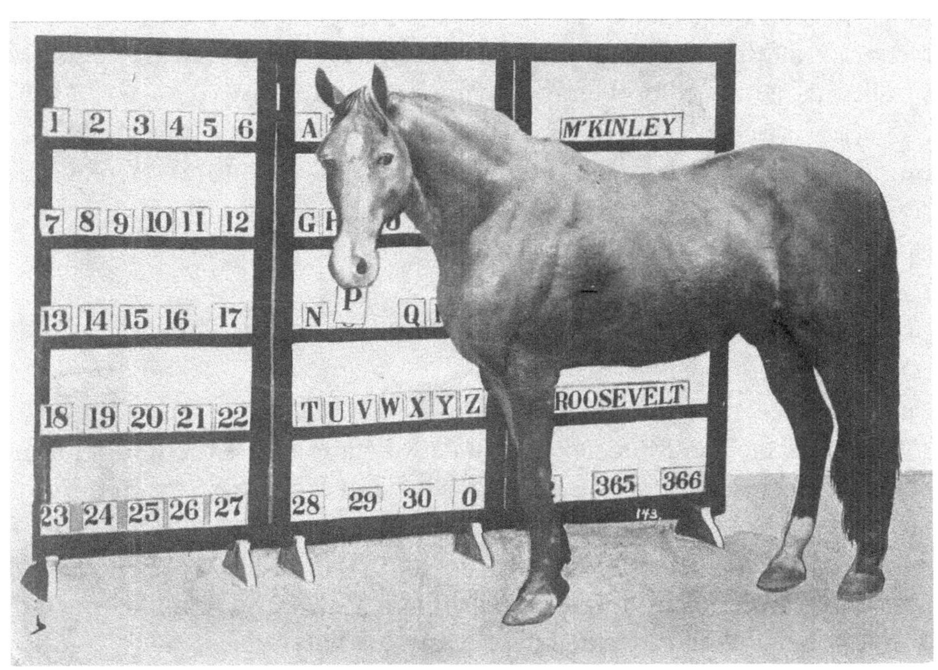

liniment, the horse's symptoms immediately vanished. The colt's antics helped Doc sell more liniment.

Next, Doc taught Jim to recognize the letter "A" on a tin square. He coated the square containing the correct letter with sugar, so Jim was rewarded by licking the right one. It took six months for Jim to learn to pick out that specific letter and bring it to Doc. Over the next years, Jim learned to recognize all the letters and the numbers from one to thirty. He could spell out words and solve simple mathematical problems with answers up to thirty.

Doc enjoyed reading passages from the Bible to Jim, especially those that mentioned horses. He trained the horse to pick up a card containing the Scriptural reference that matched the passage being read.

> *Jim likes the prophets. The prophets had visions of horses. John says he looked up and beheld a white horse in heaven, and what Jim wants to know is, if there are white horses in heaven, why can't a good bay horse go there also?*
>
> —Dr. William Key

In 1896, Doc and Jim Key toured county fairs across the state of Tennessee, performing a variety of the horse's tricks. Doc was a Republican, but at these events, Jim Key always claimed to be a Democrat.

The following year, Jim Key was one of the most popular exhibits at the Tennessee Centennial and International Exposition. President William McKinley attended one of their performances. Jim bowed to women in the audience. He selected letter blocks one at a time to spell his own name. The horse retrieved letters from simulated post office mailboxes and filed them in the correct drawers. He could pick out coins that added up to values called out by members of the audience. Jim could even write his name on a chalkboard. Actually, the horse held an eraser in his mouth and erased his name from the chalk-covered board.

Doc came up with a variation of Jim's old trick of feigning lameness they'd used during their days on the road, selling liniment. When someone in the crowd offered to buy the horse, Jim Key would suddenly act as though he were deathly ill. But he would miraculously recover when Doc refused to sell him.

When a presidential cabinet member's name was called out, Jim selected the card containing that man's name. Doc asked him where the president was seated, and Jim Key turned and bowed to McKinley. The Republican president was determined to change the horse's political persuasion. He asked him whether he was a Republican, but Jim Key moved his head from side to side, insisting he was not.

McKinley was quoted in a newspaper,

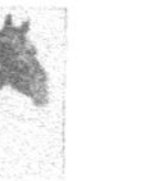

> *This is certainly the most astonishing and entertaining exhibition I have ever witnessed. It is indeed a grand object lesson of what kindness and patience will accomplish.*

When that article caught the eye of Albert Rogers, a young promoter, he decided he had to own Jim Key. Rogers met Doc Key at the Centennial Exhibition and offered $100,000 for the horse. Doc turned him down. As a former slave, Doc knew what it felt like to be bought and sold. He wouldn't do that to Jim Key. But the two men worked out a deal. A substantial initial payment went to Doc. Rogers would receive a percentage of the proceeds from each exhibit he arranged. And Jim Key would travel in his own private rail car with only the best hay.

Albert Rogers proved to be an effective promoter. Doc and Jim soon rose to national prominence. Both Rogers and Doc Key wanted to promote the ethical treatment of animals as well. As part of their events, Doc explained the gentle methods he used to train the horse.

The book, *Black Beauty*, written by Anna Sewell twenty years earlier in England, was awakening people to the plight of abused horses. Jim Key's act caught the attention of George Angell of the American Humane Education Society. He endorsed the act, making Jim Key an honorary agent of the organization. Angell gave Doc a copy of *Black Beauty*, which Doc promised to read aloud to Jim Key.

In 1901, at an exhibition in Atlantic City, New Jersey, a small black-and-white dog appeared one day in Jim's stall. The dog barked menacingly, preventing the stable help, and even Doc, from approaching the horse. The dog then leaped onto Jim Key's back.

Doc named the dog Monk, short for monkey. When no one claimed him, Monk began to travel with Jim Key. He never appeared on stage, but was a constant companion in the horse's stall. From his perch atop Jim's back, Monk served as the horse's bodyguard, threatening to bite strangers who came too close.

What was the secret of Jim Key's abilities? Did the horse really have a level of intelligence that allowed him to think and reason—or were his feats merely sophisticated tricks?

In October 1901, a group of professors from Harvard College attended two of Jim's performances. They concluded the act was not a

hoax. Neither Doc Key nor anyone in the audience was consciously giving the horse cues. Jim Key's unique upbringing and close relationship to Doc, as well as the gentle training he had received, seemed to play a role in the horse's ability to sense what Doc wanted him to do.

Doc and Jim Key were one of the most popular acts at the 1904 St. Louis World's Fair. The Silver Horseshoe Pavilion was specially constructed for their exhibit. Five million visitors attended Doc and Jim's performances. Two million children joined the Jim Key Band of Mercy and signed a pledge that stated, "I promise to be kind to animals."

After their 1906 season, Jim Key began to suffer from arthritis. Doc and his horse returned to their home in Shelbyville, Tennessee to rest. Over the next few years, Doc and Jim performed for small groups who visited their farm, but due to the declining health of both, the pair never traveled again.

In 1909, Doc died at seventy-six. Jim Key was lost without the man he'd rarely been apart from. Mrs. Key's brother, Stanley Davis, who had traveled for years with the show, took over Jim's care. Three years later, at twenty-three, Beautiful Jim Key passed away.

21

Clever Hans

H ans, what is two and three?" asked Wilhelm von Osten.

Tap, tap, tap, tap, tap. Clever Hans, a tall, thin Orlov Trotter, pawed five times with his right leg. Wilhelm von Osten, born in 1838, was a retired math teacher. At times, he must have compared his equine protégé's ability to that of his former students. Some of his fellow Germans estimated Hans' mathematical abilities to equal that of a fourteen-year-old human.

In 1888, Wilhelm had purchased the first Hans, a stallion he used as a carriage horse. He recognized the animal's intelligence by the horse's ability to maneuver the carriage with little or no assistance from his driver. Believing the intelligence of animals was greatly underestimated, Wilhem began an unusual experiment with the horse. The first Hans learned to tap out numbers up to five when Osten called them out. Before Wilhelm got any further with his project, the twelve-year-old Hans died from colic.

Von Osten traveled to Russia to select a new horse. He chose a five-year-old Orlov Trotter stallion, black with two hind socks and a star. Wilhelm named this one Hans, as well. The horse's later fame resulted in plain old "Hans" being altered to "Clever Hans" or in German "der Kluge Hans."

Wilhelm resumed his training experiment with this new incarnation of Hans. After four years, the horse could perform an amazing variety of feats, and Wilhelm put Hans on display in Berlin. Von

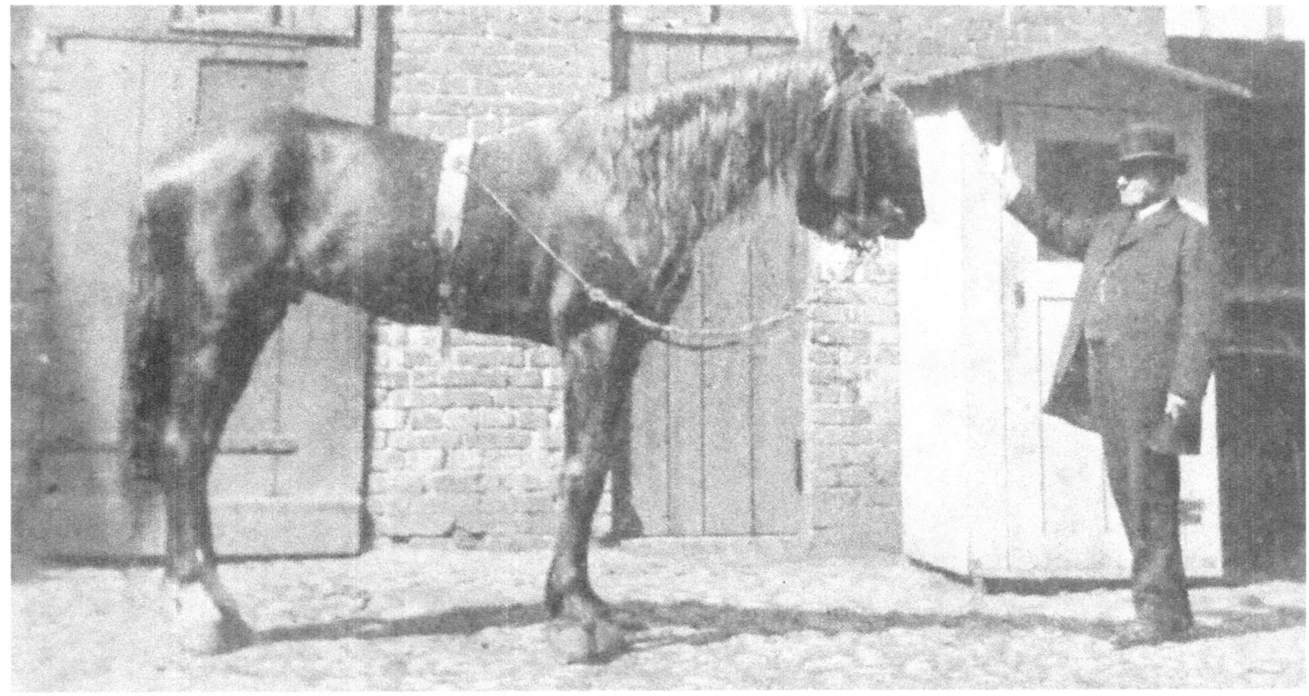

Osten never charged for these performances. He simply wanted the scientific world to recognize the horse's intelligence and abilities.

Crowds were astonished when the horse displayed seemingly human intelligence by answering various types of questions asked of him in German. Hans responded by selecting items in his mouth or by tapping with his right hoof.

Hans could:

- Move his head to indicate yes or no
- Identify colors
- Distinguish between right and left
- Count
- Add, subtract, multiply, and divide
- Work with fractions
- Tell time
- Spell using lowercase letters (he was not taught capitals)
- Identify musical notes
- Understand the value of German coins
- Understand the calendar
- Tell time
- Recognize people from photos
- Count groups of people from among the spectators—for example, the number of children or girls in the audience

During his exhibitions, Hans stood untied. Mr. Osten never used a whip with the horse but rewarded him for correct behavior with a treat of bread or carrots. If Hans understood a question, he nodded his head—if not, he shook it from side to side. Hans could also indicate directions by turning his head up, down, left, or right.

"If the first day of the month is a Wednesday," Von Osten would ask Hans, "what is the date of the following Monday?"

Six hoof-taps followed.

Hans could pick out a requested color from a row of colored cloths. He could recognize a musical note sounded or sung to him, such as C, D, or E. He mastered the numbers from 1 to 100.

When asked a fraction problem, such as, "How much is 2/5 and 1/2?" Hans first tapped the numerator (9) then the denominator (10) to show that the answer was 9/10.

Hans spelled words using a special table created by Mr. von Osten. Each letter of the alphabet, and some letter

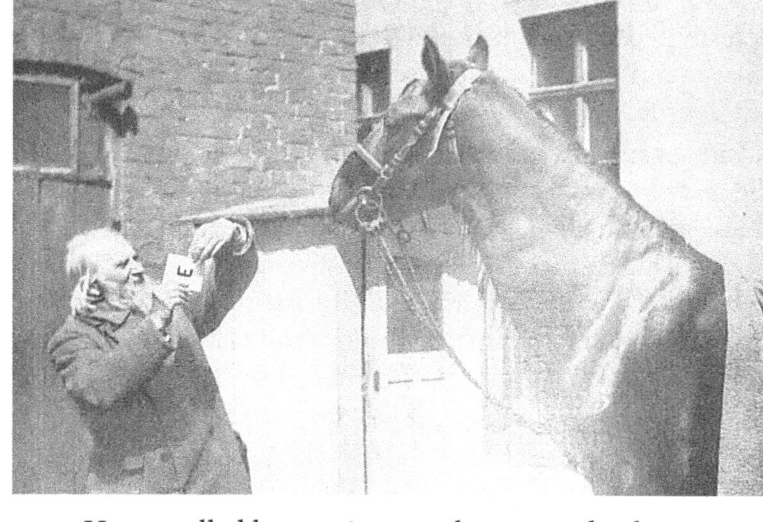

combinations, were in fixed rows and columns. Hans spelled by tapping out the row and column numbers for each letter in a word.

Tasks that were given once could be repeated correctly upon request. The sentence: "Brücke und Weg sind vom Feinde besetzt." (The bridge and the road are held by the enemy) was given to Hans one day. The following day, he was able to correctly tap out the numbers that spelled the sentence.

Hans became the subject of poetry and songs. His likeness appeared on children's toys and postcards. Articles were printed in German newspapers and magazines extolling the horse's intelligence. News of Hans even traveled to the United States. In September 1904, a New York Times article described Hans as "Berlin's wonderful horse! He can do almost everything but talk."

After observing him in person, many leading psychologists and animal trainers were convinced of the horse's intelligence. Others remained skeptical.

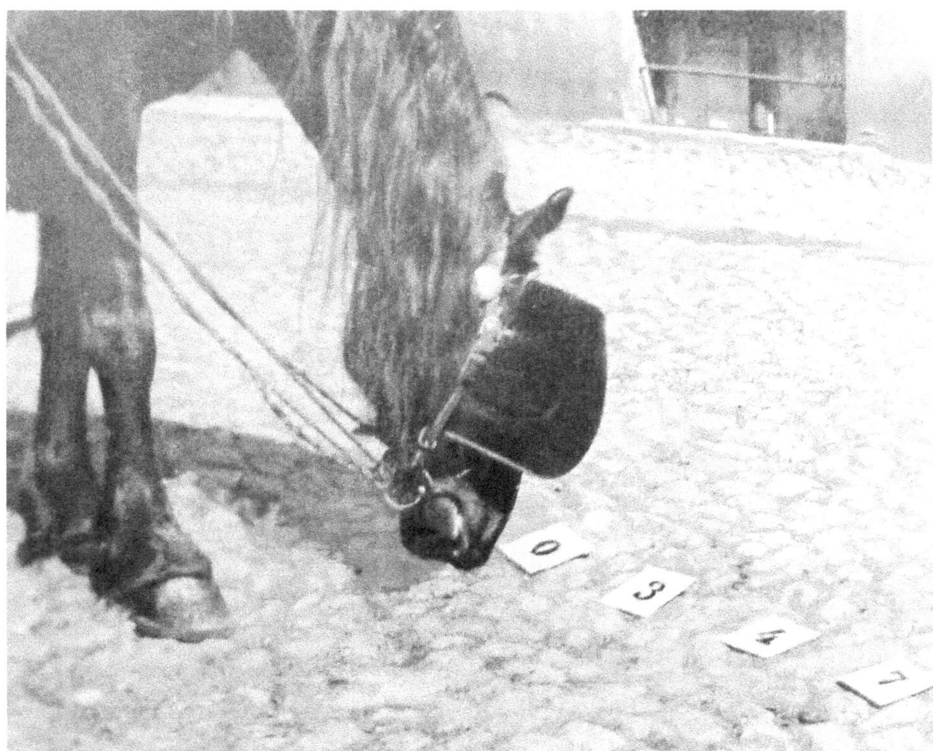

In 1904, a scientific committee headed by C. Stumpf (director of the Institute of Psychology at Berlin University) included a circus proprietor, army captain, veterinary surgeon, and zoo director.

The committee studied Hans' performances to determine whether the horse was responding to signals from von Osten. After observation, the commission concluded there was no trickery involved in the performances.

Still not convinced, psychologist Oskar Pfungst, headed another investigation in 1907. Pfungst determined Hans came up with the right answer 89% of the time when von Osten knew the correct answer and the horse could see him. If von Osten did not know an answer, Hans was correct only 6% of the time.

Pfungst realized he was on to something. Somehow, von Osten was communicating answers to the horse. Upon examining Wilhelm von Osten more closely, Pfungst detected almost imperceptible changes in the man's posture or facial expression when the horse approached the right answer. Given a horse's nearly 360 degree field of vision, and the ability to see separately out of each eye, Hans could observe his handler while remaining focused on the task at hand. This allowed him to respond to the tiny, involuntary cues of von Osten's body language. Some even believed Hans was capable of detecting a slight change in the man's heart rate.

While for most people, the mystery of Clever Hans' intelligence was solved, von Osten was certain his horse really could read and count. He continued trying to convince the world of Hans' intelligence.

Some speculated von Osten died of grief from the suggestions that he engaged in fraud or trickery. In reality, he died of liver cancer in June 1909. Wilhelm requested that upon his death, Clever Hans be given to Karl Krall in Elberfeld, Germany.

Krall was training his own horses in a manner similar to von Osten's. For several years, Krall worked with Clever Hans. But in 1916, Hans, as well as Krall's other horses, were conscripted into the army to serve in World War I. It's believed Krall's animals, including Hans, were used as artillery horses and died in battle in Flanders, Belgium.

22

The Talking Horses of Elberfeld

Hans was not the only clever horse in Germany. Upon his owner's death, Clever Hans was given to Karl Krall, a jeweler. Krall used methods similar to Wilhelm von Osten's to train his own equine menagerie. Besides Hans, Krall owned two donkeys, a Shetland pony named Hänschen, a blind stallion Berto, an elephant, and several other horses. Collectively, they were known as the Talking Horses of Elberfeld.

Other than Hans, the most famous among Krall's group were the Arabian stallions Muhamed and Zarif. Muhamed liked to solve complex arithmetic problems while Zarif's skills were in the area of reading. Muhamed could find the cube roots of numbers. He tapped out answers with his hooves. The horse used his left leg for the part of the answer to the left of the decimal point and his right leg for the digits to the right of the decimal.

Krall considered Muhamed the most intelligent of his horses. He even believed Muhamed would tell him if the other horses were being lazy or when any of the animals were abused.

Krall was as convinced as von Osten that the horses possessed intelligence at a higher level than was previously recognized. Also like von Osten, Krall was determined to prove it. Berto was blind, therefore unable to see visual cues, but he was still able to perform mathematical calculations.

Krall attached blinders to the other horses so they couldn't see the trainer. He even gave performances in the dark. To exclude the possibility of mind reading, questions were sometimes asked by telephone, placing the receiver near the ear of the horse.

Author Maurice Maeterlinck was one whom Krall and his horses convinced. The following is an account of Maeterlinck's introduction to the horses.

> *The master, standing beside the blackboard, chalk in hand, introduces me to Muhamed, in due form, as to a human being, "Muhamed, attention! This is your uncle" —pointing to me— "who has come a long way to honor you with a visit. Mind you don't disappoint him. His name is Maeterlinck."*
>
> *"Do you understand: Maeterlinck? Now show him you know your letters and that you can spell correctly like a sensible child. Go ahead, we're listening."*
>
> *Muhamed gives a short neigh and on the small, movable board as his feet strikes first with his right hoof and then with his left the number of blows which correspond with the letter M in the conventional alphabet used by the horses. Then, one after the other, without stopping or hesitating, he marks the letters A D R L I N S H, representing the unexpected aspect which my humble name assumes in the equine mind and phonetics. His attention is called to the fact that there is a mistake.*
>
> *He readily agrees and replaces the SH by a G and then the G by a K. They insist that he must put a T instead of the D; but Muhamed, content with his work, shakes his head to say no and refuses to make any further corrections. [ending with MADRLINK]*
>
> *— Denkende Tiere*

Krall volunteers to leave the area and encourages Maeterlinck to test the horse by giving him any two or three syllable German word for the horse to spell.

Behold Muhamed and me by ourselves. I confess that I am a little frightened. … However, I summon my courage and speak aloud the first word that comes to me, the name of the hotel at which I am staying: "Weidenhof."

At first, Muhamed, who seems a little puzzled by his master's absence, appears not to hear me and does not even deign to notice that I am there.

But I repeat eagerly, in varying tones of voice, by turns insinuating, threatening, beseeching and commanding: "Weidenhof! Weidenhof! Weidenhof!"

At last my mysterious companion suddenly makes up his mind to lend me his ears and straight-way blithely raps out the following letters, which I write down on the blackboard as they come: W E I D N H O Z. It is a magnificent specimen of equine spelling.

But probably to many of us the most astonishing thing that Herr Krall reports is that upon two different occasions on his return from a business trip, one of these horses spelled out to him information of things that had happened in his absence:

"One morning, for instance, I came to the stable and was preparing to give him [Muhamed] his lesson in arithmetic. He was no sooner in front of the spring-board then he began to stamp with his foot. I left him alone and was astounded to hear a whole sentence, an absolutely human sentence, come letter by letter from his hoof: 'Albert has beaten Hänschen,' was what he said to me that day."

"Another time I wrote down from his dictation, 'Hänschen has bitten Kama.'"

Of this Maeterlinck says: "Krall, for that matter, living in the midst of his miracle, seems to think this quite natural and almost inevitable. I, who have been immersed in it for only a few hours, accept it almost as calmly as he does. I believe without hesitation what he tells me; and in the presence of this phenomenon which, for the first time in man's existence, gives us a sentence that has not sprung from a human brain, I ask myself whither we are tending, where we stand and what lies ahead of us."

— *The Presbyterian of the South, Atlanta, Georgia, October 28, 1914*

As with Clever Hans, Krall's horses were tested by scientists and psychologists, many of whom were convinced of the animals' intelligence and believed no trickery was involved in their performances. Professor H. E. Ziegler of Stuttgart observed the equines in action.

The pony Hänschen was the most willing of the horses to work alone with strangers, but that in no case could the horse see its master or anything but the board on which the problems are written, as they wear blinkers.

Ziegler described the way they tapped out the solutions as rapid and elegant, adding,

the horses are so friendly they lick your hands all over—all except old Hans, now sixteen years of age, whose temper is very bad although he still calculated extremely well.

In 1912, Krall published the book, *Denkende Tiere*, (Thinking Animals), which focused on his experiments with Clever Hans, Muhamed, and Zarif.

But after Oskar Pfungst's testing seemed to prove Clever Hans was being unconsciously signaled by von Osten, much of the public and the scientific community no longer believed in the idea of human-level intelligence in horses.

With the outbreak of World War I, the Talking Horses of Elberfeld were requisitioned by the German government. Initially, Krall protested so vehemently that they were not taken. But later, they were demanded again, and Krall was forced to give them up.

According to a January 6, 1915 article in The Princeton Daily Clarion, the Elberfeld horses were used in the artillery and were killed in battle in Flanders, Belgium.

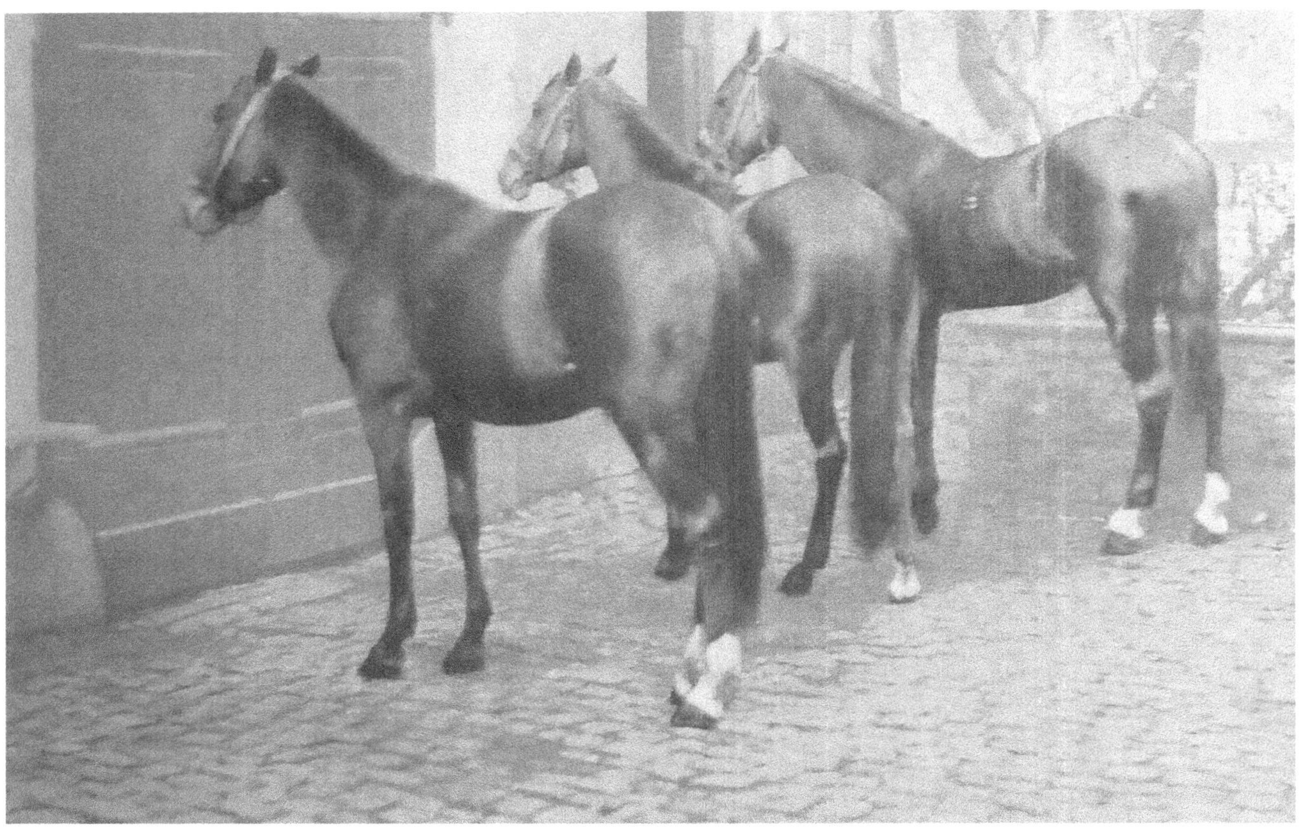

l. to r. - Zarif, Muhamed, Hans

23

Captain

Even though George Wharton James wrote a detailed book about Captain, the horse is perhaps the least familiar of the "intelligent" equines of the late 1800s/early 1900s. Captain was owned and trained by Mr. W. A. (Captain) Sigsbee.

Sigsbee grew up in the horse business, helping his father and uncles raise and train trotting horses in Wisconsin. By eighteen, he had his own business training and selling horses and dogs. After marrying, he continued in that line of work. Sigsbee knew his neighbors would pay extra for a horse, who in addition to being well trained, could perform a few tricks.

His reputation as a trick trainer spread, and circus men came to him to purchase his trained horses and dogs. In time, Barnum and Bailey, Ringling, and other famous circus owners asked Sigsbee to train horses for them.

Always on the lookout for unusually intelligent young horses, Sigsbee found a great prospect in Princess Trixie. He trained the part-Arabian filly to perform a variety of tricks and exhibited her at county fairs before selling Trixie to another showman.

Sigsbee worked for four years as the director of a traveling circus. His duties included keeping the animals in good condition and training new stock. Initially, the show traveled with sixteen wagons. Later, they used eleven rail cars. Sigsbee's wife tired of the nomadic lifestyle, and they returned home to rest.

While searching for another horse the caliber of Trixie to train, Sigsbee heard of a colt in Illinois. There, he found a 15.2 hand chestnut, owned by Judge Cartwright. Born in 1905 and known then as Sid Bell, the colt was fast and had a promising future in harness racing as a pacer. But, more important to Sigsbee, he was friendly, playful, and showed keen intelligence.

Judge Cartwright wasn't interested in parting with his star colt, so it took some persuading on Sigsbee's part. He explained the colt would have an easier life than that of a racehorse. His purpose in training the horse was to demonstrate that animals could reason and were capable of thought. He appealed to the pride the judge would feel when the colt he had raised became world famous. Those persuasive words, along with a check for a thousand dollars, did the trick, and Sigsbee returned home to Chicago with his next project.

From the start, Sigsbee believed he could go farther with the colt he named Captain than anything he'd done before, even with the remarkable Trixie. Sigsbee gave Captain time to adjust to his new surroundings. He worked to gain the horse's trust and affection. Captain received plenty to eat, the best of care, was treated kindly, and given treats such as carrots, apples, and sugar.

I never disappointed him. I never lied to him—that is promised him anything I did not intend to perform, and thus he soon learned I was to be trusted.

— The Story of Captain, How I Bought And Trained Captain

Captain became very uneasy when left alone, so Sigsbee hired a groom named Chili, who remained with the horse night and day. The groom didn't teach Captain anything, but simply cared for him and was his companion. Captain became fond of the man, but due to Chili's carelessness, Sigsbee had to let him go. Jasper replaced Chili and remained with the horse long term.

Captain still resented being left alone. Each night, he listened for his groom. If he was absent, the horse would paw and whinny, making a continual ruckus until Jasper returned and talked to him. Then content, Captain could sleep.

One day, Jasper was given a pigeon. He brought the bird to the stable where it perched on a partition of the stall. Captain was greatly interested in the pigeon and nuzzled it affectionately. The bird wasn't afraid and seemed to enjoy the attention. The two became nearly inseparable. Captain spent hours resting his head upon the partition, close to the bird.

People often ask me how I train an animal. Personally I would not use the word "train," in speaking of such a horse as Captain, not because it is the wrong word, but because it conveys a wrong idea. I would say "educate," for I firmly believe that horses and dogs and elephants and other animals possess the power of reason, though, of course, in a limited degree. And I believe that by patient and kindly treatment we can "draw out,"—educate—the intelligence possessed.

Though you must be kind you must also be firm. Many people confound and confuse kindness with mushiness. No animal must be allowed to have his own way, when that way conflicts with his master's will. There should be no attempt to "break the will." It is to be trained, disciplined, brought under control.

When it comes to actual teaching always be very patient, never excited, always talk gently and keep your voice pitched low, and remember that all animals are curious, possess more or less of the imitative faculty, and have good memories. To remember these things is of great importance. Never lose sight of them. Talk to your animal as you would to a child. Whether you think or believe he understands you, or not, act and talk as if he did. Then show him what you want him to

do. Do it before him, again and again. Thus you will excite his imitative faculties and at the same time, train his memory.

Remember always, in all you do, that you are dealing with an animal whose brain power is far less than that of an ordinary child, and be patient, kind and persevering. Never allow yourself to believe the animal does not possess intelligence. Believe he has it, hope he has it, trust God that he has it and work in that belief, hope, trust, and you will accomplish wonders.

In his book, George James also described Captain's experience from the horse's perspective:

For five whole years my master kept me at school. Every day he came to my stable, or took me out into the yard, to give me my lessons. I guess I was a slow learner, and it took a great deal of patience to make me remember, for I was only a horse—not a boy or a girl, with human intelligence. We had to go over the same lessons scores, hundreds of times, until I knew them by heart. But my master was kind all the time, seldom spoke angrily to me, and never whipped me, though he kept a small switch in his hand with which he gave me a gentle reminder, once in a while, when I was inclined to be a little more frolicsome than usual.

One day he came to me and said: "Now, Captain, you and I are going to travel and see the world. Do you know what I have been educating you for? I am going to let people all over this country see you, and what you can do, so that they will no longer be able truthfully to say that a horse has no intelligence. When we are on the trains, your groom will remain in your stall and travel with you, and when we stop anywhere to 'show' he will spend his nights with you as he has done all the time."

    — The Story of Captain, Captain's Own Story

George Wharton James with Captain

And travel they did, Captain performed many of the same "tricks" of the other "educated" horses like Clever Hans and Muhamed. As had been the case for the other horses, many people were skeptical about how Captain could do so many amazing things.

The author describes his first encounter with the horse.

> *I was introduced to CAPTAIN, the educated horse, or, as he has been termed, "the horse with the human brain." His appearance was pleasing. He looked well cared for, contented, happy and willing to go through his exhibition. There was none of the holding back, the whipping, the sharp orders, the ugly looks one so generally sees on the faces of "trained animals" when they are being put through their tricks.*
>
> *After a little pleasantry his master asked him to count the number of ladies on the front row. Captain's eyes at once began at one end, followed the row, down to the other end, and, by pawing, he told the number. Several similar questions were asked, as, for instance, how many gentlemen in the second row; how many women along the aisle; how many girls, or boys, in the second or third rows, etc., and in every case Captain gave the answer correctly.*
>
> *Then a standard was brought forward containing numbers, to which were attached leather lugs or holders. Here he showed his familiarity with numbers, bringing from the rack any one called for. Then tests in arithmetic were applied, such as the addition of numbers as 9 plus 6 plus 7. Captain at once picked out the figure 2 and then after dropping it, picked it up and showed it again. Subtraction was equally well performed, and multiplication up to 12 times 12, and the answers given were invariably correct.*
>
> *When told to pump water he would swing his head up and down continuously, and he would swing his head to right and left as commanded. When asked to laugh he opened his mouth and showed his teeth, and he wiggled his ears with equal readiness. When told to put out his tongue it came out immediately, and when commanded to make a hobby-horse of himself he planted his hind feet firmly and then proceeded to stretch himself by planting his forefeet as far ahead as he could.*
>
> *Then came an exhibition of Captain's recognition of colors. A rack containing ten or fifteen colored cloths was placed before the audience. The horse was asked to go and pick out, say, the third lady in the second row, look at the color of her hat (or shawl, dress, gloves or other article of apparel), and then take up the cloth from the rack which corresponded to the color of the article worn. In this he seldom made mistakes.*
>
> *The exhibition with the Cash Register then followed, Captain being asked to get a paper dollar, then change it for small silver, when he brought out half a dollar and two quarters.*
>
> *Then he was called to the chimes and the audience was informed that Captain could play "Nearer, My God to Thee," or "The Suwanee River," and it could make its choice. The former tune was called for and Captain played it correctly.*
>
> *These, in the main, were his achievements. They delighted, yet, at the same time, puzzled me. How did he accomplish them? By the kindness of his owner, Mr. W. A. Sigsbee, I was permitted to visit Captain in his stall as often as I chose. As I got to know him better my interest increased, until I decided that I should like to write his story.*
>
> — *The Story of Captain, Introduction*

Captain was tested by a veterinarian, Dr. G. V. Hamilton. Based on his observations, Hamilton reached the following conclusions.

I am convinced that Mr. Sigsbee is sincere in his belief that Captain is capable of abstract thought, and that he resorts to no trickery in his public performances.

My observations, although incomplete and inconclusive in many respects, have convinced me that Captain can give correct answers in entire independence of directive visual stimuli. There was no trickery about his blindfold: Captain wore a leather mask which so well excluded the light that he had to be led from place to place on the stage.

This animal may receive auditory cues that are given involuntarily by his master. It is not only conceivable but even likely that Captain is sensitive to changes in his master's respiratory sounds. A spasmodic inspiration, a faint sigh or a sudden quickening of respiration might easily serve as cues for Captain.

Captain first performed in Chicago in 1913. Some of his larger exhibitions included the Panama-Pacific International Exposition at San Francisco in 1915, and the Panama-California International Exposition at San Diego in 1916.

A "Horse's Prayer" requesting kind treatment from his master was printed in many newspapers at the time. George James included a long prayer that he believed was more suitable to Captain. Rather than being abused or neglected, Captain had been well-treated his entire life. In Captain's prayer, he thanks his master for that kind treatment. The prayer ends with these words.

And, though I am a horse, I am sure you have remembered that God is my Father and Creator as well as yours, or I should not be here, and that His Son said that His Heavenly Father cared even for the sparrows, two of which were sold for a farthing, and that He himself ever sanctified a stable by the fact that He was born in one and cradled in the manger at Bethlehem. So, In His Name, I give you thanks for all your kindness to me, recalling to your memory His words that "inasmuch as ye have done it unto the least of these, my brethren, ye have done it unto Me."

Amen.

24

The Great Cowboy Race

Due in part to railroad expansion, refrigerated rail cars, and barbed wire, the ways of the cowboys and the Old West were fading. In a desperate attempt to hold on to the excitement of the past, nine cowboys gathered in the small town of Chadron, Nebraska, each determined to win a 1,000 mile race across the prairie. The finish line of the Great Cowboy Race was the entrance to Buffalo Bill's Wild West show next to the 1893 Chicago World's Fair.

The idea for the race began as a hoax, dreamed up by Chadron news reporter John Maher. A story spread to the Eastern newspapers that there were 300 entries, including Native Americans, outlaw cowboys, and even one woman, who would all race across several states to Chicago.

In the East, no one suspected the event was a figment of Maher's imagination. The eastern papers built up the outlaw aspect of the race. To save face, the people of Chadron decided to go through with The Great Cowboy Race; otherwise, they feared they would become the laughingstock of the country.

The following rules governed the event.

- The race would start on June 13, 1893, from the Blaine Hotel in Chadron and end at the entrance to the Wild West show in Chicago

- Cowboys could ride no more than two horses

- Horses must have been western bred and raised

- Only western stock saddles weighing at least thirty-five pounds could be used

- Rider, saddle, and blanket were to weigh at least 150 pounds

- The entrance fee for each rider was $25, paid no later than June 1

- The race would be open to anyone in the world

- Each horse would be given a commemorative brand

- Riders were required to register at twelve checkpoints along the route

- Anyone sneaking off to ride a train would be disqualified

- Each rider would be given a map just before the start of the race

The prize for first place was $1,000. In addition, the first place winner would receive:

- Another $500 from Buffalo Bill Cody

- A revolver with a gold-plated cylinder and carved ivory handles from Colt Firearms

- A saddle from the Montgomery Ward store in Chicago

Arrangements were proceeding better than expected until George T. Angell, president of the Massachusetts Society for the Prevention of Cruelty to Animals, heard about the race. Angell immediately sent a letter of opposition to newspapers and animal rights organizations throughout the country.

> *Some three hundred cowboys are proposing to race more than seven hundred miles from Chadron, Nebraska to the Chicago World's Fair.*
>
> *If these semi-barbarians were to pass through Massachusetts we could take care of all of them without difficulty, but as it is we have written a letter to our friend John J. Shortall, Esq., president of the Illinois Humane Society, who will unquestionably do all in his power to prevent this proposed outrage.*
>
> *The time of starting the race is fixed at about June 25th, (perhaps the hottest part of the summer), and each rider is allowed only two horses.*
>
> *Under these circumstances we do most earnestly pray all of the about ten thousand American editors who will receive this paper and all humane citizens, will prevent by the power of the press and the enforcement of laws, this disgrace to American civilization so that if the race is begun no rider shall ever be permitted to enter Chicago having ridden two horses day and night, under whip and spur, to win these purses.*
>
> *And we do most earnestly ask all humane people who may reside in any city through which these men pass to receive them with hisses and cries of "Shame."*
>
> *On behalf of the dumb beasts whom it is proposed to ride in this terrible race, I earnestly pray the assistance of all who are able in any way to assist in saving them from this torture and our country from this disgrace.*

Of course, there never had been 300 "semi-barbarians" preparing to race to Chicago. And the cowboys who had entered the race didn't appreciate Angell's opinion of them.

James Middleton Riley, "Doc" Middleton, was perhaps the truest outlaw of the nine men in the race. Middleton stole his first horse at fourteen, and would steal perhaps 2,000 in his lifetime. He had once been convicted of murder but escaped from the prison.

The nine participants and their horses included:

1. Emmett Albright riding Outlaw (buckskin) and Joe Bush.

2. Joe Campbell riding just one horse, Boomerang (gray gelding).

3. "Little Davy" Douglas riding Wide Awake and Monte Cristo. Davy was in his teens.

4. Old Joe Gillespie riding Billy Mack (chestnut gelding) and Billy Schafer (dapple gray). Joe was the oldest rider, at fifty-eight, and the heaviest at 185 pounds.

5. George "Stub" Jones riding Romeo (bay) and George (black).

6. Charley Smith riding Dynamite and Red Wing (chestnut).

Doc Middleton

7. James Stephens "Rattlesnake Pete" riding General Grant and Nick. The wife of the Chadron sheriff sewed seventy-two rattlesnake rattles into his hat band. The twenty-five-year-old was the smallest of the riders at 5' 4". He'd trained General Grant in one week, then ridden him from his home in Kansas to Nebraska for the race. Pete kept dried beef to feed his horses.

8. Doc Middleton riding Geronimo and Jimmy (bay). Doc was the village of Chadron's favorite.

9. John Berry riding Poison (chestnut stallion) and Sandy (bay gelding).

Berry was part of the committee that laid out the "secret" race route through Nebraska, across Iowa, and into Illinois. Some believed his horses weren't western range horses. Berry claimed he was only in the race because Poison's rider had gotten sick and dropped out. The organizational committee decided they couldn't keep Berry out of the race. But because he had prior knowledge of the route, he wouldn't be eligible for the prizes.

The morning of the race, each of the participating horses was branded with a "2" on the right side of his neck to prevent the riders from switching to new horses during the race.

Although they'd planned for an early morning start on June 13, agents from the National Humane Society arrived in Chadron, determined to stop the race. After some discussion, everyone agreed to allow a Humane Society veterinarian to examine the horses prior to the start of the race and at each checkpoint. (Long Pine, O'Neill, and Wausa in Nebraska; Sioux City, Galva, Fort Dodge, Iowa Falls, Waterloo, Manchester, and Dubuque in Iowa; Freeport, Dekalb, and Chicago in Illinois.)

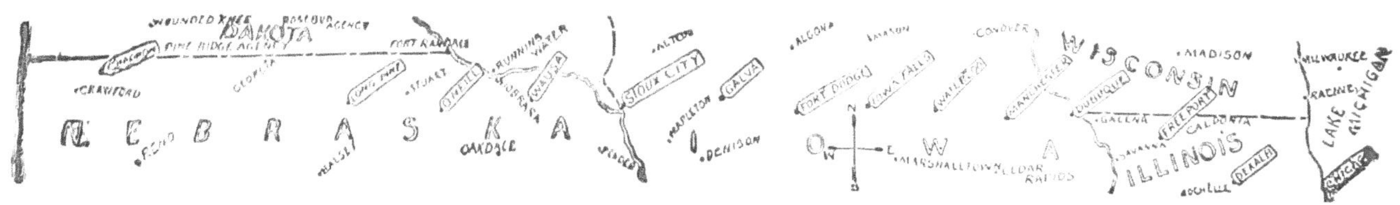

It was evening before they were ready for the race to begin. Sheriff Dahlman read the race rules to the contestants. He stressed that,

a rider cannot have his horse drop dead at the goal line and gain a prize. He must see to it that his horse is in fairly good condition on arrival.

At 5:30 PM, James Harzell, chief of the Chadron volunteer fire department, spoke to the nine riders.

Gentlemen, the time for the Great American Cowboy Race to start is upon us. Be kind and take care of your horses. Conduct yourselves as gentlemen and uphold the good name of Chadron and Nebraska.

He raised the gold-plated Colt revolver and fired the shot that started The Great Cowboy Race. Despite the humane societies' concerns about the riders abusing the horses, all nine left Chadron at a walk or jog. The race wasn't a sprint; the cowboys were in it for the long haul.

As the days progressed, the riders started early in the morning, rested during the heat of the day, and resumed riding into the night to take advantage of the cooler temperatures. At each stop, the riders saw to the needs of their horses before addressing their own hunger and thirst.

After four days, Doc, Joe, and Pete were the early leaders. On day six, young Davy Douglas became sick and dropped out near Atkinson, Nebraska.

They ferried the horses across the Missouri River on a barge. Fifteen hundred spectators showed up to welcome the racers to Iowa. Despite George Angell's letter, none of the spectators cried out, "Shame!" to the cowboys.

As they entered Iowa, Humane Society veterinarian, Dr. Tatro, reported to his surprise, that most of the horses were fine.

There has not been any sign of cruel treatment of the horses. In fact, quite the reverse is the case, and they are well cared for and are not being over ridden. A stop is made every night, giving both the horses and men a good night's rest, and stops are made during the day from 3 to 5 hours.

Doc's horse, Geronimo, came up lame and was left behind. But, for the most part, the horses fared better than their riders. Rattlesnake Pete began coughing up blood, but he continued on, self-medicating with a bottle of whiskey.

John Berry reached Dubuque, Iowa first and crossed the High Bridge over the Mississippi River into Illinois.

After thirteen days and sixteen hours, at 9:30 AM on Tuesday, June 27, John Berry arrived at the Wild West show in Chicago. He slumped off of Poison's back and collapsed on the ground, saying, "Look after my horse."

Poison and Berry had traveled the last 150 miles in twenty-four hours. Two of Buffalo Bill Cody's staffers led Poison to a stable where they sponged the exhausted horse and rubbed liniment on his joints. Poison eagerly dove into the hay and oats they provided.

Emmett Albright arrived at 11:15, claiming to have finished second behind Berry. But when it was learned he had shipped himself and his horses part way to Chicago by train, Albright was disqualified.

Joe Gillespie came in at 1:30 PM on Billy Shafer, the real second-place finisher. He said of Billy Shafer, "He's the best hoss I ever throwed a leg over. Give him a little rest and two quarts of oats and he'll throw off another fifty miles this afternoon." After the race, Joe was offered $1,000 for his horse, but he refused to sell him for any price. Joe had lost thirty pounds on the two-week ride. Gillespie might have won the race if he hadn't stopped at a circus in a small Iowa town where he amused the spectators by riding a mule.

Charlie Smith on Dynamite finished third, fifteen minutes behind Gillespie.

Coming in fourth was Rattlesnake Pete on General Grant. His other horse, Nick, had suffered a bout of colic. Pete was followed by George Jones, Joe Campbell, and Doc Middleton. Middleton also shipped his horses part of the way when both came up lame.

With John Berry's surprising entrance into the race and his eventual win, there was much haggling between the participants regarding who would receive the prizes.

Since Berry was ineligible for the Chadron prize money, as agreed upon at the start of the race, the $1,000 was distributed as follows:

- $200 to Gillespie
- $200 to Smith
- $187.50 each to Stephens and Jones
- $75 each to Campbell, Middleton, and Albright

Buffalo Bill Cody's $500:

- $175 to Berry
- $50 to Gillespie
- $75 each to Smith and Jones
- $50 to Stephens
- $25 each to Campbell, Middleton, and Albright

John Berry received the Montgomery Ward saddle. Joe Gillespie received the gold-plated revolver which today is the property of the Dawes County (Nebraska) Historical Society. Only Davy Douglas, who had dropped out of the race early on, received nothing.

The fact that the horses held up so well during the race surprised The Humane Society representatives. Dr. Tatro pronounced the race a success.

It started in foolishness and was foolish business all through, but it has been an educator of the people, showing them that the so-called cowboys are not a set of horned animals, all wild brutal men, and the Humane Society discovered it was wrong in supposing that the riders would treat their horses badly. We consider the race a big success in every way.

— W. W. Tatro, Humane Society veterinarian

The finish line for The Great Cowboy Race was Buffalo Bill's Wild West (technically not "at" but "near") the Chicago World's Fair. The official name for the Fair was The 1893 World's Columbian Exposition. Dedication services were held in October of 1892, but the Fair, which celebrated the 400th year of Christopher Columbus' discovery, didn't open to the public until the following year.

The Exposition featured 200 new buildings on 690 acres, along with man-made canals and lagoons. More than twenty-seven million people attended the event during its six-month run from May 1 to October 30, 1893. The U.S. Census population for 1900 was about seventy-five million, so one in every three Americans attended the Exposition.

Buffalo Bill wasn't about to miss out on the biggest American event of his lifetime. When he inquired about bringing his show, he learned the required payment was half of each ticket sold. (There was a general admission ticket to the Exposition, but many exhibits within the Fair charged additional fees.)

Cody didn't want any part of that deal, so he leased fourteen acres of adjoining land to the west of the Exposition. He started his shows a full month before the Fair opened and closed down one day later. The Wild West averaged sales of 18,000 tickets per day for the Fair's duration.

Chicago Mayor Carter Harrison requested that a day be set aside for poor children in the area to attend the Fair for free, but Exposition officials turned him down. Buffalo Bill stepped up and offered every Chicago child free admission to his Wild West, including train tickets and all the candy and ice cream they could eat. Fifteen thousand children took advantage of his generous offer.

25

The Great Horse Manure Crisis

Those who love horses are likely guilty of a romanticized view of life in the horse-drawn vehicle era. The reality was that relying on millions of horses for transportation created a unique set of problems.

- Each horse produced twenty to fifty pounds of manure a day. That's roughly nine tons a year per horse along with untold gallons of liquid waste.

- In dry weather, traffic pulverized the manure into dust that floated onto people and through open windows.

- In wet weather, the manure became a mucky mess no one wanted to walk through.

- Decaying manure created a strong odor.

- In the past, farmers paid stable owners for the manure to fertilize their fields. But by 1900, the "fertilizer" was so plentiful, stable owners had to pay farmers to haul it away.

- Horses sometimes died on the streets, and it might be awhile before someone removed the bodies. Disease-carrying flies multiplied profusely in the standing manure and horse carcasses.

By 1900, there were twenty-four million horses in America. Many of those worked in cities, pulling carriages, streetcars, delivery wagons, and other vehicles.

Young "crossing sweepers" worked at street corners, offering to clear a path through the manure-covered streets for pedestrians, especially wealthy women, to walk through. In the days when women's attire reached the ground, this was an important service.

London, then the largest city in the world, had eleven thousand horse-drawn cabs, several thousand buses manned by teams of twelve

horses, and countless single horses pulling vehicles of all kinds.

One writer for The Times of London, 1894, stated that in fifty years, every London street would be buried under nine feet of manure. Not to be outdone by that dire prediction, some New Yorkers claimed that by 1930, horse manure would block third-story windows lining their city's streets.

The larger a city became, the more horses were required to keep everything functioning. The more horses—the more manure.

All those horses needed to be fed. Hay grown in the countryside was brought to the city by horses—who created—more manure. Even hauling the manure away by the wagon-load required additional horses—which produced even more manure!

People feared there was no solution to the Great Horse Manure Crisis.

In 1898, the first international urban-planning conference convened in New York City. Manure was the chief topic. Although scheduled to last ten days, the conference shut down after three. When the delegates could come up with no solution to the manure problem, they all packed up and went home. As it turned out, the dismal predictions of the Great Manure Crisis never materialized. No cities were ever buried in horse manure.

What was the miraculous solution, and who came up with it?

The crisis resolved itself as millions of horses were gradually replaced by motorized vehicles. By 1912, there were more cars than horses in London and New York City.

26

Horse vs. Bike

The year 1816 is known as the "Year Without a Summer." Temperatures in Europe were the coldest of any summer on record. The resulting crop failures caused the starvation and death of many horses. This loss of horsepower motivated a German, Karl von Drais, to find an alternative to horse-drawn transportation. In 1818, Drais received the first patent for a two-wheeled, steerable, human-propelled bicycle, known in German as a laufmaschine (running machine).

Drais constructed the forty-eight-pound bicycle primarily from wood. It was also called a draisine or velocipede. The bicycle's wooden wheels were wrapped with iron. It had no pedals; the rider simply pushed it along.

Some were certain the invention would never become popular. They scoffed, calling it a hobby or dandy horse. Those who rode it gave it a more fitting name—bone-shaker. Its rigid frame and iron wheels, combined with the rough roads, resulted in an uncomfortable "bone-shaking" ride.

For those accustomed to modern bicycles, it seems odd that no one thought to attach pedals to the velocipede until much later. Pedals didn't seem to appear until 1864.

In 1871, James Starley, a British engineer, created a modified velocipede. His design included a tall front wheel with attached pedals, and a small rear wheel. The size of the front wheel was limited to

the length of a man's legs, since the rider rode directly over the high wheel. These bikes, known as penny farthings or ordinary bicycles, were lighter and had rubber tires.

Although popular in the 1880s, the ordinary bicycles were dangerous. The high position of the rider meant his feet could not reach the ground. In the event of an accident, the rider was thrown over the front wheel. Two broken wrists were common as the rider reached out with both hands to break his fall.

Later in that decade, major improvements hit the cycling world. These changes produced the safety bicycle. As their name indicates, these bikes were much safer than the high-wheelers they soon replaced. Safety bicycles were close to today's version of the bike with smaller, equal-size tires, the seat positioned between the wheels, and a chain-driven pedaling system that powered the rear wheel.

Up to this time, bicycling had been almost entirely the province of well-to-do males. The poor couldn't afford the new inventions, and women's long, bulky dresses were certain to become entangled in the wheels. Also, it was inappropriate for women to be seen in public, attempting such an indecent thing as riding a bicycle.

However, a few brave women ventured out during the bicycle craze of the 1890s. These female bicyclists took advantage of new women's clothing styles, such as split-skirts and the pant-like "bloomers" which gave women more freedom of movement.

Annie Cohen Kopchovsky provided a boost to the acceptance of women cyclists when she became the first woman to bike around the world in 1894/1895. She was also known as Annie Londonderry after one of her early sponsors, the Londonderry Lithia Spring Water Company.

Returning to the premise of Karl von Drais and his original laufmaschine. Could bicycles replace horses? Certainly, a human riding a bicycle would have nowhere near the pulling power of a single horse, let alone a team of four or more.

The author of the following 1895 newspaper article fiercely defends horses in his rebuttal of a previous editorial extolling the virtues of bicycles over horses.

The horse-attacking editor has evidently learned to ride the bicycle and also evidently has never mastered the horse. His soul has never soared above the delirium of riding a "bike" over street-car tracks. If he had ridden a good horse over a picket fence he would know more about real life and excitement than he does now.

Suppose that a bicycle can go faster or further than a horse. Does that dishonor the horse? Why, you poor bicycle-pushing scribe, do you not know that an $8 typewriter can write faster than Shakespeare? Is the typewriter greater than Shakespeare?

Of course the horse has many diseases. So has the whale. The finer the animal the more complicated his organism and the more numerous his diseases. The horse-attacking editor has or could have more diseases than the horse or the whale. Shall we therefore despise him and replace him with something rubber-tired?

The horse is a man's animal. Well treated he keeps his health. Well handled he never shies, he never runs away, he never refuses to pull to the last ounce of strength in his body.

He is no more afraid of bullets than the horse-attacking editor is afraid of thistles. He is the fit associate of heroes. Can you see Napoleon or Alexander riding to victory on a "safety?" No. The horse is for heroes and the "safety" for horse-attacking editors. Bicycles and flying machines may come and carry the horse-fearing editor far and safely, but they will not destroy the horse.

— *The Sacramento Bee, Saturday, June 22, 1895*

The article illustrates the strong feelings on both sides about the superiority of their preferred mode of transportation. As the popularity of bicycles increased, horses were forced to share streets and roads with the two-wheeled machines.

It was inevitable that challenges would emerge to prove which was faster. In the 1890s, racetracks across America held exhibition races, pitting horses against bicycles. A popular format was a race of ten to thirty miles. Jockeys could switch off between multiple horses while the bicyclist often remained on a single bike.

Buffalo Bill Cody, always on the lookout for events to draw a crowd, was involved in organizing many races of this type. In November 1887, during a tour of England, Bronco Charley Miller and Marve Beardsley competed on horseback against two cyclists, Richard Howell and W. M. Woodside. Beardsley had been a Pony Express rider. Bronco Charley also claimed to have ridden for the Pony Express when he was eleven years old.

The six-day race took place on indoor tracks at the Agricultural Hall in London. As many as 20,000 spectators watched the event. The contestants raced for eight hours a day. Thirty horses were used by the cowboys who switched off on them every hour. The horses and cowboys came out on top, beating the cyclists by two miles. The cowboys completed 814 miles and 4 laps. The cyclists rode 812 miles and 3 laps.

In Milan, Italy, Buffalo Bill Cody raced the famed European cyclist, Romulus Buni, on March 9, 1894. Buni was known as "The Little Black Devil," because he always wore a black sweater when he raced. Both Cody and Buni

rode for three hours. Cody had the use of up to ten horses. At the end of the three hours, Buffalo Bill was the winner, traveling sixty-three miles to Buni's sixty-one.

Even when the bicycle craze began to die down, the popular horse versus bike races lasted well into the 1930s. Olympic bicyclist, Eddie Testa, lost to a horse named Brick in a one-lap race in Los Angeles in 1934.

In recent years, a few bicycle against horse exhibitions have resurfaced, mainly in Europe. In 2014, at Leopardstown Racecourse in Ireland, jockey Pat Smullen rode Moonbi Creek in a fund-raising race, the Beast vs. Bike Challenge, against Tour de France cyclist Nicolas Roche. Moonbi Creek won the two furlong (1,320 ft.) sprint quite easily.

Did races pitting horse against bicycle prove anything? The consensus seems to be when competing without relays, a horse will usually win at shorter distances, but in longer races, the bike will win. Even if true, that doesn't make a bicycle better than a horse. As the Sacramento Bee article concluded—

> *No pneumatic-tired arrangement, however valuable to the poor, timid, busy, aged, or obese editor, can take his [the horse's] place. He is first, now and forever, in the heart of normal, healthy men.*

THE VELOCIPEDE.

27

Rural Free Delivery

In 1775, the Second Continental Congress established the first official postal system in the American colonies, naming Benjamin Franklin the first postmaster general. Franklin improved mail delivery times by establishing more efficient delivery routes.

When America became independent, its new constitution gave Congress the power "to establish post offices and post roads." In 1792, the Post Office Department was created to deliver mail weighing up to four pounds. Newspapers formed the bulk of early mail deliveries. Private delivery companies handled heavier packages.

The Pony Express only operated for nineteen months (April 1860 to October 1861), but its horses and riders delivered mail from St. Joseph, Missouri, to Sacramento, California, in as little as ten days.

Free mail delivery within cities began in 1863. But sixty-five percent of Americans lived in rural areas at that time. Rural residents traveled to the closest post office to pick up their mail. Congress frowned upon free delivery to rural areas; fearing the extra cost would bankrupt the post office. They finally decided to offer a test service in 1896, beginning with five routes in West Virginia, covering ten miles each. The deliveries were so popular, Rural Free Delivery (RFD) became a permanent part of the postal service in 1902 with rural routes averaging twenty-five miles.

Most of the first RFD mail carriers made their rounds on horseback or by horse-drawn wagons. The carriers provided their own horses and vehicles. They were also responsible for the food, care, and stabling of the animals. In wintry weather, they sometimes used a sleigh for deliveries.

One carrier, Leroy J. Caldwell of Craig County, Virginia, was proud of his equine delivery partner. His horse carried the mail 56,000 miles over his career. The animal knew every mailbox on their route and stopped at each one without any signal from Caldwell.

In 1903, journalist Max Thrasher rode with a rural carrier in Michigan and described the experience.

We left the post office at Cassopolis at 8.30 AM and were back there at 5 PM There were 109 boxes on the route over which we drove, and we stopped at over one hundred of them. Into those boxes we distributed 264 papers, 37 letters, 8 postals, 12 circulars and 2 packages.

We made the trip in a small, light, covered wagon, built expressly for this purpose, so as to secure the comfort and convenience of the carrier with the least possible weight.

In the bottom of the front end of the wagon and in easy reach of the driver's seat is a set of pigeon holes in which he arranges his mail as he drives, so as to have it convenient for delivery. This man must have had between fifty and seventy-five pounds of mail when he started out that morning. Delivery begins about two miles out from the post office.

The exterior of the cart is painted a light blue, and from its size and color the vehicle is conspicuous a long way off on the country roads. The carrier wears the gray uniform of the regular postal service. Each carrier is required to furnish his own wagon and the horses to draw it, and to provide for the keep of the horses. Two horses are necessary, so that they may have alternate days in which to rest. It takes a pretty good horse to draw such a wagon over twenty-five to thirty miles of country roads in all kinds of weather, at all seasons of the year, making a hundred or

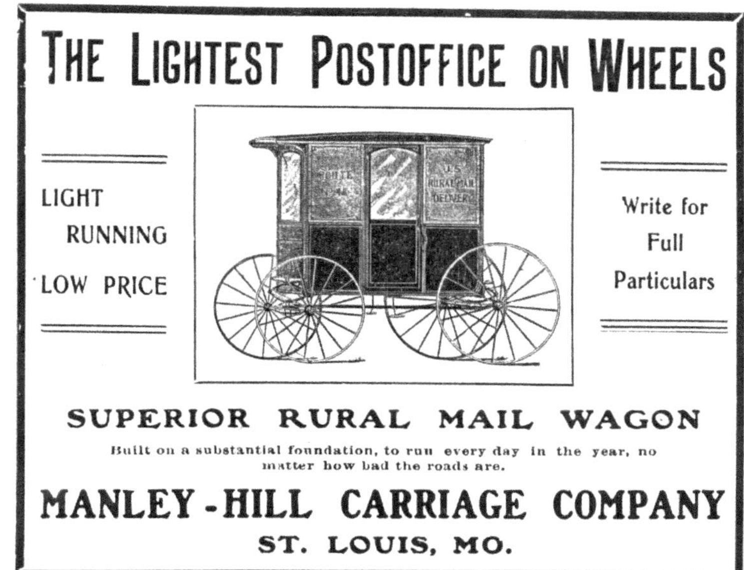

Post offices began accepting parcels over four pounds on January 1, 1913. This was a big boon to mail order companies like Montgomery Ward whose first catalog in 1872 listed 163 items for sale. By 1883, the catalog, known as the "Wish Book," had grown to 240 pages and 10,000 items.

An early competitor to Montgomery Ward in the mail order business was Sears & Roebuck. The company, founded in 1892 by Richard Warren Sears and Alvah Curtis Roebuck, initially offered watches and jewelry, but expanded to include additional items.

No regulations specified what type of parcels could be sent through the mail. Several children were mailed via the post office as it was cheaper than alternate modes of travel, such as train.

In February 1914, a five-year-old Idaho girl, May Pierstorff, was mailed by her parents for fifty-three cents to the girl's grandparents, seventy-three miles away. They attached the postage stamps to May's coat. The postal worker, who delivered her by mail train, was related to the girl's mother. Michael O. Tunnell created a picture book of May's story, *Mailing May*.

Edna Neff of Pensacola, Florida, had the record for the longest distance a child was mailed. She was six when mailed 720 miles to her father's home in Christiansburg, Virginia.

After word of these "packages" spread, the postmaster general added a rule that humans could not be sent through the mail. But people still attempted it for a number of years.

Although horses were the primary means of local delivery in the early RFD days, the mail arrived at the local post offices by train. Special rail cars, known as Railway Post Offices or RPOs, were included in passenger trains. Since passenger trains didn't always stop at every station, they devised a way to exchange incoming and outgoing mail without the train having to stop or even slow down.

The station's postal agent hung his mail bag on a "mail crane" alongside the track. The RPO car had a mail hook or catcher located beside its door. As the train passed a station, a clerk on the train rotated the hook arm out to catch the bag. The mail bag coming from the train to the local post office (incoming mail) was often just flung out the RPO door.

This system didn't always work perfectly. If the RPO clerk moved the catcher arm out too soon, it might bash something close to the track or the arm might be ripped off the side of the train. If the incoming mail bag wasn't tossed far enough, it could be run over by the train. A bag bursting open, with letters and other mail flying everywhere, was known as a snowstorm.

Mail Bag Catcher

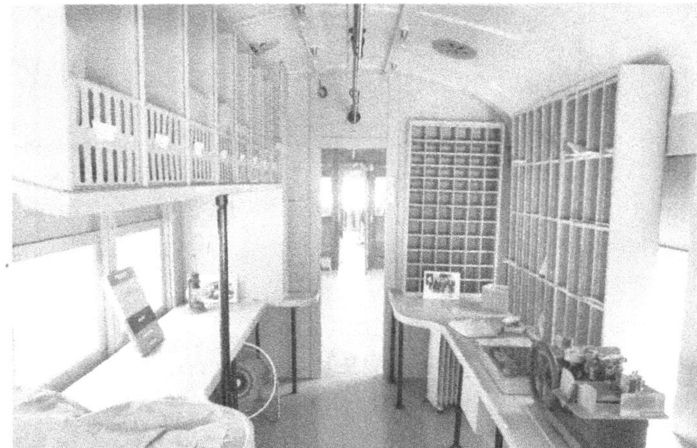

Railway Post Office Interior

Larger cities began to use entire trains devoted to mail service rather than just a single car in a passenger train. In 1875, a five-car mail train began delivering mail between New York and Chicago.

Just as the stagecoaches out West were targets for criminals wanting to make easy money, so the mail trains were subject to robbers.

The worst mail train robberies were committed by two sets of brothers. On October 11, 1923, Hugh, Ray, and Roy DeAutremont ambushed a Southern Pacific train in Oregon as the train emerged from a tunnel. They believed there was $40,000 in gold on the train. The brothers dynamited their way into the mail car but used so many explosives the car was nearly destroyed as were most of its contents. A mail clerk died in the explosion, and the brothers killed three other crew members. The brothers escaped, with nothing. They were apprehended three years later, convicted, and sentenced to life in prison.

Between 1919 and 1924, the "Newton Gang" robbed eighty-seven banks and six trains. In 1924, the four Newton brothers, Doc, Jess, Joe, and Willis, stole $3 million in cash, jewelry and securities from a mail train in Illinois. It was the largest train robbery in history. A corrupt postal inspector, William Fahy, was part of the scheme. No one was injured in the robbery, except Doc, who was shot but survived. They all received prison sentences with Fahy receiving the longest at twenty-five years. All but about $100,000 from the robbery was recovered.

126

28

Equine Moving Company

For centuries, horses have pulled carts, wagons, sleighs, and cannons, but in the past, they pulled something even bigger—houses! In fact, in the late 1800s, horses moved fifty-five houses from the old location of the village of Katonah, New York to its new location a half mile away. What made an entire village move?

It wasn't totally voluntary. Either they moved or the village would be underwater. Katonah, about forty miles north of Manhattan, stood in the middle of the construction site for the new Croton Dam and reservoir. They needed the larger system to provide water to New York City—home to more than a million people and growing.

City administrators paid the village residents for their land and houses, taken by the process known as eminent domain. Rather than lose their community as well, they formed the Katonah Village Improvement Society. Most of the townspeople chose to remain together by moving to a nearby location on higher ground, safely away from the dam and reservoir. The main street of the new Katonah was one hundred feet wide with a flower-filled center strip. "The selling of liquor was not to be allowed nor the keeping of swine, vicious dogs or poultry."

Residents bought their houses back at auction so they could be moved to the new village site. The houses began their trek in 1897 with a few buildings being moved as late as 1901. Other buildings in

New Katonah, such as the schoolhouse, were constructed on site. The official date of the founding of New Katonah is April 5, 1897.

It's difficult to imagine horses being able to move a house, but the determined villagers and their strong equines used a slow but effective process.

Jacks lifted the house up from its foundation. Next, they laid heavy timbers to serve as a track. A tow rope, connected to the house, was attached to a pulley, and then to a capstan. The capstan was anchored to something strong, such as a nearby tree. A team of horses were hooked to long bars extending out from the capstan. As the horses walked in a circle, the tow rope wound around the capstan, causing the house to inch forward on the timber track extending from under the house.

Laundry soap greased the timbers to help the house slide more easily. When the house passed over one set of timber rails, they were picked up and moved to the front to extend the track. When the house reached the capstan, the horses and capstan were moved ahead. It was a slow process, but it worked.

James Clark has arrived in Katonah with H. W. Kellogg's house and barn. They are now sliding down Bedford Road and in another week will be near their foundation next the residence of E. B. Newman. June 10, 1898

Some families continued to live in their houses during the move. Dr. F. H. Williams arrived in Katonah to serve as the best man in an on-the-move wedding. It wasn't uncommon for children to leave for school in the morning and return to find their house in a different place.

Katonah, named for a 17th-century Ramapo Indian chief, has remained small. The population of the village in the 2010 census was 1,679. In 2007, representatives of Katonah opposed an attempt by Martha Stewart to trademark the name of their village for her furniture line. Stewart gave up on the "Katonah Collection" and her trademark application was abandoned.

Katonah wasn't the only place where horses moved houses. This photo shows a similar process where a Victorian home was moved in San Francisco, California, in 1908.

For smaller houses, a capstan might not be necessary. Teams of ten or more horses could pull some buildings without one.

It's not as common to move houses today. When one is moved, horses are no longer used. The route has to be clear of overhead electric or utility lines. State or local permits can cost $10,000 or more. The cost of the move depends on the size of the building and the distance it will be moved. It can sometimes be as much or more than the cost of new construction, so moving is often used only for historic buildings.

29

Rough Walkers

Remember the Maine!" was the slogan of Americans calling for war against Spain. Since the early 1500s, Cuba had been part of Spain's empire. Although other Latin American countries gained independence from Spain, Cuba had not. In 1895, Cubans renewed their efforts for freedom.

To support Cuba, the U.S. sent the battleship, the USS Maine, to Havana. The ship sat anchored in the harbor for several months. On February 15, 1898, the Maine exploded, killing 262 American sailors. The ship sank in Havana Harbor.

Although Spain denied blowing up the Maine, American journalists and Assistant Secretary of the Navy, Theodore Roosevelt, called it a Spanish act of war. On April 25, 1898, Congress declared war against Spain.

A volunteer cavalry regiment was authorized to fight in Cuba. Leonard Wood resigned as White House physician to command the regiment. Roosevelt resigned his naval position to serve under Wood as second in command.

Colonel Wood and Lt. Colonel Roosevelt began recruiting and organizing the 1st United States Volunteer Cavalry, later known as the Rough Riders. The regiment trained at Fort Sam Houston in San Antonio, Texas.

Volunteers poured in from Arizona, New Mexico, Oklahoma, and Texas—cowboys, prospectors, hunters, gamblers, Native Americans, and a few college students from the East. They were skilled horsemen, eager for combat. The regiment's uniform was a slouch hat, blue flannel shirt, brown trousers, boots, and a handkerchief worn around the neck.

Two mounts were procured for Roosevelt at $50 each—a small bay called Little Texas and a larger horse, Rain-in-the-Face, named after a Lakota chief. Roosevelt said of the two, "The animals were not showy; but they were tough and hardy, and answered my purpose well."

Although the quartermaster put out a call for horses that were "well broken to saddle," many of the animals that arrived at the fort were not trained. The first time the troopers mounted, many of the horses bucked, tossing riders in all directions.

Meanwhile we were purchasing horses. Judging from what I saw I do not think that we got heavy enough animals, and of those purchased certainly a half were nearly unbroken. It was no easy matter to handle them on the picket-lines, and to provide for feeding and watering; and the efforts to shoe and ride them were at first productive of much vigorous excitement. Of course, those that were wild from the range had to be thrown and tied down before they could be shod. Half the horses of the regiment bucked, or possessed some other of the amiable weaknesses incident to horse life on the great ranches; but we had abundance of men who were utterly unmoved by any antic a horse might commit. Every animal was speedily mastered, though a large number remained to the end mounts upon which an ordinary rider would have felt very uncomfortable.

— *The Rough Riders, Theodore Roosevelt, 1899*

The horses hadn't the slightest idea of what was wanted. Some of the horses seemed to think we were getting ready for a race while others considered it a free-for-all and proceeded to pitch, bite, strike and kick at everything near them.

— *Rough Rider, Royal A. Prentice*

On May 29, 1898, after several weeks of training at Fort Sam Houston, 1,060 Rough Riders and 1,258 of their horses and mules made their way to the Southern Pacific railroad to travel to Tampa, Florida where they would set off for Cuba.

According to Roosevelt, "There were no proper facilities for getting the horses on or off the cars, or for feeding or watering them; and there was endless confusion and delay among the railway officials."

Four days later, they arrived in Tampa.

Once on the ground, we speedily got order out of confusion. For thirty-six hours we let the horses rest, drilling on foot, and then began the mounted drill again. There were but four or five days at Tampa, however. We were notified that the expedition would start for destination unknown at once, and that we were to go with it; but that our horses were to be left behind, and only eight troops of seventy men each taken.

The Rough Riders, although they received the most attention, were a small part of the U.S. force which included sailors, regular Army soldiers, and African American Buffalo Soldiers.

Ironically, the Cavalry regiment went horseless, except for officers' mounts. Most of the horses were left behind in Tampa, and the Rough Riders became known as the "Rough Walkers" or "Weary Walkers."

There was barely room aboard the ships to carry the soldiers, let alone their horses. A transport ship, the Yucatan, carried 940 men. The officers' horses, including Roosevelt's Little Texas and Rain-in-the-Face, were in the hold of another boat.

When the transports arrived in Cuba on June 22, they had no good way to get the horses and mules off the ships. The frightened animals were simply shoved out the side hatches. The animals plunged into the sea, uncertain which way to swim.

Meanwhile, from another transport, our horses were being landed, together with the mules, by the simple process of throwing them overboard and letting them swim ashore, if they could. Both of Wood's got safely through. One of mine was drowned. The other, Little Texas, got ashore all right. I had succeeded in finding Texas, my surviving horse, much the worse for his fortnight on the transport and his experience in getting off, but still able to carry me.

— The Rough Riders,
Theodore Roosevelt, 1899

Mosquitoes proved to be a formidable enemy, attacking soldiers on both sides of the war, spreading yellow fever and malaria. Dirty drinking water sickened the men as well, causing dysentery and typhoid fever.

When Colonel Wood left to replace a sick officer, Theodore Roosevelt took command of the Rough Riders. They joined the Buffalo and regular troops in two important battles. First was the

Battle of Las Guasimas on June 24, where the Spanish were driven back. The second was the battle Roosevelt and the Rough Riders became famous for. Some refer to it as The Battle of San Juan Hill.

On July 1, Roosevelt, mounted on his horse, Texas, led a charge up Kettle Hill toward San Juan Heights. Roosevelt called this "the great day of my life." Waving his men forward, the Rough Riders (on foot) stayed put, hugging the ground. Roosevelt challenged them, "Are you afraid to stand up when I am on horseback?"

While it might seem an advantage to have a horse, it made Roosevelt a more visible target. Ironically, the first soldier to stand was shot and killed. The remaining Rough Riders followed on foot while Roosevelt rode up and down the hill, encouraging his men to fight. Partway up the hill, Roosevelt encountered a barbed wire fence, forcing him to dismount and continue on foot himself.

> *Some forty yards from the top I ran into a wire fence and jumped off Little Texas, turning him loose. He had been scraped by a couple of bullets, one of which nicked my elbow, and I never expected to see him again.*
>
> *— The Rough Riders, Theodore Roosevelt*

Within ten weeks, Cuban and American victories brought the war to an end. On July 17, Spain surrendered, and in August, Cuba was freed from their control. The Treaty of Paris officially ended the war. Roosevelt returned a war hero and national celebrity and was elected governor of New York the following year. Roosevelt believed he deserved the Medal of Honor for his part in the Cuban battles, but the War Department refused to give it to him. Secretary of War Russell A. Alger believed Roosevelt was only following orders and had done nothing extraordinary.

> *In charging up San Juan Hill, Colonel Roosevelt was carrying out the orders of his superior officers. If we were to award him a medal it would be necessary to reward in like manner every officer and man who participated in that charge, and, carrying out the same principle, it would only be just to award a medal to every officer and man who did his duty in the campaign before Santiago de Cuba.*

One thousand of the unit's horses, who had been left behind in Florida, were auctioned by the War Department in September 1898. The animals sold for $25 to $30. A few Rough Riders were successful in purchasing horses they had ridden.

Little Texas survived the war and retired at the Roosevelt's summer residence in New York. He died in 1903 and was buried in a pet cemetery behind the main house.

30

Rodney

We know little about the millions of horses who served in wars around the world. The few who are remembered are most often officers' mounts. Rodney is one of the exceptions. He served as an artillery horse.

A beautiful bay, they drafted Rodney into the Army in 1896 at the age of eight. Believed to be a Thoroughbred and Clydesdale cross, Rodney stood almost 16 hands tall and weighed 1,250 pounds. Because of his size and strength, he served with the artillery. In the days before motorized vehicles, artillery horses pulled large guns or cannons onto battlefields. A team of six horses was usually assigned to each gun.

Rodney's position was the left wheel horse, directly in front of the two-wheeled cart or limber the team pulled. His partner, Shaw, was hitched to Rodney's right. Two swing horses were ahead of them, with the lead pair at the front. As a wheel horse, Rodney not only pulled the heavy limber and gun, he and Shaw served as the brakes for the unit via the breeching strap around their hindquarters.

An artillery team was harnessed to the two-wheeled limber which had a single box or ammunition chest on top. At the back was a quick connecting system known as a pintle. This allowed other equipment to be towed behind the limber—a gun or cannon, the caisson, a battery wagon carrying spare parts, or a traveling forge for a blacksmith.

Guns had their own two-wheeled carriages, each towed by a limber. The gun was pulled backwards with the firing end pointing away from the horses. The gun and its carriage could be quickly "unlimbered" or detached from the limber.

After the gun was detached, the horses remained harnessed to the limber and were moved to a safer area. They usually stood behind the gun, facing toward it. Each pair of horses was held by their driver. When the gun needed to be moved, the horses and limber returned to the gun and "limbered up" or reconnected to it.

A caisson was similar to a limber but bigger. It connected behind a limber. A caisson had two ammunition chests as well as an extra wheel and other spare parts.

Each horse on the near (left) side was ridden by a "driver." The riders were known as postilions and the ridden animals as post horses. Traditionally, horses are mounted from the left. The left horses in the artillery team are ridden since there is no easy access to the near side of the right-hand horses. Other soldiers in the unit rode on the limber or walked.

Once Rodney's training was complete, his first battle experience came in 1898 when he was shipped to Cuba during the Spanish American War. Rodney and Shaw were most likely involved in the early phase of the Battle for San Juan Hill, in which Teddy Roosevelt and the Rough Riders fought.

> *Rodney was the pet of every driver who sat him and the pride of every battery with which he served. He was never sick and never refused a feed or a task. Intelligent, strong, and willing, he pulled so hard that sometimes he broke his harness. His great moment came at El Pozo, Cuba, in 1898.*
>
> *When the guns of Light Battery A, 2d Artillery, badly needed on the firing line, became mired in a churned-up, almost impassable slough, Captain George S Grimes ordered all teams unhitched. Rodney and his teammate, Shaw, alone were kept in draft. Urged by their driver, the mighty pair, belly-deep in mud, threw their weight into their collars, tugged for dear life at traces, and hauled limber and gun out onto firm ground. Then they extricated all the rest of the stalled carriages, and the battery galloped forward into action. The same day they rescued another bogged-down outfit, much to its chagrin, and later, before Santiago, repeated their feat.*
>
> *— Sound of the Guns, p. 200-201*

Although wounded, Rodney survived the war. After returning from Cuba to the United States, he was transferred to the 3rd Field Artillery at Fort Myer, Virginia. There, he participated in military drills, exhibitions, and was used to help train young horses.

At twenty-eight, Rodney showed his age. He could no longer pull the limber, even in exhibitions. But he remained a favorite of the men at Fort Myer. One day, while Rodney's outfit was on a hike, an inspector condemned the old horse and ordered that he be sold.

> *The men of the battery heard of the matter just in time to have a representative at the sale and bid the horse in, as they could not bear to see the old fellow sold outside the service. He brought something like $120, which was subscribed and paid for by the men of the organization.*
>
> *Since that time this horse has remained a pet and an inspiration to the men of the battery and a favorite among the officers, and has been fed, groomed and cared for by the battery.*
>
> *This horse is an inspiration and though unable to accompany the battery in the field, should be cared for at the post, as has been done in the case of other "retired" animals (old "Putnam" and old "Foxhall," both of the 3rd Field Artillery).*
>
> *It is requested that the authority be granted to stable, forage and care for this animal wherever he may be for the balance of his life.*
>
> — *letter written by the battery commander, Capt. Charles G. Mortimer, to the Adjutant General*

In his retirement, Rodney was given a new job—helping raise hay into a loft, using a rope with block and tackle. Not as eager to work as he'd been in his youth, the white-muzzled Rodney often galloped away from the stable when he spotted a load of hay arriving.

Rodney died at Fort Myer at thirty.

Rodney was the inspiration for a short story by Leonard Nason for The Saturday Evening Post, January 21, 1933. The story was so popular it was made into a motion picture the following year. Initially titled *Rodney*, as the Post story had been, the seventy-two minute film was released March 2, 1934 as *Keep 'Em Rolling*.

Apparently, there was some difficulty in finding a horse suitable for the role of Rodney.

Of course there is Rodney, the equine lead, yet to be found. And Radio [RKO] is having a hard time finding the right animal to play the role. It's easy enough for an author to cause a horse to do things in a story, but it's another thing to find one that is smart enough to do those things in real life, as Brower [the director] feelingly remarked.

— *The Los Angeles Times, August 29, 1933*

They filmed the RKO movie at Fort Myer in Virginia. The War Department authorized the use of Fort Myer troops in the film. During filming, a cannon slipped backward and rolled down a hill, killing cameraman William Casel and seriously injuring his assistant.

The Post story and the movie play loosely with the facts of Rodney's life, beginning with a change in the setting. Both are set during World War I rather than the Spanish American War. What remained true was that after experiencing how faithfully Rodney served in the war, his men couldn't bear to see him sold off in his old age.

In addition to Rodney, two other artillery horses mentioned by Fairfax Downey in *Sound of the Guns* were Putnam and Foxhall. Putnam was taller than Rodney. He was a Percheron/Thoroughbred cross who not only served in the Spanish American War but spent a year fighting in the Philippines. In 1900, Putnam was in China for the Boxer Rebellion. There, he was part of a ninety-mile march to Peking.

The team of the first piece hit the grade. Lead, swing, and wheel pairs had scrambled up and over when a trace spring snapped just as the limber wheels reached the top. Five horses out of the six quit pulling and began to slide back. Old Put alone dug in his hoofs and kept the remaining trace taut. Then without a word from his driver he virtually crawled up the slippery slope. Unaided, the splendid wheeler hoisted the carriages on to the level plain, averting a crash which would have disabled both gun and team. That fine performance and his service in the storming of the city won the horse the new name of "Peking."

— *Sound of the Guns, p. 202*

Putnam or "Peking" returned to the Philippines where, after completing his career as an artillery horse, he was retired. He was honored at his death with a military funeral.

Foxhall was one horse that was pushed out of the ship when it arrived in Cuba in 1898. The confused horse swam far out to sea but was herded back to shore by a boat crew. He survived the Spanish American War and later worked delivering bread at an Army base. He pulled the driver-less cart from the commissary to the kitchen, ate his share—four loaves, then galloped back to his stable. Foxhall passed away at the good old age of forty.

138

The 3rd United States Infantry Regiment, also known as The Old Guard, is the oldest infantry regiment still active in the U.S. Army. One of its special units, the U.S. Army Caisson Platoon, is used for military funerals, ceremonies, and parades. The unit has teams of all gray and all black horses who perform up to eight funerals a day.

Artillery horses vanish except for a team to draw a caisson and its flag-draped burdens in military funerals. They yielded to the efficiency of the age of motors, and even surviving artillerymen of the horse-drawn days, who knew the thrill of a battery galloping into action, are resigned, content to cherish the memories of four-footed companions that served them so gallantly and so well.

— *Sound of the Guns, p. 197*

In 1956, "The Army Goes Rolling Along" was designated the official song of the United States Army. Originally, the song was "When the Caissons Go Rolling Along," written in March 1908 by Brigadier General Edmund Louis Gruber, a descendant of Franz Gruber, the composer of "Silent Night."

The original version of the song.

Over hill, over dale
As we hit the dusty trail,
And those caissons go rolling along.
In and out, hear them shout,
Counter march and right about,
And those caissons go rolling along.

Refrain:
Then it's hi! hi! hee!
In the field artillery,
Shout out your numbers loud and strong,
For where e'er you go,
You will always know
That those caissons go rolling along.

The modified lyrics.

March along, sing our song,
With the Army of the free
Count the brave, count the true,
Who have fought to victory
We're the Army and proud of our name
We're the Army and proudly proclaim

Refrain:
Then it's Hi! Hi! Hey!
The Army's on its way.
Count off the cadence loud and strong,
For where e'er we go,
You will always know
That The Army Goes Rolling Along.

31

Lifeboat Horses

S ir William Hillary devised a plan to save the victims of shipwrecks along the coast of the United Kingdom and Ireland. In 1823, he proposed a lifeboat service to be manned by

a large body of men in constant readiness to risk their own lives for the preservation of those whom they have never known or seen, perhaps of another nation, merely because they are fellow creatures in extreme peril.

The priorities of the lifeboat service were as follows:

- *preservation of human life from shipwreck*

- *assistance to vessels in distress*

- *preservation of vessels and property*

- *prevention of plunder and depredations in case of shipwreck*

- *succour and support of those persons who may be rescued*

- *bestowing of suitable rewards on those who rescue the lives of others from shipwreck or who assist vessels in distress*

When the British Navy ignored Hillary's proposal, he sought non-military support. For a year, Hillary appealed to prominent citizens, politicians, bankers, and shipping merchants. William Wilberforce, who was instrumental in abolishing slavery in England, was one who backed the founding of what would become the Royal National Lifeboat Institution (RNLI).

Lifeboats were rowed by a crew of twelve or more men into the stormy seas out to shipwrecks. But first, those boats had to be moved to a site along the shore where they could be safely launched. That was the horses' role in a rescue.

Teams of up to twelve or more horses hauled the heavy boats on trailers across sand and mud to the best launching point with respect to the wreck. Since shipwrecks often occurred during horrible storms, the horses endured severe weather as they pulled their boat. The launch point might be several miles from the boat's storage location.

Lifeboat stations didn't keep their own horses. Animals were provided by the community or by paid contractors. The Merchant Shipping Act of 1854 gave lifeboat stations the right to demand horses, paying the owners an hourly rate for their use.

The average time to collect all the animals, gather a crew, and launch the lifeboat was an hour and a half. The work was strenuous and dangerous. Sometimes, horses were washed out to sea. Consequently, owners were reluctant to hand over their best horses for lifeboat work.

One of the most amazing rescues was that of the Forrest Hall, a 1,900-ton ship sailing from Bristol to Liverpool with thirteen crew members and five apprentices. On January 12, 1899, a violent storm threatened the ship and its crew.

At 7:52 PM, the Lynmouth lifeboat station received a telegram that the Forrest Hall was in danger of running ashore. Unable to put to sea at Lynmouth, their only chance to save the ship was to tow their lifeboat, Louisa, to Porlock Weir.

The leader of the lifeboat's crew, Jack Crocombe, proposed a thirteen-mile overland journey to get the Louisa to a safe position for launch. A local farmer, Tom Jones, provided eighteen horses. Tom Willis was the driver. The team, with the boat carriage, stretched to one hundred and thirty feet.

The treacherous terrain from Lynmouth to Porlock Weir climbed from sea-level to over 1,400 feet. Six men with shovels went ahead to widen parts of the road so the team and boat could pass through. In the muddiest areas, they lined up wooden skids for the team to walk across. Once over them, the men picked up the skids and placed them in front of the horses again. At one point, a wheel came off the carriage, and they had to stop to repair it—all this in a driving rain and snow storm.

C. Walter Hodges lists the horses as:

> *Daisy and Ben closest to the boat trailer, Busko and Lady as the leaders, "difficult" Margie and Grace, Charcoal and Jake, Sailor and Samson, Betty and Barnstable, Sue and Alice, Beauty and Stamper, Molly and Tomboy.*
>
> *— The Overland Launch, p. 55*

The lifeboat arrived at the launch point at 6.30 AM on the thirteenth after a grueling eleven-hour journey. The crew launched the lifeboat immediately. It took an hour to row out to the Forrest Hall. Between the lifeboat crew and men from two tug boats, all eighteen passengers aboard the ship were saved.

Volunteers re-enacted the Forrest Hall rescue one hundred years later, on January 12, 1999. Although the re-enactment was during the daytime, the weather was nearly as bad as it had been in 1899.

Many horses performed this vital rescue role for nearly a hundred years. Little is known about the individual horses or the men who trained and cared for them. As with horses that pulled fire engines, machines later replaced the lifeboat horses. The RNLI experimented with tractors using caterpillar tracks in 1920. Horses were phased out over time in various locations.

THE OVERLAND LAUNCH

Written and illustrated by

C. WALTER HODGES

Penguin Books

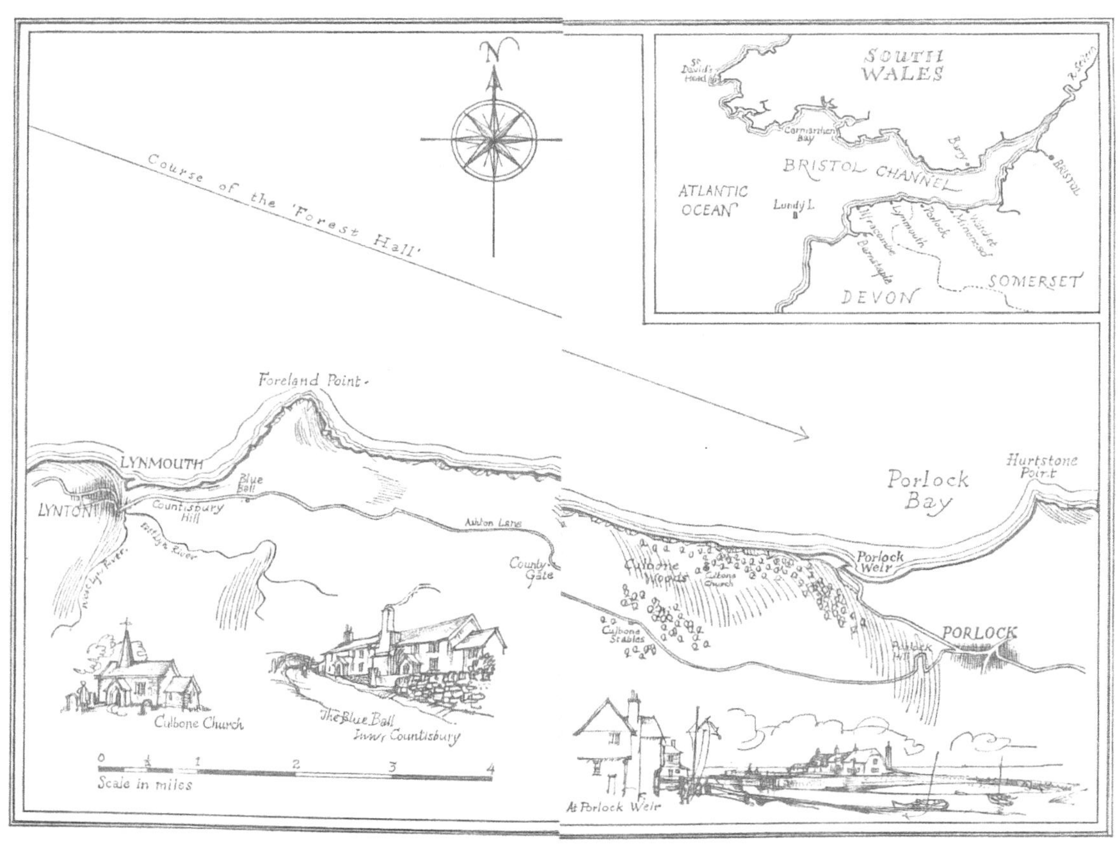

32

Horse Fountains

One of the early campaigns for animal welfare organizations was the creation of public water fountains for working horses. Cities designed ornate fountains, often in the middle of a busy intersection, for easy access by multiple horses. It became an unofficial contest to see which city had the most, or the most elaborate, fountains. Washington, D.C. had over 150 public fountains. London, England had over 1,000.

When Hermon Lee Ensign, a wealthy animal welfare advocate, died in 1899, he left his fortune to the National Humane Alliance, an organization he founded. Ensign's money was designated for the creation of animal drinking fountains. The only cost to a city was the shipping fee from the quarry in Vinalhaven, Maine where the granite fountains were made.

People contacted the Alliance to request a fountain for their city. The city needed to have a suitable location, a public water supply, and they must agree to maintain the fountain. Between 1902 and 1915, 125 fountains were donated.

One of the cities that received a Humane Alliance fountain was Grand Junction, Colorado. The seven-foot-tall fountain weighed five tons and had a six-foot bowl hewn from a single piece of granite. Water flowed from three sides out of brass lion heads. Eight horses could drink from the fountain simultaneously. Bowls around the base held water for dogs. A street light was mounted at the top. On March 29, 1911, Grand Junction residents held a ceremony to dedicate the fountain.

Cleveland, Ohio received their fountain in 1906. The following summer, it was reported 700 horses a day were drinking from it. But the era of public horse fountains didn't last long. In 1914, there was an epidemic of glanders in the horse population. Glanders is a fatal bacterial disease that causes skin lesions and respiratory infections. It is one of only a few zoonotic diseases (transmissable

from horses to humans). Fortunately, the last recorded case of glanders in the United States was in 1937.

In 1914, over a thousand horses died of glanders in Massachusetts alone. Many cities shut down or removed their horse fountains. The fountain closures caused a heated controversy. One side argued the fountains were spreading the disease. The other side wanted the fountains to remain open. They reasoned that if the water was continually flowing and diseased horses were euthanized, the spread of glanders could be controlled. Another argument in favor of using the fountains was that the harm to horses from not having adequate water during the workday would cause more deaths than the disease.

In 1916, Cincinnati, Ohio, which had closed its fountains, had an outbreak of glanders, anyway. The controversy over the fountains raged, but most cities kept them closed. Women in some towns formed crews stationed at water hydrants to fill buckets of water for horses to drink.

The invention of the automobile meant the gradual disappearance of most horses from the cities. This issue with the water fountains may have hastened that transition. Without the public fountains, workers found it challenging to provide their horses with enough water during the day. At about that

same time, old cobblestone and brick streets were being replaced with pavement that provided a smooth ride in a car. But the paved surfaces provided less traction for horses, making it more likely for them to slip and injure themselves. These factors all worked against using horses in the cities.

As more automobiles appeared on the streets, the fountains became traffic hazards. Fountains in busy intersections were removed. In recent times, some of the horse fountains have been restored. At least seventy NHA fountains are still publicly viewable. The Cherry Hill Fountain in New York City was restored in 1998. The fountain is located at the center of a circular concourse in Central Park that was once used as a carriage turnaround.

33

The First Cowgirl

Although cowgirl is a common word in English today, it wasn't widely used until 1899 when Teddy Roosevelt applied it to fourteen-year-old Lucille Mulhall.

Lucille was born on October 21, 1885 in St. Louis, Missouri. By the age of four, the family had moved to a ranch north of Guthrie, Oklahoma. At its peak, the ranch consisted of 80,000 acres.

The daughter of Zack and Agnes Mulhall, her family claimed Lucille was "born in the saddle." Lucille didn't remember a time when she couldn't ride a horse.

> *I've ridden all my life. I expect my father gave me a horseback ride before I was a month old, probably took me for a 24-26-mile ride to show me to our nearest neighbor.*
>
> *— Tulsa World, June 28, 1931*

Lucille wasn't the only Mulhall child. Agnes was her older sister. The two younger siblings were Mildred and Charles. An older brother, Logan, died of diphtheria at thirteen.

When Lucille was thirteen (some accounts say seven), her father promised her all the calves she could rope and brand herself. He had to retract his offer when the girl branded over 300 (some say 20) with her "LM" brand. (It's difficult to separate truth from hype for many of these early western stars.)

In July 1900, Theodore Roosevelt, then governor of New York, attended a Rough Riders reunion in Oklahoma City. Zack Mulhall arranged a wild west show for the Rough Riders' entertainment.

Roosevelt was impressed with Lucille's riding skills. He urged Mulhall to allow his daughter to perform publicly, but Zack was reluctant.

In the years after the reunion, Roosevelt returned several times to visit the Mulhall ranch. At some point, the topic of wolves came up.

"Did you ever rope a lobo wolf?" Roosevelt asked Lucille.

I said I had not but I knew I could do it. He challenged me to rope one and bring it in for him. I did so while he was there. I ran it down,

Lucille had the wolf mounted and presented to Roosevelt.

Zack Mulhall started his own western show, "Mulhall's Congress of Rough Riders and Ropers." He remembered Roosevelt's suggestion that Lucille be allowed to show off her talents to the public, and he allowed his daughter to perform. Lucille's sisters Agnes and Mildred were also excellent horsewomen and participated in the show, but they were overshadowed by their daredevil sister.

Weighing only ninety pounds, Lucille performed in a gray, divided skirt, white silk shirt, and hat. She always rode astride—never sidesaddle. The girl was a favorite with the spectators as she competed, and often won, against men in roping, shooting, and riding contests. Lucille's fame never went to her head; she remained modest throughout her life.

Charley Mulhall also starred in the show, as well as young Tom Mix (future cowboy actor), and Will Rogers (entertainer, humorist, and newspaper columnist). Mulhall's show traveled around the United States even performing at Madison Square Garden in New York in 1905.

Lucille performed with a white horse named Eddie C. She also trained her own trick horse, Governor.

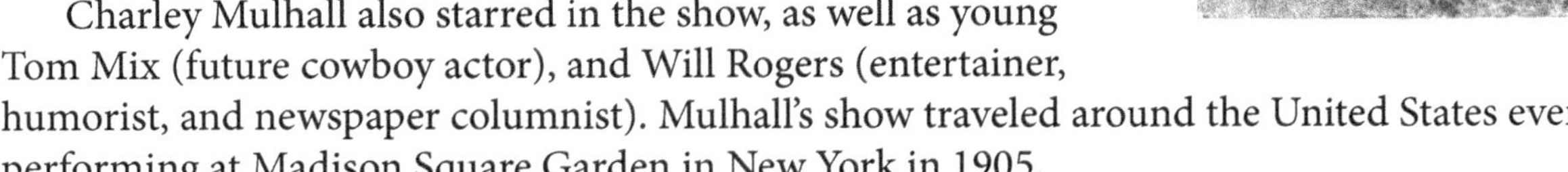

> *My system of training consists of three things: patience, perseverance, and gentleness. Gentleness I consider one of the greatest factors in successful training. Governor, the horse I ride in our exhibitions has nearly forty tricks. He can shoot a gun; pull off a man's coat and put it on again; can roll a barrel; can walk upstairs and down again—a difficult feat; is perfect in the march and the Spanish trot; extends the forelegs so that an easy mount may be made; kneels, lies down and sits up; indeed, he does nearly everything but talk.*
>
> — *Tulsa World, June 28, 1931*

President Roosevelt had a bridle with silver trim custom made for Lucille. Later, he gave her the saddle he used when fighting as a Rough Rider in Cuba.

Mulhall thoroughly enjoyed her cowgirl life.

> *I feel sorry for the girls who never lived on a cattle ranch and have to attend so many teas, and be indoors so much, with never anything but artificiality about them.*

Besides her father's show, Lucille performed in many other rodeos and wild west shows over the years in the U.S. and Europe. She was known by a variety of titles—Rodeo Queen, Daring Beauty of the Plains, Queen of the Western Prairie, Deadshot Girl, Queen of the Saddle, and America's Greatest Horsewoman. She is almost universally recognized as America's First Cowgirl.

Lucille was married in 1908 to Martin Van Bergen. They had a son, but she and Van Bergen divorced. In 1920, Lucille married Tom Burnett, a multimillionaire from Burkburnett, Texas. Lucille and Tom were briefly known as the King and Queen of Rodeo, but after just two years, they also divorced.

Zack Mulhall retired his wild west show, and Lucille returned to the family's ranch in 1922. When her mother passed away in January 1931, Lucille became the caretaker for her father, who by then had lost most of his sight. Zack Mulhall died in September of that same year.

On April 22, 1935, in Guthrie, Oklahoma, Lucille rode a horse named Old Red to lead the five-mile '89ers parade commemorating the Oklahoma Land Rush of 1889. Here is one reporter's description.

on a horse. She knew every trick of the "wild west rodeo" trade and knew it better than most men.

"I rode in this parade because I thought maybe it would be the last time I'd have a chance. In any event, it'll be my last. Of course, it won't be the last time, I'll get on a horse. I'll ride as long as I can throw a leg across."

— *The Daily Oklahoman, April 23, 1935*

Although not quite fifty at the time of the parade, past injuries had aged and stiffened Lucille's body.

Once she was a vivacious, devil-may-care blonde in a divided skirt and white silk shirt which enhanced her charms as she passed in review before presidents, kings, and worshiping throngs. The thoughtless observer might see her now as only a gray, time-penciled old woman.

— *The Daily Oklahoman, April 23, 1935*

Five years later, Lucille Mulhall was killed when the car she rode in collided with a truck, less than a mile from the Mulhall Ranch. Her nephew, Jean Breezley, driver of the car, was also killed in the accident.

34

Horses, Dogs, And Diphtheria

Bessie Baker suffered from a sore throat, fever, and swollen glands in her neck. It was October 1901, in St. Louis, Missouri. In those days, doctors made house calls. Dr. R.C. Harris diagnosed the girl with diphtheria, a bacterial infection. Diphtheria was fatal in as many as twenty percent of the cases in young children due to airway blockage or heart failure.

In 1883, Edwin Klebs identified the specific bacteria that caused the disease. Building on Louis Pasteur's work on anthrax and rabies vaccines, scientists experimented with injecting small doses of the lab-grown bacteria into animals. The animals' immune system produced antibodies to diphtheria. That discovery led to the development of a vaccine to prevent the disease. However, the vaccine wasn't effective for people who already had diphtheria.

Further experimentation showed that a serum could be created from the blood of the infected animals. Injecting this serum into human patients who suffered from diphtheria cured the disease.

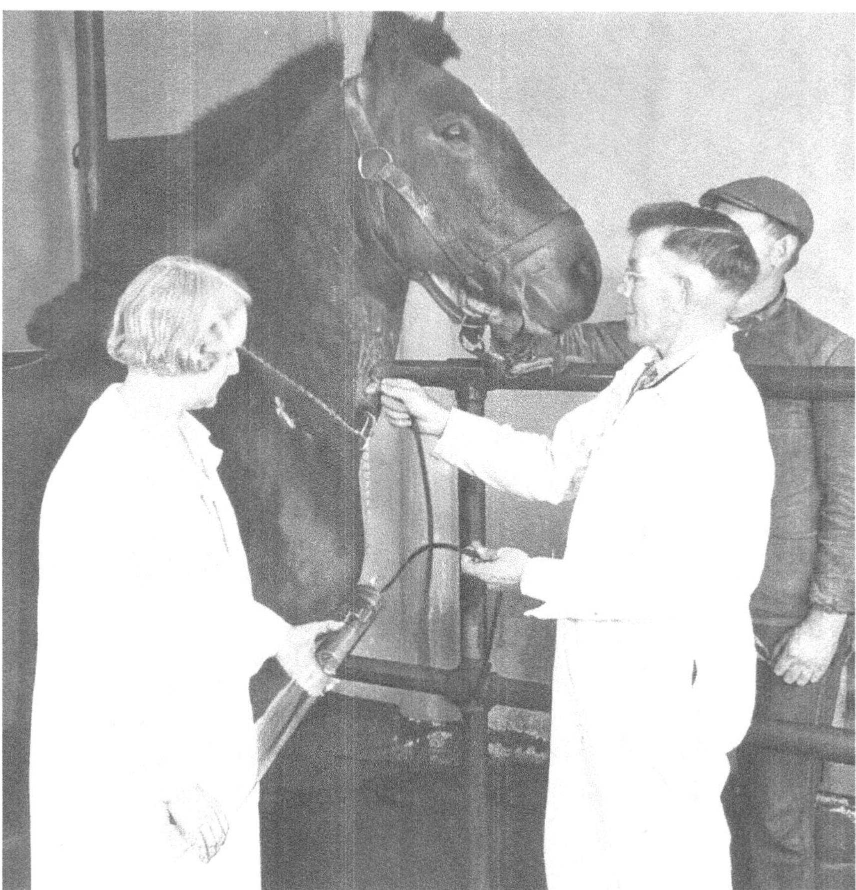

Sheep, goats, and dogs were used in the early testing. But horses were least impacted by the injection of the diphtheria toxin. Most horses suffered only a low fever as a side effect of the injections, however, some did die.

Because they are large animals, horses contained more blood to be used for creating serum. Three to six months after an injection, the horse began producing antibodies.

The first horse antitoxin laboratory in America was established in New York, producing doses of the serum in January 1895. Lab workers recorded information about each horse, including its color, gender, price, age, and final disposition.

For example, they listed one horse as Animal Number 111, a bay gelding of at least seven years. Purchased for $215, he was at the facility just over a year before he died. In that time, he underwent nine rounds of bleedings.

By 1901, the use of the diphtheria antitoxin was quite successful. Amand Ravold, a physician who had studied in Paris under Pasteur, was the director of a laboratory in St. Louis. Jim, whose previous job was pulling a milk wagon, was one horse used in Ravold's lab to produce the serum. Over his career, Jim produced seven and a half gallons of diphtheria antitoxin.

This is where the stories of Jim, and Bessie Baker, converge. Dr. Harris injected the girl with diphtheria antitoxin, courtesy of Jim. As a preventative, the doctor also injected Bessie's two younger siblings. Four days later, Bessie's condition was worse. Dr. Harris returned to the Baker's home to discover the girl was suffering from tetanus (lockjaw). The doctor could do nothing for her, and Bessie passed away the following day. Her two siblings also died of tetanus within the week.

By November 7, thirteen tetanus deaths were reported in the area. All the deaths traced back to serum dated September 30 that Dr. Ravold produced from Jim's blood. When lab workers realized the horse had tetanus, Jim was euthanized. But the contaminated serum was already in use.

The tetanus deaths were reported nationwide. People panicked and refused the diphtheria vaccine and antitoxin.

In December, the St. Louis Board of Health held an inquiry. Dr. Ravold insisted he and a janitor, Henry Taylor, destroyed the September 30 batch of serum after Jim's death. However, the janitor contradicted him, confessing that he released some of the September 30 serum. He thought it was safe, and they had run out of other batches.

The Health Department found Dr. Ravold negligent. Both he and Mr. Taylor were dismissed. The city stopped their production of diphtheria antitoxin. In 1902, Congress passed the Biologics Control Act which subjected companies making antitoxin or vaccines to inspections and regulations.

Today, cases of diphtheria in the United States are very rare. Horses are no longer involved in the production of antitoxin serum in the U.S., but they are used in other countries, particularly India.

In addition to horses, dogs played a role in the treatment of diphtheria. An outbreak occurred in 1925, in Nome, Alaska. Nome needed additional antitoxin, but the closest supply was in Anchorage, a thousand miles away by dog sled. The relay of the serum by dog teams became known as the "Great Race of Mercy."

A twenty-pound cylinder of serum traveled by train to Nenana. On January 27, the cylinder was passed to the first musher and sled dog team headed toward Nome. Balto was the lead dog for musher Gunnar Kaasen on the last stretch, arriving in Nome on February 2 at 5:30 AM.

Although twenty men and 150 dogs participated in the delivery, Balto received the most attention in news reports, making him a canine celebrity. A statue of Balto was erected in Central Park in New York City later that year.

But Kaasen and Balto didn't deserve all the credit. In fact, Leonhard Seppala's team, with lead dog Togo, carried the serum 261 miles over some of the most hazardous terrain, the longest distance of any of the teams. Balto's team covered only fifty-three miles.

Seppala actually owned Balto as well as Togo. He believed Togo was the better dog and resented the fact that Balto received all the glory.

> *I hope I shall never be the man to take away credit from any dog or driver who participated in that run. We all did our best. But when the country was roused to enthusiasm over the serum run, I resented the statue to Balto, for if any dog deserved special mention it was Togo.*
>
> *— Leonhard Seppala*

The 1925 serum run was an inspiration for the Iditarod, a 1,049-mile sled dog race, first held in 1973. The race, held each March, runs from Anchorage to Nome, Alaska.

Gunnar Kaasen with Balto

Leonhard Seppala with Togo (far left)

35

Black Jockeys

Many people are not aware that black jockeys dominated the early days of horse racing. In the first Kentucky Derby, thirteen of the fifteen jockeys were black. Black riders won fifteen of the first twenty-eight Derbies.

We know little about those men. Contemporary news reports gave the credit for wins to the horse owners or even to the horses themselves rather than to the skillful jockeys who rode them.

Before the Civil War, male slaves were stable hands, grooms, trainers, and jockeys. Many of those jockeys began racing as small, light, eleven or twelve-year-old boys. Using slaves meant all the prize money went to the horse owner.

Horse racing was one of the few areas where black slaves competed on equal footing with whites. For the brief duration of a race, the only color that mattered was that of the stable's racing silks.

After the war, some of the freed slaves moved North to work as jockeys—and finally be paid.

Black Kentucky Derby Winners:

Oliver Lewis, 1875 Aristides

The nineteen-year-old native Kentuckian rode Aristides to victory in the first Kentucky Derby. The chestnut colt was trained by former slave Ansel Williamson. Lewis never rode in another Derby.

William "Billy" Walker, 1877 Baden-Baden

William had his first victory at eleven. At fifteen, he finished fourth in the initial Kentucky Derby on the horse Bob Wooley. In 1876, he finished eighth on Bombay. The following year, at seventeen, Walker won the Derby by two lengths on Baden-Baden. African-American trainer Edward Brown trained the horse.

James Carter, 1878 Day Star

James and Monica Saunders, authors of *Black Winning Jockeys in the Kentucky Derby*, claim James Carter, the winning jockey in 1878, was black. If true, this would mean sixteen of the first twenty-eight Derby winners were African-American. The kentuckyderby.com website does not include Carter in their list of African American jockeys.

George Garrett (or Garrett Davis) Lewis, 1880 Fonso

A few weeks after his Derby win on Fonso, Lewis rode Bravo in a Missouri race. The horse stumbled and fell, throwing Lewis. Although badly injured, he rode in a few more races before returning to his home in Kentucky. He passed away at eighteen due to his injuries.

"Babe" Hurd, 1882 Apollo

Hurd was riding Thoroughbreds at thirteen. It's believed his nickname came because of his young appearance. Hurd's mount in the Derby, Apollo, had not raced as a two-year-old. Hurd had only ridden the horse one time, but the pair came from behind to win by half a length. This was Hurd's first and only Derby run.

Isaac Burns Murphy, 1884 Buchanan

Isaac was born into a free black family in Lexington, Kentucky, in 1861. His father died in the Civil War. Isaac's first horse experience came at twelve when he was placed on an untrained yearling colt. The colt promptly threw him, and Isaac was understandably reluctant to get back on. But he did, and two years later, he won his first race.

In the 1884 Derby, Murphy rode Buchanan, a bad-acting colt. The horse had thrown Murphy before the race. "Gentlemen, if you say 'ride him,' I'll ride him. But, I don't want to. I sure don't want to ride that crazy horse."

Buchanan reared and plunged and was left far behind at the start. But by the halfway point, he was closing in. He pulled ahead at the three-quarter mark and won by two lengths. Murphy gained international fame and was the nation's top jockey for many years.

Erskine "Babe" Henderson, 1885 Joe Cotton

At fourteen, when Henderson began his racing career, he was small, even for a jockey. Before his Derby win, he'd run in the race twice, finishing 9th (1882) and 7th/last (1883). He won the Derby by a neck on the horse Joe Cotton, who was trained by African-American Abraham Perry.

Isaac Lewis, 1887 Montrose

Isaac was the brother of George Garrett Lewis. He began riding, and winning, at eleven. He raced in four consecutive Derbies with the following results.

Sixth in 1886 on Grimaldi

First in 1887 on Montrose

Fifth in 1888 on The Chevalier

Sixth in 1889 on Sportsman

Isaac Burns Murphy, 1890 Riley

Isaac Murphy was one of the most successful jockeys of all time. He rode in eleven Kentucky Derbies.

James "Jimmy" Lee won all six races at Churchill Downs on June 5, 1907

After his win in the Derby on Riley, Murphy rode in a famous match race. The contest pitted the dominant black jockey from the south against the popular northern white jockey for a $10,000 prize. Murphy rode a horse named Salvator against Edward "Snapper" Garrison, on Tenny. Most considered these the two best horses in the country. The race was held on June 25, 1890, at Sheepshead Bay Racetrack in Brooklyn, New York.

> *When the head of the home stretch was reached, Garrison had Tenny within three lengths of the flying Salvator. Then came a battle royal for a quarter of a mile, the vast crowd going almost crazy while it was being fought out. Garrison rode Tenny like a very demon, but Murphy and Salvator would not be caught. … Salvator managed to get first past the judges, beating Tenny by a head only, and an infinitesimal part of a second in that remarkable time—2:05.*
>
> *— New York Times, June 26th, 1890*

Isaac Burns Murphy, 1891 Kingman

Kingman was co-owned by former slave Dudley Allen, the first and only black man to own a Kentucky Derby winner. Isaac Murphy rode in 1,412 races in his career with 628 wins. He was the first jockey to win three Kentucky Derbies. He likely would have won more, but Murphy died in his mid-thirties. Some attribute his death to pneumonia, others to heart failure caused by the extreme measures he took to maintain a low weight for racing.

(Bill Hartack and Eddie Arcaro currently have the record of five Derby wins each.)

Alonzo Clayton, 1892 Azra

At twelve, Alonzo "Lonnie" Clayton ran away from home to join his brother at a racing stable. By fourteen, Clayton had progressed from exercise rider to jockey. At fifteen, he became the youngest Kentucky Derby winner. There were only two other horses in the 1892 Derby—Huron and Phil Dwyer—the smallest field in the race's history up to that time. Unfortunately, Azra collapsed later that year and died of an unknown cause. Clayton competed in three more Derbies, finishing second in 1893 and 1897 and third in 1895.

James "Soup" Perkins, 1895 Halma

James came from a racing family. His father worked with trotting horses, and two of James' brothers were jockeys. He worked with horses from the age of ten and began racing at eleven. James earned the nickname "Soup" because it was his favorite meal to keep his weight down. He won the Kentucky Derby at fifteen, the second-youngest winner. James died at the young age of thirty-one.

Willie Simms, 1896 Ben Brush, 1898 Plaudit

Despite Ben Brush stumbling and almost throwing Simms at the start of the race, the pair managed to win by a nose. It was said that when he saw Ben Brush's sides spattered with blood from his spurs, Simms cried with shame.

It seems amazing, but prior to Willie Simms, jockeys rode sitting straight up as any rider would. Two-time Kentucky Derby winner Simms introduced the crouched style of riding.

Simms was the first American jockey to shorten his stirrups and ride the monkey-on-a-stick style, or crouch, which afterward was universally adopted by American jockeys.

— *Chicago Tribune, October 31, 1954*

Jimmy Winkfield, 1901 His Eminence, 1902 Alan-a-Dale

Jimmy Winkfield raced in four Derbies with back-to-back victories in 1901 and 1902. After His Eminence's racing career, the horse died in a steeplechase event.

In the 1902 Derby, Alan-a-Dale was ahead by six lengths when he became lame down the final stretch. Somehow, the horse kept running and won by a nose. Along with Isaac Murphy, Winkfield is considered one of the best jockeys of all time.

Although most of the early Kentucky Derby winning jockeys were African American, by the early 1900s, black riders had nearly disappeared. As horse racing became more lucrative, whites vied for the jockey positions, and some wanted to eliminate the competition from blacks. The Jockey Club, formed in 1894, often denied licenses to blacks.

The Supreme Court decision, Plessy v. Ferguson (1896) ruled that racial segregation laws did not violate the constitution as long as equal facilities were provided for each race. This policy was known as "separate but equal."

Black jockeys who continued to race were sometimes subjected to violence by white riders. In a race, the white jockeys might box in a horse and rider, bump or whip another jockey's horse, or slip their foot under the rider's stirrup and attempt to flip him out of the saddle.

> *The white boys retaliated by ganging up against the black riders on the rails. A black boy would be pocketed, thrust back in a race; or his mount would be bumped out of contention on a white boy's stirrup, and toss him out of the saddle … those white fellows would slash out and cut the nearest Negro rider … they literally ran the black boys off the tracks.*
>
> — *For Gold and Glory, Charles B. Parmer, p. 150*

These "rough riding" techniques kept black jockeys out of the winner's circle. Since owners hired jockeys based on their performance, the demand for black riders declined.

William Hicks

Alonzo Clayton

Isaac Murphy

According to a May 21, 1966 article in the Pittsburgh Courier, "Non-Whites Now Too Big to Ride Horses," the absence of black jockeys was attributed to black men growing too large to meet the low weight requirements. That claim is debatable, but increases in size, regardless of race, could be attributed to stricter regulations about the age for becoming a jockey. Today, most states set the minimum age at sixteen.

After dominating the Derby in the 1800s, black jockeys rarely won or even raced again. In 1911, Jess Conley finished third in the Derby, and in 1921, Henry King placed tenth. But after 1921, there were no black riders in the race until Marlon St. Julien rode in 2000.

36

Wink

S orry, you can't come in."
"But we—"

The elderly man stared at the wood grain in the door that had been slammed shut inches from his face. When the wave of humiliation faded, he turned to his daughter.

Her eyes flashed with anger. "They have to let us in. You're the guest of honor." She reached up to bang on the door, but he caught her hand. Taking a deep breath, he straightened his suit and knocked calmly.

The doorman frowned when he saw the woman and the short, thin man still standing at the entrance. "We don't allow you people to come in." He started to close the door again.

The small man gripped the edge of the door with surprising strength. "Wait! You don't understand. I have an invitation."

The doorman paused.

"Sports Illustrated," the woman added. "They invited my father. He's a guest of honor at the banquet."

The doorman looked from the woman to the man. "Wait here." He closed the door.

The man squeezed his daughter's hand and smiled at her, but her face remained stormy. Tantalizing odors drifted out from the hotel banquet room as they waited—split-pea soup, baked potato, and prime rib. After what seemed an eternity, the ornate wooden door opened, and they were quietly ushered inside to a table by themselves.

That day, something stronger than a door separated them from the other guests.

The preceding is a fictionalized account of the racial prejudice that nearly kept the eighty-year-old James Winkfield and his daughter, Liliane, from a banquet where he was the honored guest.

It was May 1961, the Brown Hotel in Louisville, Kentucky. Sports Illustrated had recently published a feature article on Jimmy Winkfield (Wink), the last black jockey to win the Kentucky Derby.

Although almost not allowed inside, Jimmy Winkfield enjoyed the fine food at the banquet. He and fellow jockey, Roscoe Goose, reminisced about the days when they competed against each other. Goose was the only white person to speak to Winkfield and his daughter that night.

Even as late as 1971, racial prejudice was evident when Marjorie Weber, a Kentucky journalist, visited the Winkfields and wrote:

> *Mr. Winkfield is a gentle, dear, elderly little man. They all have so much culture and fineness that it is difficult to think that … you know what I am trying to say … they are colored or partly so. I mean nothing vicious about this at all … please, believe me.*

In 2000, Marlon St. Julien became the first black to ride in the Kentucky Derby since Henry King in 1921. St. Julien finished seventh out of nineteen riders. His appearance in the Derby attracted considerable media attention. In response to questions about his skin color, St. Julien stated, "I just want to be considered as one of the best riders in the country, whether black, white, purple, blue, or brown."

Wink would have agreed.

Born in Chilesburg, Kentucky, in 1882, Wink was the youngest of eighteen children. He began racing at fifteen. After his two Kentucky Derby victories, when racing opportunities disappeared in the U.S., Winkfield raced in Europe and Russia. He won the Russian Derby four times, the Czar's Prize three times, the Russian Oaks five times, and the Warsaw Derby twice.

In the midst of his successful racing career in Russia, Wink escaped the Bolshevik Revolution in 1917. From Russia, he moved to France and raced in Poland, France, England, and Spain until retiring as a jockey in 1930 at fifty with more than 2,500 wins. He didn't leave racing altogether, though. He started his own stable outside of Paris and trained racehorses.

When Germany invaded France in 1940, Winkfield once again was forced to flee, this time back to the United States. After the war, Winkfield returned to France and rebuilt his training stable with the help of his son Robert. They worked together, training horses and jockeys until Wink passed away at ninety-one.

Thirty years after his death in 1974, James Winkfield was inducted into the Hall of Fame of the National Museum of Racing.

37

The Midnight Ride To The Presidency

The rugged Rough Rider, Teddy Roosevelt, began life as a sickly child confined indoors much of the time.

> *I was a sickly, delicate boy, suffered much from asthma, and frequently had to be taken away on trips to find a place where I could breathe. One of my memories is of my father walking up and down the room with me in his arms at night when I was a very small person, and of sitting up in bed gasping, with my father and mother trying to help me. I went very little to school.*
>
> — *Theodore Roosevelt: An Autobiography,* chapter 1

Doctors didn't have a cure or any effective treatments for asthma. Some of their more unusual suggestions were for the boy to smoke cigars and drink coffee or whiskey. When those remedies proved unsuccessful, Teddy determined to overcome his weakness by engaging in strenuous physical activities, including boxing and horseback riding.

> *I was fond of horseback-riding, but I took to it slowly and with difficulty, exactly as with boxing. It was a long time before I became even a respectable rider, and I never got much higher.*
>
> — *Theodore Roosevelt: An Autobiography,* chapter 2

After leaving college, Roosevelt enjoyed fox hunting in New York. He related one memorable experience with an interesting horse.

> *My purse did not permit me to own expensive horses. On this occasion I was riding an animal, a buggy horse originally, which its owner sold because now and then it insisted on thoughtfully lying down when in harness. It never did this under the saddle; and when he turned it out to grass it would solemnly hop over the fence and get somewhere where it did not belong. The last trait was what converted it into a hunter. … On the hunt in question I got along very well until the pace winded my ex-buggy horse, and it turned a somersault over a fence. When I got on it after the fall I found I could not use my left arm. I supposed it was merely a strain. … So we pounded along at the tail of the hunt, and I did not appreciate that my arm was broken for three or four fences. Then we came to a big drop, and the jar made the bones slip past one another so as to throw the hand out of position. It did not hurt me at all, and as the horse was as easy to sit as a rocking-chair, I got in at the death.*
>
> — *Theodore Roosevelt: An Autobiography,* chapter 2

In 1880, Theodore Roosevelt married Alice Hathaway Lee. A daughter, Alice Lee, was born to the Roosevelts in 1884. Two days after Alice's birth, Theodore's wife died of kidney failure. His mother had died earlier that day in the same New York house. Roosevelt wrote in his diary, "The light has gone out of my life."

Roosevelt grieved his losses deeply. Leaving his newborn daughter with his sister Bamie, he spent two years working at his Elkhorn and Maltese Cross ranches in North Dakota. When he returned, Roosevelt took custody of Alice.

Although he never considered himself an expert rider, Roosevelt spent many hours in the saddle during the time at his ranches. Those years strengthened him physically and helped him overcome his grief. His ranch horses had a variety of dispositions and training.

> *I was on a favorite horse, Manitou, who was a wise old fellow, with nerves not to be shaken by anything. … The time I smashed my rib I was bucked off on a stone. The time I hurt the point of my shoulder I was riding a big, sulky horse named Ben Butler, which went over backwards with me.*
>
> *— Theodore Roosevelt: An Autobiography, chapter 4*

In 1899, the year after the Rough Riders returned from Cuba, Roosevelt was elected governor of New York. William McKinley's vice president, Garret Hobart, died that same year.

McKinley selected Theodore Roosevelt as his running mate for his second term in 1900. The pair won the election. But Roosevelt didn't serve as vice president for long.

On September 6, 1901, Leon Czolgosz shot President McKinley. When Roosevelt heard the news, he hurried to McKinley's side in Buffalo, New York. After surgery, the president seemed to improve, and Roosevelt went to the Adirondacks in New York where, on September 12, he and his family hiked Mt. Marcy, New York's highest peak.

McKinley's condition suddenly took a turn for the worse, and a message was sent to the Tahawus Club where the Roosevelts were staying.

> *The President appears to be dying and members of the Cabinet in Buffalo think you should lose no time coming.*

A search party ventured into the mountain wilderness to find the vice president. Once located, Roosevelt returned to the Tahawus Club, intending to spend the night there and depart for Buffalo the following morning. But a sudden sense of urgency compelled him to leave the club at midnight.

David Hunter, driving a buckboard wagon, took Roosevelt on the first leg of what some have called "the midnight ride to the presidency" or "the ride heard around the world."

Next, Orrin Kellogg took him to Aiden Lair Lodge, owned by Michael Cronin.

Cronin was the last of the three drivers to transport Roosevelt. His team of Morgans, Frank and Dick, carried Roosevelt sixteen miles through the darkness over muddy, winding, cliff-side roads. They arrived at the North Creek train station at 4:45 AM on September 14.

Although Cronin knew McKinley had died, he didn't tell Roosevelt. It wasn't until they reached the rail station that Roosevelt learned the president had died at 2:15 that morning. Roosevelt completed his journey to Buffalo by train. After paying his respects to the deceased McKinley, Roosevelt was sworn in as the twenty-sixth president of the United States.

At forty-two, he remains the youngest U.S. president. John Kennedy was the youngest elected president at forty-three.

Roosevelt had six children: Alice (1884, first marriage), Theodore III or Ted (1887), Kermit (1889), Ethel (1891), Archibald (1894), and Quentin (1897).

Michael Cronin with his Morgans, Frank and Dick

His youngest, Quentin, was only three years old when Teddy Roosevelt became president. The Roosevelt children filled the White House with a menagerie of pets, including dogs, cats, guinea pigs, and rabbits. More exotic animals found their way to the White House as well—a black bear (Jonathan Edwards), a badger (Josiah), a snake (Emily Spinach), a blue macaw (Eli Yale), kangaroo rats, a flying squirrel, a hyena, and a zebra.

In 1903, the Ethiopian emperor sent Roosevelt a lion, later named Joe. Joe, like the other exotic animals, didn't remain at the White House but lived at the National Zoo.

Of course, Roosevelt brought his love of horses with him to the White House. Although offered the use of an automobile during his presidency, he refused, claiming, "The Roosevelts are horse people."

38

The Roosevelts Are Horse People

William McKinley was the first American president to ride in an automobile—a private ride in a Stanley Steamer, in 1899. An electric ambulance transported McKinley to the hospital when he was shot in 1901. But Teddy Roosevelt was the first president to ride publicly in a motor vehicle while in office.

On August 22, 1902, President Roosevelt began a tour of New England with a car ride through Hartford, Connecticut, the first presidential motorcade. Army veterans on horseback and police officers on bicycles escorted the president.

Automobiles were in their early stages. About half of them were electric, as was the model Roosevelt rode in, a Columbia Victoria Phaeton. The driver sat on an elevated box at the rear and used a tiller rather than a steering wheel to steer the car. Top speed for the Phaeton was thirteen miles per hour.

Roosevelt was the first president to own a car, but he was not a fan of them.

> *Motor cars are a trial, aren't they? I suppose that ultimately we will get them into their proper place in the scheme of nature, and when by law and custom their use is regulated in proper fashion their objectionable features will probably be eliminated; but just at present I regard them as distinct additions to the discomfort of living.*
>
> *— Letter to Charles Hughes, October 8, 1905*

As he had stated, "The Roosevelts are horse people."

That extended to his children as well. The Roosevelt children not only enjoyed their pets in Washington, D.C. but also at the Roosevelt home in New York. Sagamore Hill served as the "Summer White House."

General Grant, named after the Civil War general and president, Ulysses S. Grant, was a sorrel Shetland pony the children used for driving.

> *Sedate pony Grant used to draw the cart in which the children went driving when they were very small, the driver being their old nurse Mame … They loved pony Grant. Once I saw the then little boy of three hugging pony Grant's forelegs. As he leaned over, his broad straw hat tilted on end, and pony Grant meditatively munched the brim; whereupon the small boy looked up with a wail of anguish, evidently thinking the pony had decided to treat him like a radish.*
>
> *— Theodore Roosevelt: An Autobiography, chapter 9*

When older, General Grant began to lie down unexpectedly in the road. A "calico" pony, Algonquin, took his place with the younger Roosevelts.

Algonquin, called a calico, was a brown or black and white coloring known as pinto today. Although some sources refer to Algonquin as an Icelandic, he seems too small for that breed. The pony was likely a Shetland.

Once, when eight-year-old Archie was quarantined in his bedroom, recovering from the measles, Quentin came up with a plan to hasten his brother's recovery, or at least improve his mood. With the help of a coachman or his brother Kermit, Quentin smuggled Algonquin up to the second floor via the White House elevator. Algonquin shivered nervously as the elevator moved.

In his delight to see the pony, Archie let out a loud whoop that startled Algonquin, causing him to slip and fall on the bedroom floor. The loud crash brought the entire family running.

During his presidency, Roosevelt had nine personal horses who lived in the south wing of the White House stable built during President Grant's administration. Seven additional horses were stabled there who were available for government business. Roosevelt paid for his own horses' feed and for his coachman's salary.

The President's horses are fortunate animals, enjoying every luxury that can appeal to the equine appreciation. Straw so clean that any man might be willing to sleep on it is spread two feet deep in their stalls and even in the aisle that runs between. Snowy fly sheets defend them from annoyance by winged insects, and their coats are kept sleek and smooth by the constant attentions of skilled grooms.

One of the nine horses is a pensioner, named Diamond, which was brought to Washington just because he was a dear old friend and for no other reason. He is thirty years of age and of not much use any longer, but he was Mr. Roosevelt's pony long ago when the President was a youngster, and for the rest of his life he can count on a comfortable stall with unlimited supplies of oats and hay. Every one of the children, from Miss Alice down, learned to ride on him; in fact, he has furnished an education in the equestrian art to all of the younger generation at the White House.

The pair of horses driven customarily by the President are fine big animals, full of vigor and "high steppers"

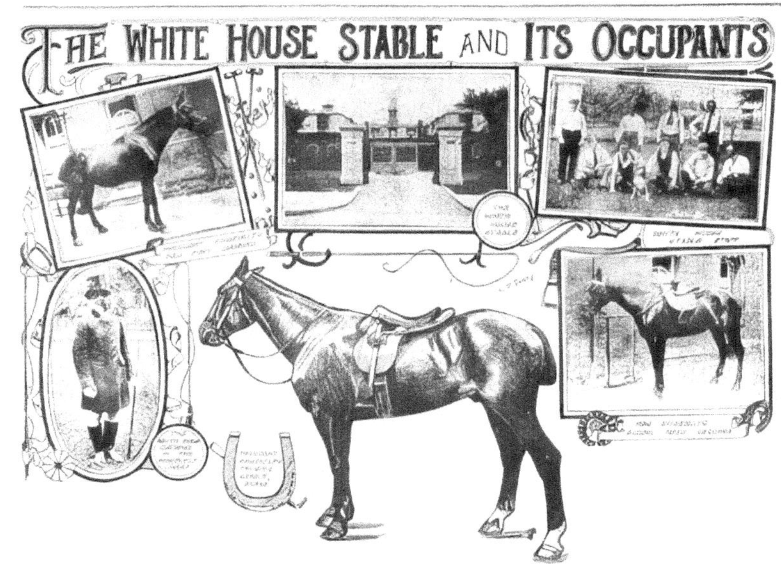

Yagenka

Yagenka, a bay mare, was a favorite riding horse of the president's wife, Edith. The mare was named after a heroine in a medieval Polish novel.

> *Poor mother has had a hard time with Yagenka, for she rubbed her back, and as she sadly needs exercise and I could not have a saddle put upon her, I took her out bareback yesterday. Her gaits are so easy that it is really more comfortable to ride her without a saddle than to ride Texas with one, and I gave her three miles sharp cantering and trotting.*

> *— 1901 letter*

> *Edith is very well this summer and looks so young and pretty. She rides with us a great deal and loves Yagenka as much as ever.*

> *— 1903 letter*

In June 1904, Roosevelt wrote, "Ethel gives sick Yagenka a bottle of medicine." After that, the horse isn't mentioned again in his letters.

The increasing presence of automobiles was a serious challenge for many horses. In an October 4, 1903 letter, Roosevelt wrote of **Renown**, a bay hunter,

> *By the way, I am working hard to get Renown accustomed to automobiles. He is such a handful now when he meets them that I seriously mind encountering them when Mother is along.*

Roosevelt shared details of his training approach which relied on positive reinforcement. One day, Renown performed better than expected and Roosevelt rewarded him.

> *Renown is behaving better about automobiles and the like. I think the difference is largely in the way I handle him. He is a very good-natured and gentle horse, but timid and not over-wise, and when in a panic his great strength makes him well-nigh uncontrollable. Accordingly, he is a bad horse to try to force by anything. If possible, it is much better to give him a little time, and bring him up as gently as may be to the object of terror. When he behaves well I lean forward and give him a lump of sugar, and now the old boy eagerly puts around his head when I stretch out my hand.*

Wyoming

The citizens of Douglas, Wyoming gave a horse to President Roosevelt on June 1, 1903. In a letter thanking them, Roosevelt said he was going to rename the horse "Wyoming" in honor of their state. Initially, Wyoming, a smooth-gaited horse, did well.

Kermit was with us this morning and got along beautifully till we galloped, whereupon Wyoming made up his mind that it was a race, and Kermit, for a moment or two, found him a handful.

— August 25, 1903

Yesterday Ethel went off riding with Lorraine. She rode Wyoming, who is really turning out a very good family horse.

— September 23, 1903

But later, Wyoming, along with several other Roosevelt horses, continued to have difficulty adjusting to encounters with automobiles.

I have no hope for Wyoming or Renown. Fortunately, Rusty is serving us well.

— May 28, 1904

At forty-eight, Roosevelt wasn't eager to tackle hard-to-manage horses, as he revealed in this letter to his daughter Ethel. It's unclear who the two new horses he mentions are.

I haven't heard a word from the two new horses, and I rather believe that if there had been any marked improvement in either of them I should have heard. I gather that one at least and probably both would be all right for me if I were twenty years younger, and would probably be all right for Ted now; but of course as things are at present I do not want a horse with which I have an interesting circus experience whenever we meet an automobile, or one which I cannot get to go in any particular direction without devoting an hour or two to the job. So that it looks as if old Rusty would be good enough for me for some time to come.

— Letter to Ethel, April 1, 1906

Yet, a few days later, Roosevelt writes of riding a young, green horse, **Roswell**.

Yesterday I took a first ride on the new horse, Roswell, Captain Lee going along on Rusty as a kind of a nurse. Roswell is not yet four and he is really a green colt and not quite the horse I want at present, as I haven't time to fuss with him, and am afraid of letting the Sergeant ride him, as he does not get on well with him, and there is nobody else in our stable that can ride at all. He is a beautiful horse, a wonderful jumper, and does not pull at all. He shies pretty badly, especially when he meets an automobile; and when he leaves the stable or strikes a road that he thinks will take him home and is not allowed to go down it, he is apt to rear, which I do not like; but I am inclined to think that he will get over these traits, …
— To Kermit, April 12, 1906

Roswell bruised his knee in a jump. When he had healed, Roosevelt decided to sell the horse.

Uncle Douglas has been riding Roswell several times this last week, usually in my company, but has not wished to pay the price I have asked, $500. However, I do not think I shall get that price and if not I shall sell him at auction Thursday next, and then Uncle Douglas may be able to get

him cheaper. Of course I should like to have him get old Roswell, for I don't want to sell the old fellow unless I am sure he will have a good home.

— February 13th, 1909

Fidelity

Did you hear of the dreadful time Ethel had with her new bull terrier, Mike? She was out riding with Fitz Lee, who was on Roswell, and Mike was following. They suppose that Fidelity must have accidentally kicked Mike. The first they knew the bulldog sprang at the little mare's throat. She fought pluckily, rearing and plunging, and shook him off, and then Ethel galloped away. As soon as she halted, Mike overtook her and attacked Fidelity again. He seized her by the shoulder and tried to seize her by the throat, and twice Ethel had to break away and gallop off, Fitz Lee endeavoring in vain to catch the dog. Finally he succeeded, just as Mike had got Fidelity by the hock. He had to give Mike a tremendous beating to restore him to obedience; but of course Mike will have to be disposed of. Fidelity was bitten in several places and it was a wonder that Ethel was able to keep her seat, because naturally the frightened little mare reared and plunged and ran.

— March 15, 1908

Roosevelt's favorite horse was a 16 hand, light-bay hunter. George Bleistein had given him the horse. Roosevelt named the horse Bleistein after his friend. He expressed his thanks in a letter written in 1902, "I don't know when I have ever received a gift out of which I get so much pleasure."

Among the various horses I have owned in recent years Bleistein was the one I liked best, because of his good nature and courage. He was a fair, although in no way a remarkable jumper.

On May 3, 1902, a series of twelve photographs were taken of Roosevelt jumping fences at the Chevy Chase Club. Roosevelt declared that one of those photos was "the best picture I ever had taken or expect to have taken."

During his presidency, Roosevelt rode almost daily. Anyone invited to accompany him was given a printed copy of his "Rules of the Road."

First: The president will notify whom he wishes to ride with him. The one notified will take position on the left of the president and keep his right stirrup back of the president's left stirrup.

Second: Those following will keep not less than ten yards in the rear of the president.

Third: When the president asks anyone in the party to ride with him, the one at his side should at once retire to the rear. Salutes should be returned only by the president, except by those in the rear. Anyone unable to control his horse should withdraw to the rear.

39

Horses And Bears

During the last weeks of Roosevelt's second term, he proposed a physical challenge for all military officers to complete annually—a ninety-mile horseback ride, completed in three days. The armed forces didn't welcome Roosevelt's idea, claiming it would be a hardship for their men.

To demonstrate that the goal was well within reach, fifty-one-year-old Roosevelt decided to make the ride himself. In January 1909, he mapped out a one-hundred-mile route he would complete in a single day. Three officers accompanied him: Admiral Presley M. Rixey, Dr. Cary T. Grayson, and Captain Archibald W. Butt.

It was fifty miles from the White House to Warrenton, Virginia. Then, they would turn around and come back for a total of one hundred miles. On a bitterly cold January 13th, the four men mounted their horses at 3:40 AM and set out over frozen, rutted roads.

At 6:30, they stopped in Fairfax, Virginia to exchange horses. The group continued to Centerville, where they again received fresh mounts.

They arrived in Warrenton at 11 AM, and the travelers ate lunch at the Warren Green Hotel. By 12:15, Roosevelt and his companions were in the saddle on fresh horses and headed back to Washington.

It's unclear which horses Roosevelt rode. Some sources say one was his own Roswell. The rest were likely cavalry horses from Fort Myer. On their return, they may have switched back to horses they'd left earlier in the day.

Halfway home, a blizzard arrived, blowing sleet into the riders' and horses' faces. This was a serious problem for Roosevelt, as the ice caked his glasses, making it almost impossible for him to see.

At Fairfax, a crowd braved the weather to cheer the men on. Roosevelt had planned to complete the journey by 7:00 PM, but the darkness, snow, freezing rain, and icy streets delayed their arrival.

At one point, the President's horse went into a ditch, but both horse and rider were uninjured. As they neared Washington, a carriage approached, offering to give the

Yagenka, Mrs. Roosevelt's horse

President a ride. But Roosevelt declared, "By George, we will make it to the White House with our horses if we have to lead them."

When they turned onto Pennsylvania Avenue and spotted the White House, the group broke into a gallop. They reached their goal, covered in mud and ice, at 8:40 PM, seventeen hours after they had set out. Roosevelt showed up for work as usual the following day.

What has surprised me more than anything on this ride is the fact that no one has said a cross word, that we have had a good time, and that we returned laughing. … if we had not met this sleet storm, it would have been like taking candy from a child.

Roosevelt could have run again in 1908, but he chose not to. As president, he was proudest of his conservation work. During his years in office, the U.S. Forest Service was established, and five national parks and 150 national forests were created. Approximately 230 million acres were declared public lands. Roosevelt was also instrumental in the development of the Panama Canal.

Despite his resolve not to run for a third term, by 1912, Roosevelt was so unhappy with President Howard Taft's policies, he changed his mind and ran under the Progressive or Bull Moose party. During a Wisconsin campaign event on October 14, 1912, John Flammang Schrank shot Roosevelt at close range. Schrank was motivated by a dream, in which President McKinley appeared to him. In the dream, McKinley communicated that Theodore Roosevelt was responsible for his death, and he wanted Schrank to seek revenge.

With blood seeping from his wound, Roosevelt completed his campaign speech, assuring the crowd he was all right. "I don't know whether you fully understand that I have just been shot; but it takes more than that to kill a Bull Moose."

It wasn't until after the speech that he sought medical attention. The bullet had lodged in his chest but hadn't penetrated his lung. Doctors decided it was more dangerous to attempt to remove it than to just leave it alone. The bullet remained there for the rest of Roosevelt's life. Roosevelt said of the bullet, "I do not mind it any more than if it were in my waistcoat pocket."

Theodore Roosevelt was known as the last true horseman at the White House. He was also connected with another animal—the Teddy Bear.

During an unsuccessful Mississippi hunting trip in November 1902, guides tied a bear to a tree and invited the president to shoot it. Roosevelt declined, claiming it would be unsportsmanlike to kill a defenseless animal.

Clifford Berryman created a political cartoon of Roosevelt and the bear. The cartoon, featured in The Washington Post, received widespread attention.

Immigrant shopkeepers Morris and Rose Michtom created a stuffed fabric bear in honor of Roosevelt. They displayed "Teddy's bear" in their New York store window. The bears sold so well that in 1907, the Michtoms formed the Ideal Novelty and Toy Company, later Ideal Toy Company.

40

Billings' Banquet

What may be the most unusual banquet in all of American history was held at Sherry's Restaurant in Manhattan, New York on March 29, 1903.

Millionaire Cornelius Kingsley Garrison Billings had recently completed the construction of a stable in Manhattan. Billings made his millions from a natural gas business, but his passion was harness racing. Known as C.K.G. or "the American Horse King," Billings' new stable was near the Harlem Speedway, a racehorse track along the Harlem River.

Billings didn't approve of gambling and always raced as an amateur. He was nearly forty in 1899, when he purchased a trotting mare, Lucille, and a pacer, Bumps. In 1900, C.K.G. drove Lucille to a mile record of 2:07 in a four-wheeled wagon.

More about Billings' horses later—but back to the stable. This wasn't any ordinary stable. The $200,000, 25,000 square-foot stable was 250 feet long, 125 feet wide, and two stories tall with a full basement. Inside were twenty-two box stalls, nine straight stalls, a training arena, carriage room, sleigh room, feed rooms, hayloft, 5,000 bushel granary, gymnasium, blacksmith shop, trophy room, and in the upper story—two five-room suites. The basement contained a dynamo room to provide power for steam heat, hot water, and electric lights.

Completing something of that magnitude called for a proper celebration, and C.K.G. had an idea for a memorable one. Reporters had gotten word of the event he'd planned to hold in his new seventy-five-foot training ring. But Billings fooled the press by holding the celebration at the restaurant of a friend instead.

He invited thirty-six friends to Sherry's restaurant. As the guests arrived in black-and-white formal wear, they found the fourth-floor ballroom decorated with artificial turf, trees, shrubbery, and painted scenery. Several inches of sand covered the floor. Horses, rented from a riding stable and brought up in the freight elevator, replaced the dining tables.

Each guest mounted a horse, all facing the center of a circle. Everyone had his own waiter, dressed as a groom in a scarlet coat and white breeches. Real grooms were stationed at the horses' heads to lessen the chance of tossed food or riders.

Waiters served each course on silver trays fastened to the pommels at the front of the saddles. The dinner began with caviar and turtle soup. Subsequent courses included rack of lamb with glazed vegetables, guinea hens with lettuce-heart salad, asparagus with hollandaise sauce, and flambéed peaches for dessert. Bottles of champagne rested in ice-filled saddlebags, from which the guests drank, using rubber tubes.

Toward the end of the meal, grooms brought in large troughs of oats, so the horses weren't left out of the banquet. After dinner, the guests were entertained with a vaudeville show. The horses traveled back down the freight elevator, never to partake in such a formal affair again.

The memorable banquet cost Billings $50,000, equivalent to more than a million dollars today. Billings later held a luncheon at the stable to exhibit his facility and horses to the press.

One of Billings' most famous horses was Lou Dillon, a Standardbred trotter. Dillon's original owner, Henry Pierce, turned down Billings' offer of $20,000 for the mare, but ten days later, the man died. All Pierce's horses were put up for sale, and Billings purchased the mare for $12,500.

Lou Dillon, driven by Millard Sanders, was the first trotter to race a

Lou Dillon at Cleveland Driving Park. Cleveland, O.

mile in two minutes (October 1903 in Readville, Massachusetts). Later that year, in Memphis, Tennessee, she lowered her record to 1:58 1/2.

In October 1904, Major Delmar, owned by Elmer E. Smathers, beat Lou Dillon in the Memphis Gold Cup. Smathers had paid $40,000 for his horse.

> *If I can win the gold cup offered by the Memphis Trotting Association away from Lou Dillon, I will consider Major Delmar cheap at the price.*

Billings accused Smathers of "doping" Lou Dillon with mercury to keep her from winning. The Trotting Association investigated the charges but found no evidence of foul play. Whether doped or not, Lou Dillon was never the same after that race. She was retired in 1906 and exhibited in America and Europe. The mare died at twenty-seven in 1925.

Not wanting to be beaten by Major Delmar again, Billings purchased the horse in November 1904.

> *Mr. Billings bought the great gelding at the November Madison Garden horse sale, paying $15,000 for him—which, considering the fact of his being a gelding, outclassed and with no earning capacity, is a big price. But the horsemen on the inside are convinced that Mr. Billings would have paid perhaps double that amount before permitting anyone else to buy Major Delmar. He is anxious to ride in front, and if some other person got Major Delmar he might have to ride behind.*
>
> — Democrat and Chronicle, March 13, 1905

In November 1905, two years after his unique banquet, Billings decided to travel abroad. He sold all but three of his horses at auction in Madison Square Garden. Eighteen horses brought $46,270. The three Billings kept were Lou Dillon, Major Delmar, and Hontas Crooke. Billings' disillusionment with racing, because of what he believed was the poisoning of Lou Dillon, may have been a factor in his decision to sell the horses.

In 1907, Billings, his wife, two children, and twenty-three servants moved into the Tryon Hall mansion built near the stable. The mansion was 25,000 square feet and included a swimming pool and two bowling lanes. Built on the site of Fort Washington/Fort Tryon from the Revolutionary War, the home was situated on Manhattan's highest point, 250 feet above sea level, with beautiful views of the Hudson Valley.

C.K.G. Billings moved to California in 1917, selling his entire twenty-five-acre Tryon estate to John D. Rockefeller, Jr. The mansion burned down in 1926. Rockefeller later donated the property to New York City, and it was developed as Fort Tryon Park.

Billings health declined over the next ten years. He died on May 6, 1937, at seventy-five.

41

Horse Correspondence School

Horses are quite intelligent, but this correspondence school wasn't for the animals. It was for those that trained them. In 1905, Jesse Beery formed The Beery School of Horsemanship, the first mail order horse training program.

Beery was born in 1861 around the time the famous trainer, John Solomon Rarey, was touring England, demonstrating his amazing skill with horses. Both trainers were born in Ohio, eighty miles from each other.

Beery, the son of Enoch and Mary Beery, was born and lived his entire life in Pleasant Hill. His mother died when Jesse was seven years old. Beery farmed with his father until adulthood, but his real love was horses. From a young age, he trained horses and enjoyed teaching them tricks. As he gained more experience, Jesse took in problem horses for training.

Some of the first horses that I took to break were bad dispositioned colts and Texas ponies … and some of them were the very worst ponies in the country.

And my folks at home were terribly opposed to my handling horses, saying I would keep on until I would get killed, etc. Father finally forbade me bringing any more bad horses on the place, saying that if I wanted to farm the place any longer he would not allow me to bring any more horses there to train. I told him that I had fully made up my mind, and resolved to make a horse trainer out of myself, if I didn't get killed in learning the business.

When he saw the determination I had to master my profession, he submitted to my handling horses.

— Jesse Beery's Practical System of Colt Training and Horse Breaking Illustrated, p. 174,175

Jesse married Almeda Coppock on December 25, 1889. They had four children: Ray, Ruth, Beecher, and Lura. For sixteen years, Jesse gave exhibitions around the country, demonstrating his training methods.

People who attended the demonstrations were eager to learn his techniques. To share his teaching methods, in 1896, the trainer wrote, *Jesse Beery's Practical System of Colt Training and Horse Breaking Illustrated.*

Soon, Beery had more business than he could handle. He grew tired of traveling and being away from his family for long periods of time. In 1905, Beery returned to Pleasant Hill and established his correspondence school. Not only was "Professor" Beery a great horse trainer, he could also clearly explain his practical training techniques so students could achieve similar results with their own horses.

The first course published was Beery's *Illustrated Course in Horse Training*, consisting of eight booklets with titles such as *Colt Training, Disposition & Subjection, Kicking & Balking, Shying & Running Away*, and *Teaching Tricks to Horses and Dogs*. Beery sold the courses through mail-order advertisements placed in newspapers and equine publications.

Beery made it clear his courses weren't simply to be read; they needed to be studied until the principles were thoroughly understood. After learning the disposition of a particular horse, the student was to adapt the training methods to that animal.

Within five years, 30,000 students had enrolled in the Beery School of Horsemanship. At peak times of the year, the school received 2,500 letters and inquiries via postal mail each day.

> *Beery Correspondence School for Horsemanship is a most unusual enterprise, being the only school of its kind in the world. It was started by Professor Jesse Beery, a native of Pleasant Hill, who had been an expert trainer of horses for 20 years, giving exhibitions in all parts of the United States for many years before starting his correspondence school.*

—*Memoirs of Miami Valley (Ohio) Vol 1. 1919*

Beery defined horse training as the art of forming useful habits. He asserted that because a horse's brain is small in relation to the size of his body, he had limited reasoning power.

> *A horse is, of course, a dumb brute; and his reasoning powers are limited to his past experience. So we must reason with him by acts alone. Hence the importance of beginning every step with the colt right; for by our acts he learns. The successful school-master aims first to teach the child*

to have confidence in him. Hence the first lesson we give the colt is simply to teach it to have confidence in us and that we are its best friend and don't intend to hurt it.

— *Colt Training, Disposition, p. 10,11*

Beery classified horses into four general types based upon the shape and features of the horse's head. Horses could be a combination of two or more types.

I have classified all horses by the shape of their heads. I can tell you how to determine the natural disposition of any colt or horse by looking at its head. Each disposition must be handled differently. To train him right, you must understand his disposition. During all my years on the road, giving public exhibitions, I never attempted to handle a single horse without first sizing him up, looking at his head both from the side and front view, so I would know exactly how to handle him. As a result, I never tackled a horse I did not succeed in training.

— *pleasanthillhistorycenter.com/people/jesse*

Type 1

No. 1 has a very kind eye. The head is uniform and lean. It is broad between the eyes and with plenty of room from the eyes to the top of the head. The ears are well formed, wide apart at the base and projecting from the head at an angle, never vertical.

This type is easily trained, adapting itself quickly to various conditions. It is not easily frightened nor provoked to stubbornness and revenge. It takes the trick training easily and is the kind that soon becomes the family driver or the general purpose horse for the boy. In a few words it is teachable, kind and obedient.

Type 2

The principal marks indicating this type are, a bulge between and below the line connecting the eyes; a heavy jowl, and a thick throat latch. The fullness between the eyes is the most common mark and varies in size from a large ridge causing the eye to appear set in the side of the head, to a slight fullness breaking the uniformity of the line of the face.

No. 2 is difficult to conquer once his willfulness crops out and it usually finds occasion to do so. It requires a long time to train him, for he is persistent. He does not give up easily. You will have to work hard for he will take it easy when you allow him to do as he pleases and will resist you by lying down or sullenly standing, doing nothing, while you try to force him. In fact nearly all his resistance, except rearing, will be of that kind. When mad his senses become blunted and he apparently has no feeling.

Type 3

The third type is quick to act and acts with all the power it has. It will resist any attempt to restrain it. It will resist the harness, the appliances or anything else that limits its freedom. It fights hard from the very beginning. Where type No. 2 allowed you to do all the work, type No. 3 will do the work itself and you need but to control its movements. This type acts through fear and nervousness. It is easily frightened and, therefore, has a strong tendency to develop the habits of shying and running away. If restrained so that it can not get away it will probably kick itself loose. This type very seldom balks. Although it resists hard it is soon conquered and when once overcome surrenders unconditionally.

Type 4

Treacherous, ill-tempered, resentful. This type has a very prominent forehead, small pig eye and a dish face. His ears are usually rough and very hairy inside. The fullness of the forehead indicates a disposition to bolt. The small eyes indicate treachery and the dish face stubborn revenge. This type is the bull-dog type. He acts without any apparent cause and when you least expect it. He is the criminal of the horse race. There is nothing a horse can do that he will not do when stirred up. He will act nice once or twice just to get the opportunity to smash you. He has to be conquered not once but many times.

The Four Types of Disposition As Found Among Horses, Jesse Beery 1909

Charley was a two-year-old Standardbred Beery used in many of his exhibitions. Beery had determined Charley had the characteristics of type two and three horses. Beery trained him to pull a carriage without the use of a bridle or reins, controlling him by elaborate signals given with a whip. Beery didn't believe in using blinders/blinkers on harness horses. He wanted the horse to be able to see all around him.

In 1908, Beery wrote a novel, *The Story of Kate and Queen*. The book depicts the different horse types as well as the results of good and bad training and handling. The mare, Queen, was ill-tempered because of her negligent handling, while her filly, Kate, who received kind, patient treatment, turned into a wonderful driving horse.

In 1910, Beery began holding public exhibitions at Pleasant Hill, giving his last performance in 1913 at fifty-two.

Beery developed specialized equipment, which he called "appliances" to use along with his training methods. These included the Four-in-one Beery Bit, the Pulley Breaking Bridle, and the Beery Short Turn Buggy, a carriage that could make sharp turns and was almost impossible to overturn.

Many today would consider some of Beery's methods harsh. It's important to keep in mind the differences in the horse world from Beery's time to now. Then, horses were essential for work and safe travel, whereas today they are used primarily for recreation.

Like John Rarey before him, Beery used leg pull downs to bring a horse to the ground, subduing and convincing him that man was in control.

Most often, this was a single front leg, however, he also had a device that was used on both front legs. He only used this technique on horses who didn't respond to gentler training methods.

CONVINCING THE HORSE THAT THINGS LIABLE TO FRIGHTEN HIM ARE PERFECTLY HARMLESS.

I claim there is no horse naturally vicious. They are always made that way by bad management or ignorant trainers.

Beery passed away in 1945 at eighty-three. Family members continued to operate his school into the 1970s before it finally closed. Over his lifetime, Beery trained thousands of horses, but beyond that, he is considered the trainer with the most far-reaching influence on other horse people. Many today still find his training books useful.

42

Polar Ponies

Throughout history, people have been driven to seek adventure and explore the unknown. While likely not as eager for exploration as men, equines were often vital parts of the exploration parties.

By the early 1900s, most of the world had been explored, except for the Arctic and Antarctica, homes of the North and South Poles. The North Pole sits on an ice cap in the Arctic Ocean, while Antarctica is an ice-covered continent. Antarctica is the colder of the two with average temperatures ranging from -60 to -75 degrees Fahrenheit and a record cold of -129.

A Norwegian, Fridtjof Nansen, first used a horse to explore harsh climates when he crossed Greenland in 1888 with a horse-drawn sled. In 1903, American explorer Anthony Fiala led an expedition to the Arctic Circle with Siberian horses. "The ponies were less troublesome than the dogs and more powerful, dragging loads that astonished us all."

There is an ongoing debate over who was the first to reach the North Pole on foot. Both Frederick Cook (1908) and Robert Peary (1909) claim the honor, however, it's uncertain whether either reached the Pole. But with the prize of the North Pole seemingly achieved, the challenging adventure of being the first to the South Pole was next.

Irishman, Sir Ernest Shackleton, was one of the first Antarctic explorers. Having been a member of a previous, failed mission that used sled dogs, Shackleton believed ponies would be more successful.

Spoiler alert: they were not.

In 1907, Shackleton planned his Nimrod Expedition. Eight Husky dogs and ten Manchurian ponies joined a crew of fourteen men.

The Manchurian (also known as Yakutian) horses were the size of large ponies. The animals were especially suited for survival in extreme cold due to the following characteristics.

- exceptionally thick and long manes and tails

- dense winter coats with hair as long as three inches

- strong hooves which allowed them to paw through deep snow and ice to locate food

- smaller size meant they would lose less body heat

- fat stored during the summer was utilized during the long, cold winter months

- they were thought to have the ability to enter a state of semi-hibernation in which their heart rate and breathing slowed to conserve energy and maintain body temperature

- Manchurians have survived temperatures as low as -90°F

The ponies, purchased in northern China and shipped to New Zealand, included: Zulu (considered the leader of the herd), Doctor, Mac, Nimrod, Socks (named for the long, feathery hair at the back of his legs), Sandy, Grisi (gray), Chinaman, Billy, and Quan. At first, the animals were wild and mean—kicking, biting, and striking at the men. Training commenced during their stay in New Zealand.

As the expedition prepared to depart, the horses, one by one, entered a large wooden box that served as an elevator to hoist them onto the Nimrod. Once on board, each was placed in a stall. The ship departed on New Year's Day, 1908.

Soon after the Nimrod set out on its 2,000 mile journey from New Zealand to Antarctica, they encountered a bad storm. As the ship lurched violently in the waves, the men attempted to rig slings to keep the ponies on their feet, but the frightened animals wouldn't allow it. The trip was so difficult, Shackleton was amazed any of the ponies survived. Doctor and Nimrod didn't.

They arrived at McMurdo Sound on January 29, but ice prevented them from reaching shore until February 3. There would be no grazing for the ponies in the frozen Antarctic. Shackleton developed an unusual feed for them, consisting of dried beef, carrots, milk, currants, and sugar. The unusual rations provided concentrated nourishment without weighing much. Although horses are vegetarians, it wasn't uncommon in the bitter cold for them to eat dog biscuits or even polar bear meat. Four ponies—Sandy, Billy, Zulu, and Mac died after eating volcanic sand they were attracted to because of its salt content.

Shackleton and three of his men began their inland march on October 29 with the four remaining ponies—Quan, Socks, Grisi, and Chinaman. The surviving ponies were lighter in color, which created the misconception that light-colored ponies were more hardy. Each pony pulled a twelve-foot sled carrying 650 pounds. Shackleton wrote, "compared to the dog, the pony is a far more efficient animal, one pony doing the work of at least ten dogs and traveling a further distance in a day."

Despite Shackleton's optimism, the horses were not strong enough for the arduous journey in the frigid cold. Chinaman, Grisi, and Quan had to be put down along the way.

Socks alone, of the original ten ponies, remained to press on with the men. He came closer to the South Pole than any of the others. But on December 7, Socks fell into a crevasse, a huge crack, in the Beardmore Glacier and perished. If the pony's harness hadn't broken, he would have taken one of the men, Frank Wild, with him.

The explorers continued toward their goal. By January 9th, 1909, they were less than a hundred miles from the Pole. But almost out of food, they decided it wasn't safe to go on. Shackleton and all his men made it safely back to their base camp.

Robert Scott,
Terra Nova Expedition

After the failed Nimrod Expedition, Robert Falcon Scott gathered supplies and a crew of sixty-five men for his own effort to reach the South Pole. The Terra Nova Expedition took place from 1910 to 1913. Scott was racing against Norwegian Roald Amundsen to be the first to the Pole.

Cecil Henry Meares, a crew member in charge of the dog teams, traveled to northern China to purchase twenty ponies for the expedition. Knowing little about

horses, Meares' prime consideration, based on Shackleton's experience, was to purchase light-colored animals. The seller took advantage of Meares' ignorance. Besides being untrained, many of the ponies were old or lame. Some accounts refer to these animals as Siberian ponies, another name for Manchurians.

Lawrence Oates, an accomplished horseman, would be in charge of the ponies on the expedition. He arrived later at the quarantine station on Quail Island in New Zealand and was startled by the poor condition of the ponies. He considered the animals too old and worn-out for the trip. Oates informed Scott that the ponies were unsuitable, but his boss disagreed. One pony was suspected of having a disease and was left behind, leaving nineteen ponies for the expedition.

Apsley Cherry-Garrard, at twenty-four, was one of the youngest members of the Terra Nova expedition. In his book, published in 1922, *The Worst Journey In The World Antarctic 1910-1913*, Cherry-Garrard provides many details about the expedition's ponies.

The nineteen ponies included Blossom, Blücher, Bones, Chinaman, Christopher, Davy, Guts, Hackenschmidt, Jehu, Jimmy Pigg, Jones, Michael, Nobby, Punch, Snatcher, Snippets, Uncle Bill, Victor, and Weary Willy.

Hackenschmidt received his name because of "his vicious habit of using both fore and hind legs in attacking those who came near him." [1]

As they continued gathering supplies in New Zealand, trainers worked with the ponies, teaching them to pull large sleds. The ponies varied in strength and temperament.

> *But it was soon clear that these ponies were an uneven lot. There were the steady workers like Punch and Nobby; there were one or two definitely weak ponies like Blossom, Blücher and Jehu; and there were one or two strong but rather impossible beasts. One of these was soon known as Weary Willie. His outward appearance belied him, for he looked like a pony. A brief acquaintance soon convinced me that he was without doubt a cross between a pig and a mule.*
>
> *There were runaways innumerable, and all kinds of falls. But these ponies could tumble about unharmed in a way which would cause an English horse to lie up for a week.*
>
> — *The Worst Journey In The World*, chapter 4

In addition to the ponies, the expedition included three motorized sledges and thirty-three dogs. On November 29, 1910, Scott and his crew set sail from New Zealand for Antarctica. Two days later, a storm killed the ponies Davy and Jones and nearly sank the ship. The Terra Nova arrived at Ross Island in Antarctica on January 4, 1911. Their final destination, the South Pole, was 900 miles away.

The ponies hauled supplies from the ship to Cape Evans where the men erected a fifty by twenty-five foot building or hut to serve as the expedition's base camp.

> *The ponies' stable was built against the northern side of the hut, and was thus sheltered from the blizzards which always blow here from the south.*
>
> — *The Worst Journey In The World, chapter 4*

A stove that burned seal blubber heated the stable. The fire was also used to melt snow for the ponies' water and to heat their bran mashes.

> *Every now and then there would be a great banging and crashing heard through the walls of the hut in the middle of the night. The watchman would run out… It was generally Bones or Chinaman kicking their stalls, perhaps to keep themselves warm, but by the time the watchman had reached the stable he would be met by a line of sleepy faces blinking at him in the light of the electric torch, each saying plainly that he could not possibly have been responsible for a breach of the peace!*
>
> — *The Worst Journey In The World, chapter 6*

Although Lawrence Oates was a skilled horseman, he had no experience in the harsh conditions of the Antarctic. Snowshoes for the ponies had been unloaded from the ship and stored in the stable. But Oates refused to use them, claiming they were a nuisance and unnecessary.

The ponies' weight was so concentrated on their thin legs and hooves, the animals continually plunged through the top layer of snow and ice, making for slow and difficult travel. Using the snowshoes would have made it easier for the ponies to cross the harsh terrain.

Leaving camp on January 24, 1911, the strongest eight ponies traveled inland with twelve men on a depot mission. This initial journey set up stores of food and supplies along a route in preparation for the actual journey to the Pole which would begin later that year.

Ponies used during this mission included Blossom, Blücher, Jimmy Pigg, Nobby, Punch, Uncle Bill, Weary Willy, and Guts. They pulled sleds containing up to 900 pounds of supplies. Nobby and James Pigg were the only ponies to survive this trip.

On February 4, the depot group encountered their first blizzard.

> *It is blowing a full gale: the air is full of falling snow, and the wind drives this along and adds to it the loose snow which is lying on the surface of the Barrier. Fight your way a few steps away from the tent, and it will be gone. Lose your sense of direction and there is nothing to guide you back. Expose your face and hands to the wind, and they will very soon be frost-bitten. And this at midsummer. Imagine the added cold of spring and autumn: the cold and darkness of winter.*
>
> *The animals suffer most, and during this first blizzard all our ponies were weakened, and two of them became practically useless. It must be remembered that they had stood for five weeks upon a heaving deck; they had been through one very bad gale: the time during which we were unloading the ship was limited, and since that time they had dragged heavy loads the greater part of 200 miles. Nothing was left undone for them which we could manage, but necessarily the Antarctic is a grim place for ponies. I think Scott felt the sufferings of the ponies more than the animals themselves.*
>
> ** Antarctica's summer is from October to February.*
>
> — *The Worst Journey In The World, chapter 5*

Back at the base camp, the pony Hackenschmidt died of an unknown illness. By late 1911, eight of the original nineteen ponies remained. Two additional ponies arrived on another ship. The ten ponies that accompanied the men on their actual march to the South Pole were Jehu, Chinaman, Nobby,

Jimmy Pigg, Snippets, Christopher, Victor, Snatcher, Bones, and Michael.

Jehu was the thinnest of the ponies, described as a scarecrow. He bravely pulled a lighter load.

Chinaman was described as "Jehu's rival for last place."

Nobby had been rescued from killer whales the previous year and was one of the two ponies that had survived the depot-laying mission, along with Jimmy Pigg.

Snippets was known to eat blubber. He fell partway into a large crevasse but the men were able to pull him out.

Christopher was a man-killer if ever a horse was; he had to be thrown in order to attach him to the sledge; to the end he would lay out any man who was rash enough to give him the chance; once started, and it took four men to achieve this, it was impossible to halt him during the day's march, and so Oates and his three tent mates and their ponies had to go without any lunch meal for 130 miles of the Southern Journey.

— *The Worst Journey In The World, chapter 6*

Early on, Victor was said to be nervous but not vicious. Later, he became more steady and reliable.

He is a steady goer, and as gentle as a dear old sheep. I can hardly realize the strenuous times I had with him only a month ago, when it took about four of us to get him harnessed to a sledge, and two of us every time with all our strength to keep him from bolting when in it. Even at the start of the journey he was as nearly unmanageable as any beast could be, and always liable to bolt from sheer excess of spirits. He is more sober now after three weeks of featureless Barrier, but I think I am more fond of him than ever. He has lost his rotundity, like all the other horses, and is a long-legged, angular beast, very ugly as horses go, but still I would not change him for any other.

— *The Worst Journey In The World, chapter 9*

194

At some point during the final journey, Snatcher wore snowshoes and led the line of ponies.

Bones and Chinaman were known for kicking their stalls at night. Bones suffered from a severe attack of colic but recovered.

Michael, the most attractive of the ponies, was described as high-strung.

On October 24, 1911, sixteen men set out on the polar route. Most of the men carried additional supplies to leave at designated drop points, after which they would return to Cape Evans. A group of five would continue on the last phase of the journey to the South Pole.

The bond Cherry-Garrard felt with the ponies is clear from his book.

> *… let me add that no animals could have had more considerate and often self-sacrificing treatment than these ponies of ours. Granted that they must be used at all (and I do not mean to enter into that question) they were fed, trained, and even clothed as friends and companions rather than as beasts of burden. They were never hit, a condition to which they were clearly unaccustomed. They lived far better than they had before, and all this was done for them in spite of the conditions under which we ourselves lived.*
>
> — *The Worst Journey In The World, chapter 6*

The ponies crossed 425 miles of the Ross Ice Shelf to the Beardmore Glacier. From there, the five men would continue on foot. Once they reached the glacier, the ponies were no longer needed, and the animals were shot. The additional men and the sled dogs returned to Cape Evans.

Robert Scott continued toward the Pole with Edward Wilson, Henry Bowers, Edgar Evans, and Lawrence Oates. The men crossed the Beardmore Glacier and the Polar Plateau, reaching the South Pole on January 17, 1912. When they arrived, they learned that Roald Amundsen's team had beaten them there.

Inside the tent Amundsen left behind, was a note stating he had reached the Pole on December 14, 1911, nearly a month earlier. Amundsen's party used dogs rather than ponies.

> *The Pole. Yes, but under very different circumstances from those expected. … Great God! This is an awful place and terrible enough for us to have labored to it without the reward of priority. Well, it is something to have got here.*
>
> — *Diary Of Robert Falcon Scott*

Discouraged and defeated, Scott and his men turned around and started toward their base camp. A dog team with supplies was supposed to meet them on their way back. It did not. None of the men made it to Cape Evans. The last three, Robert Scott, Edward Wilson, and Henry Bowers, died in their tent just eleven miles from one of the supply depots. They likely would have survived if they had reached it.

Eight months later, on October 29, 1912, seven Indian mules, trained in the Himalayas, pulled the sleds of a rescue party led by Dr. Edward Atkinson. The mules were equipped with eye shades to protect them from snow blindness. No one expected to find Scott and his men alive. On November 12, the search party located the deceased men and recovered Scott's journals and photographs.

Inside one of the journals, Scott had written, "Send this diary to my ~~wife~~ widow." The word "wife" was struck out, replaced with "widow."

The heroic search party mules were Abdullah, Begum, Gulab, Khan Sahib, Lal Khan, Pyaree, and Ranee. However, when it came time for the search party to leave Antarctica, the mules weren't treated as heroes. Rather than bringing them back to either New Zealand or India, the mules were killed.

Subsequent visitors to Cape Evans found a pile of pony snowshoes in the remnants of the stable. Would their use have made a difference in the outcome of the Terra Nova Expedition? Not for the ponies, as the plan had always been to dispense with them after the animals had served their purpose. But perhaps human lives might have been saved.

---

1. The pony was possibly named after Georg Hackenschmidt. Born in 1878, Hackenschmidt was one of the earliest body builders and a heavyweight wrestling champion.

2. On the fourth day, one of the motorized sledges broke through the ice and sank into the sea. The other two covered only fifty miles before being abandoned after continual breakdowns. teuaka.org.nz/news/terra-novas-motorised-sledge

43

The Abernathy Brothers

Being raised by a father famous for catching wolves with his hands might make for an unusual childhood. Such was the case for the Abernathy boys—Louis (Bud) and Temple.

When President Teddy Roosevelt heard about "Catch 'em Alive" Jack Abernathy's unusual technique for wolf catching, he wouldn't believe it until he'd seen it for himself, so a special wolf hunt was arranged.

Mr. Abernathy greeted President Roosevelt upon his arrival in Frederick, Oklahoma, in April 1905. On the first day of the hunt, Roosevelt joined Abernathy on horseback. When a wolf was spotted, they gave chase. Having done this many times, Sam Bass, Abernathy's gray Arabian, knew just what to expect. When the horse came alongside the wolf, Jack leapt onto the wild animal's back.

The wolf snarled, but before he could attack, Abernathy rammed his gloved hand into the startled animal's mouth. Unable to open or close his mouth, the helpless wolf was caught. Over his lifetime, Abernathy captured over a thousand wolves in this manner. He sold the animals to parks, zoos, and traveling shows. Roosevelt, an avid hunter and sportsman, had no desire to try the technique himself but was content to observe from a safe distance.

Abernathy's sons, Bud and Temple, met the president when they camped with their parents at that hunt. Bud was five, and Temple just fifteen months old. Roosevelt was impressed with Jack Abernathy, and the two became lifelong friends.

Then came the five days wolf hunting in Oklahoma, and this was unalloyed pleasure… The party got seventeen wolves, three coons, and any number of rattlesnakes. I was in at the death of eleven wolves. The other six wolves were killed by members of the party who were off with bunches of dogs in some place

The following year, President Roosevelt appointed Jack Abernathy as the U.S. Marshal for the Western District of Oklahoma Territory. The Abernathys moved to Guthrie, Oklahoma, but Jack kept their Cross Roads ranch near Frederick. In 1906, in Guthrie, Mrs. Abernathy died a few months after giving birth to their fourth daughter, Pearlie Mae.

Raising six children while traveling frequently as a U.S. Marshal wasn't easy. Abernathy's father and sister helped him with the children. Being motherless might explain why Bud and Temple were permitted to embark on their daring escapades. Their mother might not have gone along with the boys' adventures.

The idea for their first trip began in June 1909. By then, the boys had heard many of their father's stories about his travels as U.S. Marshal. Bud and Temple wanted to see the extravagant governor's mansion in Santa Fe, New Mexico Territory.

Each night, by the light of a kerosene lamp, Bud mapped out their route. His hand-drawn map listed the cities the boys would travel through by horseback on their way from Guthrie, Oklahoma to Sante Fe, New Mexico and back. Surprised by his sons' idea, Jack wanted time to think about it.

They didn't have to wait long for their father's answer. The next day, Mr. Abernathy gave them his permission. He opened a hundred-dollar checking account for each boy. Bud was nine. His younger brother was only five.

Temple was so small, Bud had to saddle his pony for him. Temple couldn't even mount the half-Shetland Geronimo without first climbing onto something like a porch or fence. To dismount, he slid out of the saddle and down Geronimo's left, front leg.

Guthrie, Oklahoma to Santa Fe, New Mexico and Back (1,200 miles round trip, 1909)

Mr. Abernathy arranged to meet the boys in Tipton, Oklahoma, about a four days ride from their home. He figured by then his sons would be tired of their adventure and ready to return to their ranch with him. But when they met in Tipton, the boys had no intention of turning back. Although their father did his best to convince them, Bud and Temple were determined to complete their journey. Mr. Abernathy handed Bud a New Testament and encouraged them to say their prayers every night. The two set off—Bud on his father's horse, Sam Bass, and Temple on Geronimo.

The boys were worried about the pockets of quicksand they knew surrounded the Red River. But the wise Sam Bass helped them find a safe place to cross, and they reached Estelline, Texas, late that night. Sam and Geronimo rested in a livery stable while the boys enjoyed a peaceful night in a hotel—after remembering to say their prayers.

The next day, Temple drank some foul water that made him sick. For the next few hours, he found himself frequently sliding down Geronimo's leg as his digestive system worked overtime to correct itself. Bud, in an attempt to be helpful, gave him a dose of castor oil, but that only made matters worse. They continued on, and by noon, Temple felt better—except that he'd jumped off his pony so often his ankles were sore.

Crossing the hot, desert-like Texas panhandle was challenging. The boys were always on the lookout for rattlesnakes. Fresh drinking water was hard to find, and the water in their canteens became so hot it was undrinkable. One night, Bud saw glowing eyes about thirty feet from their camp. A pack of wolves surrounded them. Bud fired his shotgun to scare them away, then the boys built a large fire to keep the wolves at a distance.

Some people in the small towns where they stopped had heard of the boys and their journey. Most were friendly and excited to hear about their adventure. When they crossed into New Mexico, they turned south and rode to the town of Roswell. The irrigated fields and fruit orchards were as amazing as their father had described. From Roswell, they ran into a hail storm while riding north. Since they couldn't outride the storm, the boys found a cave that provided shelter.

Not long after that, a crazed donkey chased Temple and Geronimo. The pony was running as fast as his short legs would carry him—which wasn't nearly fast enough for the terrified Temple. Bud came to the rescue by herding his younger brother toward a pasture gate. Once Geronimo was safely through, Bud slammed the gate in the donkey's face.

Two weeks after they'd left home, the boys reached Santa Fe where their father arrived by train to join them. Although Santa Fe was considered the capital, New Mexico was still three years away from becoming a state. The boys stayed at the governor's mansion and were given a tour of the city.

Returning home the same way would have been too tame for the boys, so Bud and Temple took a different route home. Their

father rode along for a few days, then took a train the rest of the way. On their own again, one evening, the boys spent the night with a group of cowboys they'd come across who were branding cattle. The men were friendly, but the boys thought it odd that their house had no furniture—only wooden crates, saddles, and blankets. Bud and Temple followed the men's example and slept on the floor, using their saddles as pillows.

By the time they crossed back into Oklahoma, the boys were famous. Reporters met them in each town, peppering them with questions. The women in the crowds were not as excited about the young boys traveling alone. One demanded to know why their mother allowed such a thing. When Temple informed her that their mother was dead, the woman became hysterical. She frightened Temple more than anything he'd experienced on their trip.

When they arrived home, Jack showed Bud and Temple a letter he'd received from one of the "cattlemen" the boys spent a night with. The men were rustlers, and a few months earlier, they'd tried to kill Jack Abernathy. But the outlaws were so impressed with his sons, they protected the boys.

> *I don't like one hair on your head, but I do like the stuff that is in these kids. We shadowed them through the worst part of New Mexico to see that they were not harmed by sheepherders, mean men, or animals.*

You might think that trip was enough to satisfy the boys' desire for adventure, but it only seemed to whet their appetite. The Santa Fe trip gave them the confidence to plan an even longer journey for the following summer.

Oklahoma to New York City (2,000 miles one way, 1910)

In 1910, Teddy Roosevelt had been on an African safari and would soon return to the U.S. Jack Abernathy was invited to meet him when the former president arrived in New York. Bud and Temple wanted to meet Roosevelt also, but rather than taking a train as their father would, they decided to ride there, a distance of 2,000 miles. This time, they quickly persuaded their father.

On April 1, the boys started off on Sam Bass and Geronimo. Bud was ten and Temple six. Early in the trip, they stopped to visit the last Comanche chief, Quanah Parker, a friend of their father's. In the small town of Cache, Temple bought a beautiful Navajo saddle blanket for Geronimo even though Bud insisted it cost too much.

Before they were out of Oklahoma, the boys met with their first tragedy. While staying with Deputy Wylie Haynes in Hominy, Geronimo foundered and could not continue.

The boys thought it was because Geronimo drank too much water at a creek when he'd been hot. A heartbroken Temple didn't want to leave without his faithful pony. Deputy Haynes promised to send Geronimo back to the Cross Roads Ranch by train. He helped the boys find another horse. Temple chose a red-and-white pinto and named him Wylie Haynes after the deputy who had been so kind to them. With the beautiful Navajo blanket he'd bought for Geronimo on Wylie Haynes' back, the boys were again on their way.

Not long after that, Temple challenged his brother to a race to test his new horse's speed. Sam Bass tripped over a stump and fell. The boys feared Bud had broken his leg, but neither he nor Sam Bass was seriously injured.

When the boys left their horses overnight at a livery stable in Chetopa, Kansas, someone replaced Temple's beautiful Navajo blanket with a cheap, cotton one. Temple believed the stableman had stolen his prized blanket. He grabbed a whip from the barn wall and chased the man with it. Although Bud agreed that the man had taken the blanket, he made Temple stop. The prized blanket was never returned.

In Missouri, the boys encountered a late winter storm and spent the day playing in the snow. When they reached St. Louis, the mayor gave Bud and Temple their first car ride.

Next, they traveled through Illinois and Indiana, then Cincinnati, Dayton, and Columbus, Ohio. News of their expedition spread, and the boys received the royal treatment everywhere they went. They drove a train, rode with firefighters to fight a fire, had their fingerprints taken (a relatively new practice at the time), were made deputies for a day, and toured the Wright Brothers' airplane factory with Wilbur Wright himself.

Bud and Temple arrived in Washington D.C. on May 27 and spent a week seeing the sights. They met President Taft, who arranged for them to be on a Coast Guard cutter that would meet Roosevelt's ship when it came into the harbor.

On June 6, Sam Bass and Wylie Haynes were rested and ready to carry the boys on the last leg of their journey. At Jersey City, they ferried the horses across to New York City. People were so excited to meet the young adventurers, they pulled

hairs from the horses' tails as souvenirs. One woman even yanked out a patch of Temple's hair. Seventeen mounted officers rescued the boys from the crowd, escorting them to a nearby hotel.

On June 18, Bud, Temple, and their father were on the boat that sailed out to greet Roosevelt while their ponies were held at the dock. When Roosevelt reached shore, the boys rode in a parade between Roosevelt's carriage and the Rough Riders Cavalry unit. Over a million people lined the streets to watch the five-mile long parade. When it was over, Roosevelt gave Temple a large teddy bear with flags of many nations around its neck.

Sam Bass and Wylie Haynes were loaded into a rail car and shipped back to Oklahoma. After a few days, Jack planned to return home by train with his boys, but Bud and Temple had a better idea. They wanted their father to buy a car they could drive home. Their father promised if the boys could find a car that day that was small enough for them to handle and was reasonably priced, he would buy it for them.

New York City to Oklahoma

The boys located a suitable car called the Brush Runabout, and their father purchased it for $485. After a few driving lessons (there was no limit on driving age), Bud and Temple were both able to drive the Brush. Mr. Abernathy caught their enthusiasm for motorized vehicles and purchased a larger car for himself, a Maxwell Model E30.

The boys started for home in the Brush on July 6, followed by their father in the Maxwell driven by a chauffeur. That first night, they averted catastrophe. Once, when Bud slowed the Brush, Temple jumped out and ran in front of the car. A surprised Bud had no time to react. The car ran over Temple, but the boy was not seriously injured.

When they reached Kansas, the boys looked back to check on their father's progress. The Maxwell was on fire! Many of their souvenirs from the trip, including Temple's teddy bear from Roosevelt, were destroyed. After the Maxwell was repaired, they drove the rest of the way home. The 2,512 mile trip by motor car had taken twenty-three days.

Other Adventures

In 1911, Bud and Temple starred in heroic roles in several movies, riding Sam Bass and Wylie Haynes. Then, a promoter had an unusual idea for the upcoming presidential election. Bud, riding a 7,000-pound elephant name Judy, would race against Temple on a donkey named Jennie. The race would begin in New York City and end in Washington, D.C. William Howard Taft, the Republican candidate, was represented by the elephant. The donkey represented his Democratic opponent Woodrow Wilson.

The winner of this unusual race was supposed to predict the winner of the presidential election. By the time they reached Philadelphia, however, the elephant's feet were so sore, the Humane Society intervened and insisted the race be canceled.

If both had remained healthy, it's unclear whether Judy or Jennie would have won. However, Woodrow Wilson was elected president.

New York to California (3,619 miles one way, 1911)

The Abernathy boys' final long-distance horseback ride wasn't their idea. Promoters Fred Thompson and Skip Dundy presented a challenge to Jack Abernathy. If Bud and Temple could cross the country in sixty days or less, they would receive $10,000. The boys eagerly accepted the challenge for what would be their longest and most difficult ride.

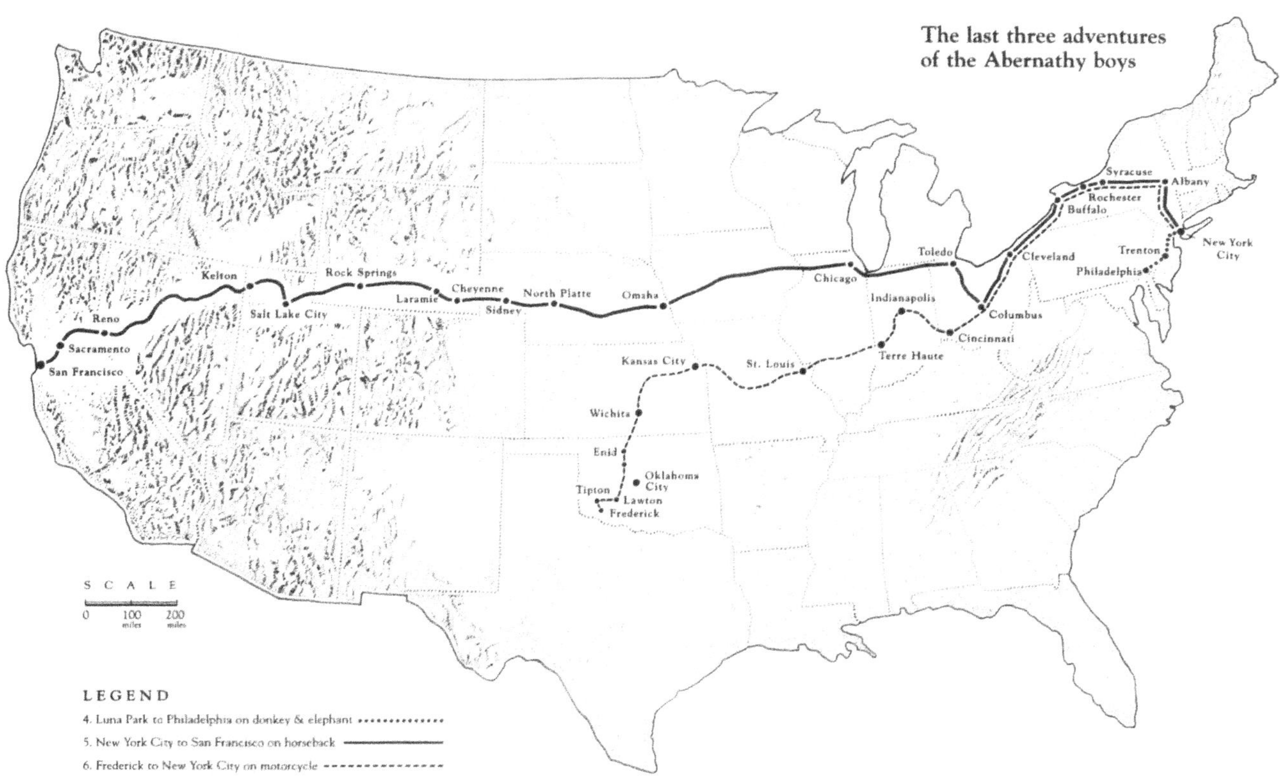

The route decided upon was 3,619 miles, from the Atlantic Ocean at Coney Island, New York to the Pacific Ocean in San Francisco, California. They needed to average sixty miles each day to complete the journey in the required time. Sundays and days of bad weather weren't counted toward the total. They were permitted only one change of horses. Also, the boys could not eat or sleep under roof at any time during the trip.

The journey began just past midnight on August 11, 1911. Bud was now eleven and Temple seven. Their starting point was knee deep in the Atlantic Ocean at Coney Island. The boys carried a flask of Atlantic sea water they would dump into the Pacific when they reached their destination.

On this journey, the boys had no time for sight-seeing and little time to rest. They slept on the ground in a makeshift tent. In some locations, people fixed meals for them, but the food was served outdoors, so the boys would not break the rules of the challenge.

The pair made good time across Ohio, past Chicago, and into Iowa. They rode so steadily Temple developed the ability to sleep in the saddle. One day, while the boy was snoozing, Wylie took a detour under a shady tree, and Temple was knocked to the ground. Bud let him sleep there for a while, then picked him up and put him back on his horse without his brother ever waking up.

Midway through Nebraska, Temple became sick. The boys lost half a day while he rested. As soon as he was able, they continued on into Wyoming. A cold snap hit near Cheyenne. A kind farmer fed the boys a warm meal and offered to let them sleep inside where it was warm. But Bud and Temple were determined to stick to the rules. The farmer showed them a haystack beside the barn, and the boys burrowed into it, pulling their blankets around them. While snowflakes fluttered down, the brothers were toasty inside the hay.

In Laramie, Wyoming, Sam Bass got into an alfalfa field. The Arabian had been their father's horse since before Bud and Temple were born. Sam had participated in countless wolf hunts with Jack and had protected the boys on their first two journeys. But Sam Bass foundered from the alfalfa and died.

Both boys were heartbroken. The horse would be sorely missed. They recalled the many times Sam had saved them, such as avoiding the quicksand on their first adventure. In the tough stretches ahead, the boys could have used Sam Bass' steadiness and experience.

Despite this significant loss, the boys didn't consider quitting. There were three more states to cross: Utah, Nevada, and California. Bud bought a new horse called Big Black. He was a good horse, but he wasn't Sam Bass, and he didn't get along well with Wylie Haynes.

The boys faced the most difficult portions of their ride, climbing to the top of the Rocky Mountains, over steep trails to a height of 7,000 feet. But even more treacherous than the climb was the descent on the other side. A wrong step by either horse could send them over a cliff.

After the boys crossed the Continental Divide, they rode along the route of the Transcontinental Railroad in Utah. They were behind schedule but still believed they could complete the ride within the sixty days.

Crossing the Great Salt Lake Desert was the most difficult and dangerous part of their journey. They were low on water and exhausted as they rode endlessly across the salt flats. One night, Bud didn't hobble the horses, figuring they were as tired as he and Temple were and wouldn't go anywhere. But the next morning, Wylie Haynes and Big Black were gone.

They searched for the horses for two days but saw no sign of them. With little food and almost no water, the boys realized they might die in the desert. On the third day, Temple was too weak to search, so Bud went out by himself. He resolved that if he didn't find the horses that day, they would start off on foot.

Temple was at his lowest point, believing he was about to die. But later, he spotted his brother riding up bareback on Wylie Haynes. The boys fed Wylie some oats. There was no water for any of them.

Bud hoisted Temple onto Wylie, and the boys rode double. Over the next hill was the small town of Kelton, Utah. Not only were they able to stock up on water and supplies, they discovered Big Black had found his way to the town ahead of them. Their trouble in the desert had put them further behind schedule, so the boys didn't remain in Kelton long.

As they followed the railroad tracks out of town, a train slowed alongside them. The men offered to take Bud, Temple, and their horses the rest of the way across the desert, promising they wouldn't tell anyone. It was against the terms of their contract, and without hesitation, Bud turned them down. Even if the men never told, Bud would know he had cheated.

The boys pushed on, over the Sierra Nevada Mountains to Sacramento, California, then to Oakland where they caught a ferry to San Francisco. There, they met their father. The boys rode their horses out into the Pacific at 6:30 PM on October 30, 1911.

They both stood in their stirrups and waved to celebrate the completion of their journey. Bud dumped the flask of Atlantic water into the Pacific. A large wave knocked Wylie Haynes off his feet, and Temple went down with him. The horse scrambled back up with Temple clinging to the saddle horn.

Bud and Temple completed their trip in sixty-two days (a total of ninety-one days, including Sundays and bad weather days when they didn't travel). The previous cross-country record was 182 days set by an army officer. Despite the young riders' amazing accomplishment, Thompson and Dundy refused to pay them any of the prize money.

Regardless, the boys were jubilant about finishing their course. Their only regret was that Sam Bass hadn't made it to the Pacific with them.

That was the last long-distance horseback ride for the Abernathy brothers. Two years later, in 1913, they had one last adventure together, riding a two-seat Indian motorcycle from Oklahoma to New York City.

As an adult, Bud became a lawyer and eventually a judge. Temple joined his father in the oil business.

In Frederick, Oklahoma, Abernathy Day is celebrated each summer on the first Saturday in June. A statue commemorating the brothers sits on the lawn of the Tillman County, Oklahoma courthouse.

Looking back from the perspective of an eighty-year-old, Temple described what the experiences had taught him and his brother.

> *We learned to endure hardship with patience, especially on those heartbreaking days toward the end of our coast-to-coast trip, when Sam Bass' death, and our trials in the desert seemed to test us more than we could bear. But we made it through, stronger for having held on. We could, we discovered, do almost anything we set our minds to.*
>
> — *Bud & Me, p. 162*

44

Stable Wrecker

William Howard Taft has the dubious honor of being the heaviest U.S. president. Taft stood five feet eleven inches tall, and at his heaviest, weighed approximately 350 pounds. However, the story about Taft becoming stuck in the presidential bathtub is not true—or nice.

A team of horses ran away with a carriage Taft rode in when he was nine. The carriage careened down a steep street in Cincinnati, Ohio, and young Taft fell out, suffering cuts and a slight skull fracture.

Despite that early bad experience and his later large size, Taft enjoyed horseback riding. He purchased a horse in February 1909 to accompany him to the White House. (Inaugurations were held in March at that time.) The bay was 16 hands tall and described as a southern plantation horse.

President-elect Taft has bought a horse—a 1,250 pound, six-year-old bay gelding. He has been named Tate Sterret, after the man from whom Gen. Clarence R. Edwards bought him.

Gov. Judson. Harmon, of Ohio, one of the president-elect's best personal friends, although a democrat, is to have the honor of riding the steed in the inaugural parade. …

Mr. Taft knows all about Tate, having ridden him while at Hot Springs. Tate carried the president-elect without sign of fatigue and without any of the frills that might make a slightly portly man a bit nervous.

— The Salina Evening Journal, Salina, Kansas, February 24, 1909

Taft is likely the last president to be thrown from a horse at the White House, according to this account by Major Archie Butt.

The President was thrown from his horse this afternoon, but luckily not hurt. I am sure he is bruised and that he will be very sore tomorrow, but it was lucky that he was not killed. We were riding near the

Although he enjoyed horses, Taft was the first president to replace them with automobiles. During his presidency, the White House stables were demolished to make room for a garage. After that, horses for White House use were kept at the nearby Army stables.

Although the horses were evicted, Taft kept two pet cows who grazed on the South Lawn—Mooly Wooly and later, a Holstein, Pauline Wayne. Pauline was the last cow at the White House. She retired to Wisconsin when President Taft left office.

Taft served one term as president, from 1909 to 1913 and was the only man to serve as both president and later, as Chief Justice of the Supreme Court.

Republican president Warren G. Harding appointed Taft to the court in 1921. Because of declining health, Taft resigned as chief justice on February 3, 1930. He died a month later on March 8th.

PAULINE · THE PRESIDENT'S COW

45

Two-Gun Nan

Nan Aspinwall was born in New York City on February 2, 1880. Shortly after her birth, the family moved to rural Liberty, Nebraska where her parents worked as storekeepers. At nineteen, Nan performed as an oriental dancer, "Princess Omene." Several years later, she marketed herself as "Montana Girl."

Her story of being raised on a Montana ranch where her father taught her to rope and ride is almost certainly fiction. However, she told it so convincingly, many newspapers reported it as fact. Given her skills as a sharpshooter, roper, and trick rider, it was easy to believe she was a ranch girl.

Aspinwall had long, wavy, blond hair. She performed wearing a divided skirt, boots, a silk blouse with a bandanna around her neck, and a Stetson hat. In 1906, she and her husband, Frank Gable, were lariat experts who performed with Buffalo Bill and Pawnee Bill's western shows. By 1910, Frank and Nan split off to tour on their own calling their act Gable's Road Show.

Some say the idea for Nan's solo ride across the U.S. originated as a way to publicize their Road Show. Others state it was a bet with Buffalo Bill. A third possibility was a challenge from a magazine who later backed out of their offer.

In 1910, a female riding over 3,000 miles alone, from San Francisco to New York City was unheard of. In fact, at that time, most women still rode sidesaddle. One of the most important preparations for her trip was locating the right horse.

> *Miss Aspinwall is an experienced horsewoman, not only on the range but also with "Wild West" shows. She says she has no fear of accident to herself on the ride, but desires to secure a horse that will be able to stand the trip without mishap. "If I do not get the right kind of a horse soon, I will send to my father's ranch in Montana and have one sent me from there. Of course, on a trip like this, I must have the best animal procurable—one that will make the trip and still look well when I arrive in New York City.*

—*Los Angeles Herald, July 9, 1910*

Aspinwall finally found that horse—a 17 hand, eight-year-old Thoroughbred mare named Lady Ellen. Some sources call the horse a chestnut, others a bay. The mare had four stockings and a star, stripe, snip. The third member of the traveling trio was Nan's border collie, Kaipo.

The thirty-year-old woman departed from the San Francisco Chronicle building at 12:30 PM on September 1, 1910 with a gun at her side. Nan carried a letter from San Francisco mayor, Patrick H. McCarthy, to be delivered to the mayor of New York City when she reached her destination in Manhattan.

Nan carried few supplies with her. In the early part of her journey, she followed the Western Pacific Rail Line. Her husband, Frank, rode ahead by train to provide additional supplies and to promote her arrival in new cities.

Nan encountered many difficulties that newspapers declared "would tax the endurance of a hardened man." The following report describes the most difficult time on her journey.

From Shafter to Proctor, in trying to take a short cut, she got on a prospector's road which led up a granite mountain. All at once she discovered she was lost. In trying to go back she could find no trail, as the horse's feet, or her own, had made no impression on the granite. She wandered all that day and finally tied her horse and climbed one of the points near to see if she could see any signs of a habitation. In coming back down the underbrush was so thick she was unable to find her horse. She sat down reduced to despair, not knowing what to do. While sitting there, the mare got restless and neighed for her rider. Miss Aspinwall feels that is the only thing that saved her life, as she had exhausted every means of finding her location and the loss of her horse took away her nerve completely.

She was in this lost condition two days and one night, with only the bunch grass for her horse, and no food for herself. It was freezing cold at night and broiling hot through the day. Miss Aspinwall finally got her mare over one of the peaks and slid down, sometimes ten and twenty feet at a time. During all this time she was on foot and got into the railroad camp of Proctor carrying what was left of her boots in her hand. The men came out and carried her into camp; her feet were bleeding from the grease-wood and granite, and there were ten cactus thorns taken from one foot.

Evening Bulletin, Honolulu, Hawaii, March 15, 1911

* Shafter and Proctor are in Nevada.

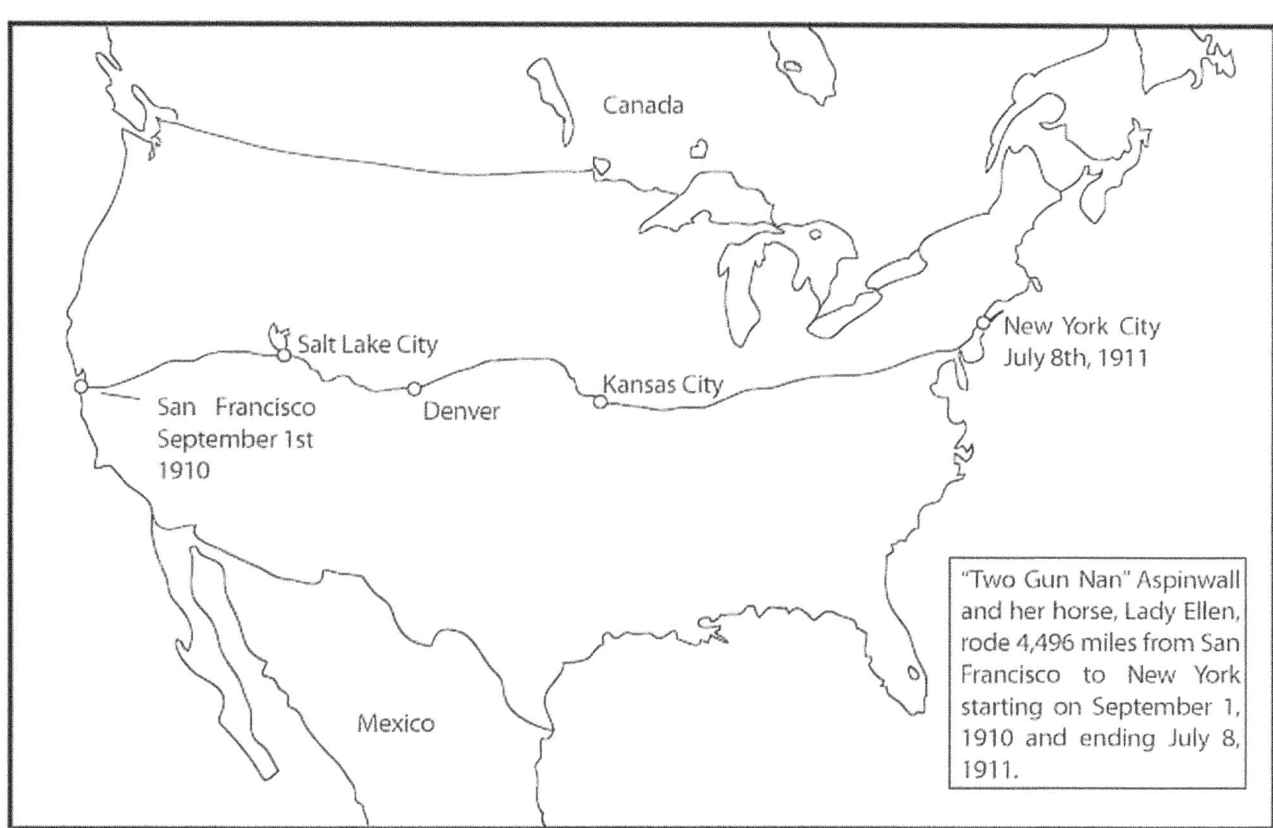

"Two Gun Nan" Aspinwall and her horse, Lady Ellen, rode 4,496 miles from San Francisco to New York starting on September 1, 1910 and ending July 8, 1911.

After three days, Nan and Lady Ellen were ready to continue. They averaged twenty-five to thirty miles each day. Kaipo doesn't seem to be mentioned after this point. It's unclear whether the dog completed the journey. Whenever possible, Nan cared for Lady Ellen herself. She shod the horse fourteen times during the trip.

One thing Nan complained about was the difficulty of finding places to sleep.

"Talk about western chivalry! There's no such thing. For weeks at a time I could find no fit place to sleep, and I had to make the best of it in railroad stations, stalls, or any other convenient place."

Denied hospitality in the town of Mitchell, at the top of the Tennessee Pass, she shot out every window she saw. "That story got around, and after that I could not draw my handkerchief without starting a panic, so I quit carrying the gun."

—The New York Times, July 9, 1911

By the time she arrived in Pennsylvania, Nan was ready to give up.

I wish Mayor Gaynor would jump on a horse and meet me halfway. I am an idiot for undertaking this trip, and I'd like to quit right here.

— Perth Amboy Evening News, New Jersey, June 11, 1911

Nan and Lady Ellen pressed on, arriving in Manhattan on July 8, 1911, becoming the first woman to cross the United States on horseback. It's estimated she rode 3,500 to 4,496 miles. She was lost several times, so it's difficult to determine an exact distance. The duration of the trip was 311 days with 180 of those spent in the saddle.

In the years following her ride, she was called "Two-Gun Nan." From 1911 to 1929, Nan and Frank continued to perform at rodeos and shows across the country. After her husband's death in 1929, Nan settled in Seattle, Washington and retired from performing in 1931.

Her story was told in a 1942 episode of the radio show, Death Valley Days. In 1958, a Death Valley Days television episode titled "Two-Gun Nan" was based on her life. Seventy-eight-year-old Nan served as a consultant for the show. Nan spent her final years in Southern California. She passed away on October 24, 1964, at eighty-four.

The month after Aspinwall arrived in New York City, the Abernathy brothers began their cross-country trip in the opposite direction, leaving New York City on August 11, 1911 on their way to California. The boys completed their cross-country trip in 91 days while Aspinwall's had taken 311.

46

The Girl from Wyoming

Although Susan B. Anthony is the most recognizable figure in the fight for women's suffrage in the United States, Alberta Claire did her part by riding a rambling 8,000 mile course around the country to advocate for women's right to vote. Claire also rode to gain acceptance for women riding astride rather than sidesaddle.

A wealthy cattle rancher bet Claire she couldn't ride the same horse from Sheridan, Wyoming to Buffalo, New York, alone, within two years. If she completed the ride on those terms, she would receive $100 and a 3,800-acre ranch. It's unclear whether that bet ever existed, but Claire's ride certainly did.

About the time Nan Aspinwall was riding East from San Francisco, Claire rode west from Wyoming, leaving on September 10, 1910. Claire traveled to Washington state and then down to San Francisco. Her eastward journey didn't begin until November 1911.

The twenty-two-year-old wore a six-shot revolver on her hip and was accompanied by a dog named "Mickie." The "Girl from Wyoming" rode a bald-faced, cow pony Bud. Some claimed the protective Mickie was more effective at keeping Claire safe than her revolver.

She decided to put Mickie on a train during her California desert crossing, as she didn't believe the dog could make it.

Mickie, my big dog, I put on the train through the desert, for the lack of water and the intense

heat would have killed him. I am sure. He is half timber wolf and half Newfoundland dog, and he weighs 114 pounds, while I weigh only ninety-eight pounds.

—*The Buffalo Enquirer, New York, April 2, 1912*

Wyoming, still a territory at the time, was the first to grant women the right to vote, in 1869. It became the 44th state in 1890.

I find that most of your Eastern women like me to tell them of suffrage in my country. You know I come from the mother country of woman suffrage, Wyoming. Women have been voting there since 1868[1], and the condition of both the women and the State is the strongest argument for the enfranchisement of the sex.

I know you have often heard men say that woman suffrage destroys the homes. I don't know where you could find better homes, more earnest housewives, more conscientious mothers, than in my State.

The women of the West are not believers in militant measures. They know that their work will be hard, even with the ballot, if the men are against them. They go about gaining their ends quietly.

Newark Star-Eagle, New Jersey, July 25, 1912

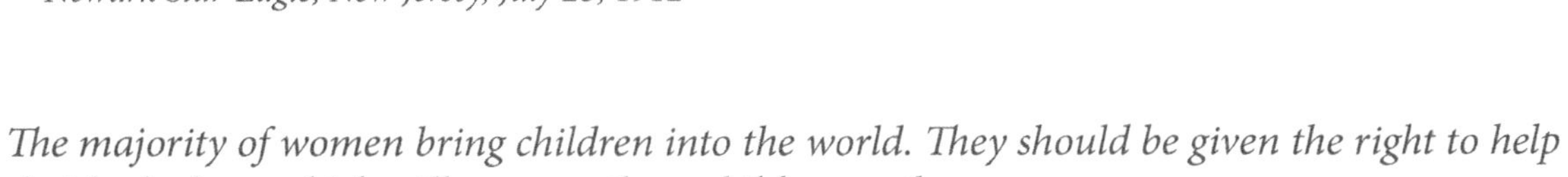

The majority of women bring children into the world. They should be given the right to help decide the laws which will concern those children as they grow up.

— *The Buffalo Enquirer, April 02, 1912*

In February 1912, Claire was caught in a snowstorm between Champaign and St. Joseph, Illinois. When no one heard from her for days, newspaper accounts predicted the worst. But Claire was later found sleeping in a barn outside of St. Joseph.

Former President Teddy Roosevelt greeted Alberta Claire in New York City where she finished her journey in June 1912.

Although standing only four feet eleven inches tall and weighing ninety-eight pounds, Claire reported that she remained healthy on her trip.

I've had just one day's illness on my entire trip of over a year and a half. The open air is my physician, and a mighty good one he is. If some of these city women who are always complaining

214

Claire wrote a brief poem about herself.

*My name's not Cheyenne, but I carry a gun,
And I ride o'er the limitless plains.
My steed is a cow pony, mean and a dun,
But chuck full of vigor and brains.
I've rounded up cattle.
My spurs have clinked
On many a different spot.
They'll tell you the cowgirl's extinct,
But, take it from me, pal, she's not.*

— *Pittsburgh Daily Post, May 23, 1912*

Claire toured the east coast for a while, then reversed directions and rode from New York to El Paso, Texas. She took a detour into Mexico and assisted a crew that was creating a film about the Mexican Revolution.

Alberta Claire's publicist, Mr. J. H. Moore, was also her husband. She never received the Wyoming cattle ranch. After her 8,000 to 10,000 mile cross-country journey, Claire traveled with various carnivals and vaudeville shows.

In later years, Mrs. Alberta Claire Moore was an actress in plays and taught dance in Pennsylvania.

---

1. *Technically, the woman suffrage law passed on December 10, 1869, and women first voted in 1870. Claire may have been referring to a local election when she stated women voted in 1868.*

47

Suffrage Riders

I nez Milholland, known as the "Most Beautiful Suffragist," rode a horse to support the right of women to vote, however, her ride was much shorter than Alberta Claire's. Mounted on Gray Dawn, Inez, wearing a crown and a long white cape, led 5,000 women's suffragists in a parade up Pennsylvania Avenue in Washington, D.C. on March 3, 1913.

The parade was planned for the day before President-elect Woodrow Wilson's inauguration in order to reach thousands of visitors with the suffragists' message.

Behind Inez was a float displaying a banner that read, "We demand an amendment to the Constitution of the United States enfranchising the women of this country."

The suffragettes hadn't gone far when a mob of opponents blocked them. Police stationed along the parade route did little to control the crowds. The suffragists were verbally and physically abused. Over 100 women were hospitalized for injuries before a U.S. Cavalry escort came to their defense.

Claiborne Catlin

Inspired by Inez Milholland, Claiborne Catlin, a thirty-two-year-old widow, decided to use horses to gain publicity for her suffrage efforts. On July 2, 1914, Catlin set out on a tour around Massachusetts to spread the word about women's suffrage. She rode a black mare, Trixie, and carried all her belongings in a pair of saddlebags.

> *When Mrs. Caitlin[1] left Boston last Wednesday she was riding a horse loaned from the Murphy stables, which are well known in this city. In Marsfield she met Mrs. Florence Harding, who has a stable and owns a stock farm in Texas. One of Mrs. Harding's jockies, the well-known "Joe" Calvert, offered for Mrs. Caitlin's use his trick mare, Trixie, and that is the horse which she is at present riding.*

> *— Fall River Globe, Fall River, Massachusetts, July 7, 1914*

Several weeks later, Mrs. Lilian Snow provided Catlin with a fresh horse, Diana, which she rode for the next six weeks.

> *Presently, in the most dramatic way, Mrs. Catlin came riding up the street from under the shade of trees—a brave young figure—on a spirited horse, sitting like a Cavalry figure. She reined up in front of the people, faced up and began.*

> *— Why They Marched, p. 150*

When one of Diana's legs became sore, Mrs. Catlin received a horse named David. Although she loved him, David was skittish when he encountered automobiles. One day, he spooked and threw her.

> *The four months' horseback tour of Massachusetts which Mrs. Claiborne Caitlin, of this city, has been making in the interests of suffrage, came to a sudden end yesterday afternoon when the animal she had been riding bucked and threw her, then fell, broke a leg and had to be shot, according to a dispatch last night from Boston.*

> *Mrs. Caitlin was thrown 10 feet into the road when the horse took fright at a passing street car. She escaped with a shaking up. Friends took her home.*

> *—The Baltimore Sun, October 27, 1914*

> *I loved my horses almost as much as I loved the cause for which I was riding, and it took a long time to recover from David's loss.*

> *— Why They Marched, p. 154*

Covering 530 miles from July to October, Catlin visited thirty-seven towns and organized fifty-nine suffragist meetings. The Nineteenth Amendment to the U.S. Constitution was ratified on August 18, 1920.

> *The right of citizens of the United States to vote shall not be denied or abridged by the United States or by any State on account of sex. Congress shall have power to enforce this article by appropriate legislation.*

---

1. *Although the newspapers spell the name "Caitlin," the correct spelling seems to be without the 'i' "Catlin."*

48

The Overland Westerners

It was a bold plan, guaranteed to be full of adventure—ride horseback through every continental U.S. State[1] and be photographed with the governor in front of each capitol building. The idea was the brainchild of George W. Beck of Bainbridge Island, Washington.

Beck, a thirty-year-old logger and carpenter, believed fame and fortune awaited him at the end of the journey. George convinced three others to join him—his brother Charles, brother-in-law J. B. Ransome (married to the Becks' sister Catherine), and a friend Raymond "Fat" Rayne. Fat was a skinny twenty-year-old, the youngest of the four. Ransome was the only married man. He would leave his wife behind for the duration of the trip.

The four, who called themselves the Overland Westerners, planned to finance their trip by selling subscriptions to The Westerner, a monthly magazine published in Seattle, Washington, as well as selling calendars and postcards they printed from their own photos. They also hoped people in the states they visited would provide meals and lodging.

The quartet set out on May 1, 1912 from Shelton, Washington, each riding a horse, with a fifth serving as a pack animal. The first segment of the trip was just eighteen miles to Olympia, Washington where Governor Marion Hay gave the men a letter of introduction to be used in the states to come.

Pinto, their initial pack horse, would ultimately become more famous than any of the men. Just days into the journey, Pinto expressed his displeasure with the role he apparently considered beneath him. The horse broke free and ran in the opposite direction for nine miles.

Started to get the pack animal to get him ready but as soon as he saw us go for him he took a hike up the road and we after him but he knew what we wanted him for so in consequence he was not so easy to catch. He ran down a road and I supposed I would never have gotten him had I not yelled to a couple of fellows coming up to stop him which they did and they turned him over to me and of course being very angry on account of the chase I gave him a licking. He did not like it and bolted and drug me about 900 feet through the mud and got away again so I had it all to do over again. But myself and another fellow caught him in a barn yard so I took him to camp where the boys were waiting for me. I got the worse of the deal having sprained my ankle a little.

Another time, Pinto was almost lost in a treacherous river crossing.

We had forded dozens of busy rivers. Jay tested the stream with a long pole, then rode over to show us how it could be done. Everything went fine until he got in midstream when Pinto, carrying our pack which slipped, flipped over and couldn't flip back. I thought he was a gone horse, but Jay hung on, flipped him over right side up, headed him upstream and snaked him to shallow water. I don't know how. We all rushed in and after slashing the diamond hitch got Pinto on his feet. We lost some grub and a few utensils but we were very glad to escape that easy by saving Pinto.

Pinto was finally promoted to a riding horse. The 15 hand, half Arabian, half Morgan weighed 900 pounds and was six years old at the start of the journey. He became the favorite mount of George Beck and was the only horse, of the eventual seventeen used, that made the entire trip.

The second state on the Overland Westerners' route was Oregon. On their way, the men found a pup that appeared to be parts Gordon Setter and Newfoundland. They adopted the dog—or perhaps the adoption was the other way around. Nip stuck with the riders to the end.

The Westerners' first significant obstacle was the snow-covered Cascade Mountains and seven-foot snowdrifts.

Got to the snow line at 5 AM and then the fun began, although it was better than we anticipated having frozen some the night before. It held us up pretty well. But the horses went through to their belly once in a while. It tired them out pretty much on the start as it was pretty tough work and new to them. But when they got their second wind they done better and got somewhat steadier. I thought once we would never make her but a fellow can do more than he thinks he can if he makes up his mind and we made up our minds to go through or bust.

They made it over the Cascades into Idaho and then Montana where three horses escaped one night. The horses attempted to cross a train trestle and fell between the railroad ties. None died, but their injuries prevented the horses from continuing. The Overland Westerners were forced to negotiate their first trade for fresh mounts.

By the time they left Montana, they realized Pinto, who had not been injured on the tracks, provided a new slant for their journey and additional marketing opportunities. The flashy horse was featured, with accompanying text, on some of their postcards.

> *The object of the enterprise is to bring one or more of the original starting horses thru the entire journey within the given time and thereby accomplish the greatest traveling feat ever known to the history of horse flesh.*

A poem was even attributed to Pinto.

> *Twenty-thousand miles I am supposed to travel,*
> *Thru mud, sand, rocks and gravel.*
> *And if I receive the proper care,*
> *you will surely see me at the fair.*

Although the plan was for The Westerner to publish periodic updates of the group's travel, the magazine went bankrupt early in the Overland Westerners' journey. Losing the income from the sale of subscriptions hurt. And the men weren't always met with hospitality in the states they rode through. Rather than a journey of enjoyable adventure, the men faced one challenge after another on

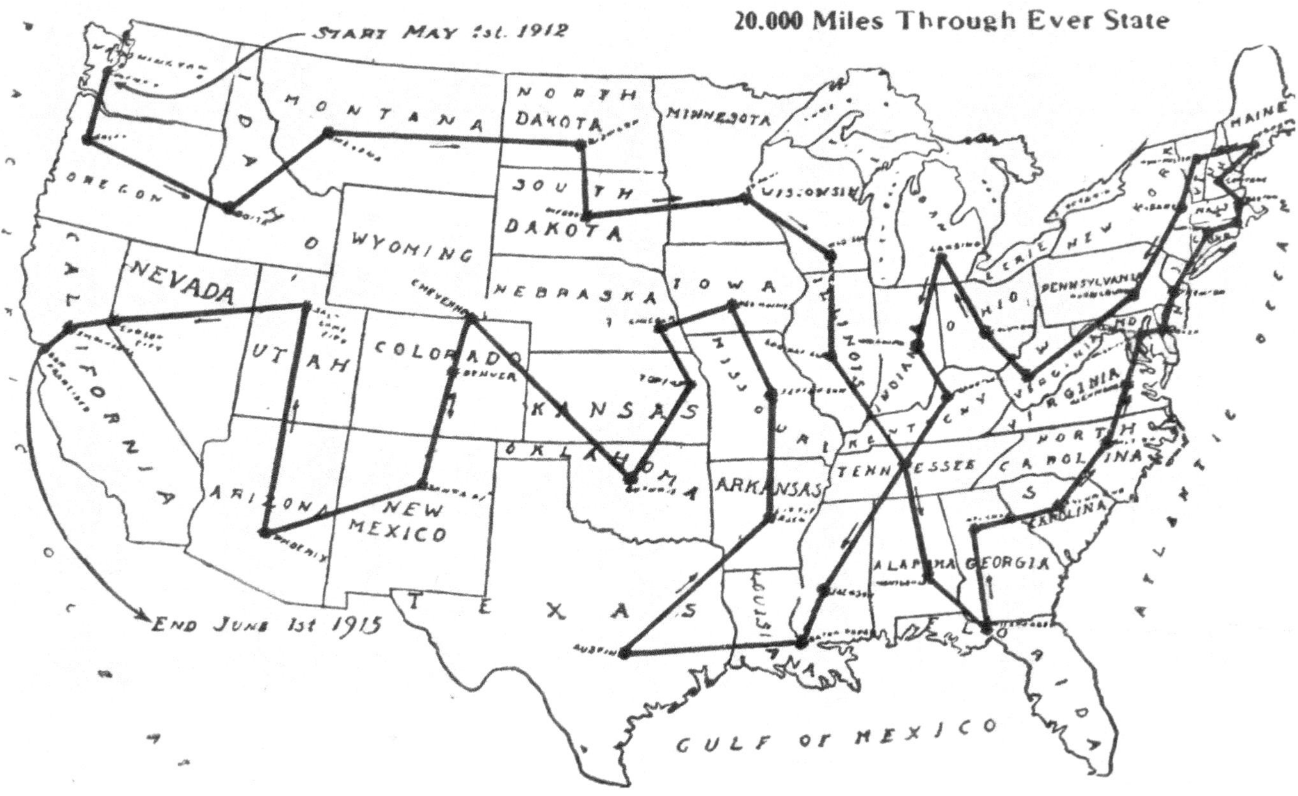

222

"the world's greatest horseback trip." The Westerners were hungry, cold, and broke for much of the three-year journey. Besides treacherous trails and rough weather, Charles was once awakened by an animal, thought to be a timber rat, biting at his head. Someone stole Raymond's saddle and tack in Montana. The men had to pay $54.00 for a new saddle and bridle. Since they didn't have that much money, they exchanged some of their equipment for the new tack.

In 1912, the Westerners rescued a child on a runaway horse.

> *One of our party also experienced the rescuing of a child from a runaway saddle horse, the child's foot being caught in the stirrup and was dragging on the ground. The horse had got under good headway when overtaken by one of our party. The child was in an unconscious state when taken into the house of a neighbor. This happened near Grant, Montana, July 2, 1912.*
>
> *—The Butte Daily Post, July 8, 1912*

What little money they earned went first to care for their horses. The men often slept in hay stacks, barns, livery stables, or out in the open under the stars. People in the southern states greeted them with the least enthusiasm. Most poor Southerners weren't impressed with four men riding horseback, but at least the cowboys were warm there.

In the summer of 1913, they reached Washington D.C. The cowboys brushed the hayseeds out of their hair and the manure off their jeans before meeting President Taft.

The Overland Westerners' route appears somewhat random, but there was a purpose to their zig-zag travel. The men rode south in the cold months and north as the weather warmed. They averaged twenty-two miles a day on the 20,352 mile, three-year journey from 1912 to 1915.

As can be imagined, putting that many miles on a horse produced fatigue, sore feet, and sometimes saddle sores, resulting in the need for fresh mounts. Beck describes one of their horse trades.

> *The rancher was a nice guy but no dummy and I figured he'd want some scratch, seein' as our two animals seemed headed for the glue factory instead of the rest of the state capitols. The first deal was open and shut, horse for horse, and we gave the fellow $10 to boot. The second deal was for a horse for Charles. The fellow wanted $25 besides his horse, but I had a rush of brains, and told him he was getting a real bargain because our horse was famous, ridden by one of the Overland Westerners. "Why he's a show piece and you can have barrels of fun showin' off." That got him and we walked away with his nag. I didn't mention sore feet, tender bellies or sore backs, just said he was a show horse maybe risin' six or seven years.*

In 1914, a story circulated that the Overland Westerners would be awarded a prize of $20,000, by the Northwestern Stockmen's Association—one dollar for each mile traveled if they reached San Francisco with Pinto by June of the following summer. It's unclear where the rumor started, but the prize money was never a reality.

The last capitol the group reached was Sacramento, California. From there, it was on to their final destination—the Panama Pacific International Exposition in San Francisco. The exposition celebrated the Panama Canal which opened on August 15, 1914.

They didn't receive the warm welcome at the Fair Beck had hoped for. When they arrived on June 1, 1915, a police officer yelled at them to "get them hayburners off the street."

Although George Beck stayed in San Francisco for a while, his three partners quickly sold their horses, tack, and other gear to pay for train tickets home. Beck, who kept a journal along the way, hoped to convince someone to write the story of the Westerners' adventure. He had a favorite writer in mind—Jack London, author of *The Call of the Wild*.

Eventually, even George had to accept that no one was interested in their story. Discouraged, he too, left San Francisco, taking a steamship to Seattle with Pinto and Nip. He returned to Bainbridge Island and worked as a logger and carpenter.

Beck attempted to write the Overland Westerners' story himself, but he was never successful. "I write it sweet enough, but it always comes out sour."

The only thing he ever had published was a short poem about Pinto in the Bainbridge Island Review.

> *Let me tell you a story that is most unique,*
> *of a little horse with a world of hidden fame.*
> *In these lines, a little kindness I'll seek,*
> *For a noble animal tried and true.*
> *Pinto is his name.*

The Overland Westerners rode a total of seventeen horses on their journey. Two are reported to have died, although it's unclear which horses they were or what happened to them.

Pinto was the only horse to complete the trip. Not to be outdone, it's estimated Nip covered twice the distance of Pinto, nearly 40,000 miles. In typical dog fashion, he didn't stick to the trail but chased birds and other animals along the way.

Although their horseback ride was the longest of the 20th century, not many of their contemporaries found it interesting. Men riding horses didn't capture the public's attention as had the young Abernathy brothers or the women who traveled alone. Also, the era of horse transportation was passing away. Instead, people were infatuated with the automobile and new technologies such as telephones, radio, and airplanes.

In 1913, Henry Ford began using one of the first assembly lines to produce a Model T Ford in just ninety minutes. This process made the vehicles affordable for the average American.

War had broken out in Europe in 1914. Although the U.S. wouldn't enter World War I until 1917, the conflict was on many people's minds.

On January 25, 1915, Alexander Graham Bell, in New York City, made the first transcontinental telephone call to his assistant Thomas A. Watson in San Francisco, repeating his famous "Mr. Watson, come here. I want you." The call traveled 3,400 miles and was the official beginning of transcontinental telephone service.

The amazing journey of the Overland Westerners is appreciated more today than it was when they completed their trip in 1915.

In 1934, Ransome decided to repeat the Westerners' trip with two friends, calling themselves the "Roaming Cowboys." They rode from Washington to Oregon, then to California, but there is no evidence the group went any farther.

George Beck died at sixty-seven in 1948, reportedly having drowned in a roadside ditch while intoxicated.

It's unclear exactly what became of Pinto. The Bainbridge Island Historical Museum (Washington) and National Cowboy and Western Heritage Museum (Oklahoma) contain the most information about the Overland Westerners and their journey. Neither source has details about what happened to the horse.

According to the Bainbridge Museum, Pinto worked in the Olympic National Forest, although when and what type of work he did is unknown.

Pinto was nine, still in his prime, when the Westerners completed their journey. Perhaps the horse was used for forestry work at first, and when older, someone in the forestry service remembered Pinto's amazing journey and returned him to live out his last days on the island.

It's unlikely that the horse outlived George Beck. Pinto would have been forty-two years old in 1948 when Beck died.

One account[2] indicates Pinto roamed freely around the south end of Bainbridge Island. He begged food from islanders and was ridden by neighborhood children. According to island resident Jack Klamm, "You whistled, and he came over. You jumped on, and he took you anywhere you wanted."

---

1. In 1912, New Mexico and Arizona became the 47th and 48th states. Alaska and Hawaii didn't become states until 1959.

2. Kitsap Sun web page, data.kitsapsun.com/projects/1961/08/28/the-longest-ride

49

The Great War

In World War I, old battle strategies, such as soldiers marching on foot or advancing by horseback met modern technology—tanks, aircraft, bombs, machine guns, and poison gas. Great Britain, alone, used over a million equines. It quickly became the bloodiest war in European history—the Great War, the one to end all wars. That didn't happen, of course, but it was the last war in which horses played a major role.

As tensions increased in the years preceding the Great War, now known as World War I, the British military conducted a census to document all the horses in the country. *The Impressment of Horses in Time of National Emergency*, a booklet published in 1912, explained that the government had the right to requisition horses for war. The census tracked the age, size, location, type of work the animal was suited for, and the proximity of the closest train station for shipment.

When they declared war on Germany in August 1914, Britain had 26,000 military horses. They needed to add more—a lot more—and quickly! Within two weeks, using the records from the horse census, military leaders requisitioned (forced) 140,000 equines into service.

According to the terms of the Impressment Order, any horses found suitable for military use had to be surrendered by the owner. They would be

> *paid for on the spot at the market value to be settled by the purchasing officer. Should you not accept the price paid as fair value, you have the right to appeal to the County Court, but you must not hinder the delivery of the horses and vehicles, etc.*

The Order also authorized the forced purchase of additional equipment such as harness and tack. Losing their horses left many farmers and businessmen in difficult situations. In 1914, motorized vehicles were in the early stages. Britain, as well as most other countries, still relied on horses for agricultural work, deliveries, and transportation. Some families wrote to the War Office requesting their ponies be spared service. The War Office agreed not to take any horse under 15 hands.

Len Whitehead was a young boy on an English farm at that time. When the army requisitioned three of his family's four workhorses—Boxer, Duke, and Violet, Len remembered crying himself to sleep that night. The Whiteheads never saw the horses again.

The requisitioned horses were moved to one of several remount depots. Army "roughriders" hastily trained any unbroken animals. All the horses were prepared for war, if such preparation is possible. A typical length of stay at a remount center was one to four months. Since they would live outdoors rather than in a stable, the horses were trained to stand tied to a picket line.

The British soon exhausted the supply of horses in their own country. During the Boer Wars, a decade earlier, the British purchased large quantities of horses from America. Once again, the U.S. became the primary provider of horses to Britain.

Often, these horses were Mustangs rounded up from the West. More American horses and mules fought with the British in World War I than with American troops.

In 1916, the United States supplied 357,553 equines to the war effort. The heaviest demand was for light draft horses for the artillery.

Sound of the Guns, p. 205

The Guyton and Harrington mule farm in tiny Lathrop, Missouri (current population 2,300) supplied most of the mules to Great Britain—70,000 mules for the Boer Wars and another 180,000 for World War I. Lathrop was known as the "Mule Capital of the World,"

Prices for horses and mules from the U.S. ranged from $175 to $250. Shipping fees were added to the purchase price, often doubling an animal's cost. Shipping included transport by rail to a seaport as well as travel across the Atlantic to England or France. At one point, 1,000 horses were arriving in Europe from the U.S. every day.

The sea voyage was dangerous for the horses. Many died from pneumonia or other diseases passed around while confined in the tight quarters. German submarines sank a few ships transporting horses. After the long voyage, the animals required several weeks to recuperate on land before being put into active service.

Anton Dilger, the son of a German immigrant, was born in Virginia in 1884. Although his father was an American Civil War hero, from a young age, Anton's loyalties were with Germany. Dilger was educated in his father's home country. He became a surgeon and germ research specialist. After the war began in Europe, Dilger, working as a German spy, returned to Virginia to wage biological warfare against U.S. horses. Although the United States hadn't entered the war yet, the shipping of horses overseas was in full swing.

In his basement laboratory, six miles from the White House, Dilger developed anthrax and glanders cultures that would be used to infect horses awaiting overseas shipment. The anthrax required injection, but the glanders culture could be rubbed inside the horses' nostrils or added to their feed or water. Outbreaks of disease occurred among the horses shipped from America, but it's difficult to determine whether any were a result of Dilger's work. Anton returned to Germany in late 1916 and later fled to Mexico. He died in 1918 at the age of thirty-four.

British equine artist, Cecil Aldin (illustrator of a *Black Beauty* edition) served as commander of an Army Remount Depot in Berkshire, England. Aldin had to surrender his own horses for use in the war. Since so many men were off fighting, Aldin decided to try using women to staff a remount center. His experiment was so successful, several Ladies' Army Remount Depots were established, the largest of which was Russley Park in Wiltshire. Twenty women at Wiltshire cared for seventy horses. Their duties included cleaning stalls, grooming and feeding the horses, as well as exercising and training them.

Aldin sketched a scene, titled "Women Working in Army Remount Depot." Another *Black Beauty* illustrator, Lucy Kemp-Welch, painted a scene from the Wiltshire Center of women exercising horses.

Even when tanks and aircraft were available, horses continued to provide a valuable service. Most of the fighting was focused along the Western Front (the northeastern border of France). Trenches used by the armies, along with mud and ruts, made travel by motorized vehicles nearly impossible in certain areas. Horses and mules were able to navigate the difficult terrain, even though sometimes they sank up to their chests in mud.

Roles for horses in World War I included:

- Cavalry horses ridden into battle
- Riding horses transporting officers
- Supply horses hauling general supplies, including food, water, medicine, and mail
- Artillery horses, often teams of six, hauling heavy artillery (guns) to battle
- Ambulance horses transporting wounded soldiers to field hospitals

Painting by Lucy Kemp-Welch

Soldiers sometimes used the bodies of horses killed on the battlefields as shields to shoot behind. French troops expanded on that by creating hollow, life-sized, papier mâché "dead" horses to use as shields and observation posts. The horse models were large enough for a man to crawl into and poke a gun through. They might even run a telephone line from the fake horse back to a trench to inform others of their observations.

Given the hazardous conditions, horses were important animals and, as much as possible, received good care. The animals were well groomed. Clean horses were less likely to develop harness or saddle sores. They were often clipped to control skin infections and infestations like lice. Since clipped coats made it difficult for the horses to stay warm, some units clipped only their legs and

other problem areas. To protect against the poison gases used in World War I, both soldiers and horses wore gas masks. Horses' noses were covered but their eyes were not.

They fed the horses from a nose bag, a canvas or leather bag with a strap that went up and around the horse's head behind his ears. The nose bags reduced waste and prevented one horse from eating another's food. Keeping the animals fed was a challenge. The horses were always hungry. At best, they received three-fourths of a normal equine ration. Of the eight million equine deaths in World War I, most were due to starvation, exhaustion, exposure, or disease rather than in battle.

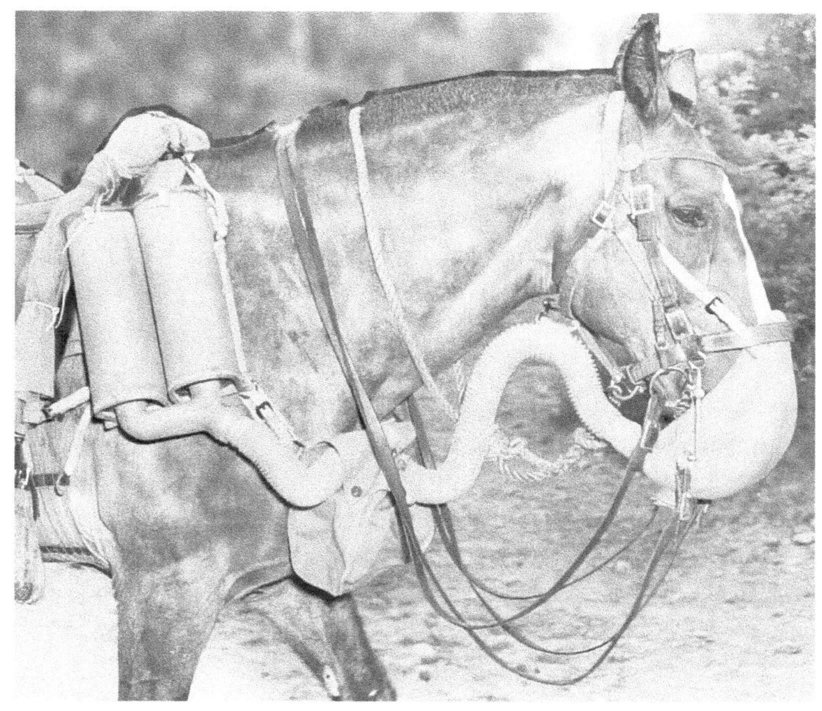

Since horses might travel up to forty miles a day, horseshoes wore out quickly. Farriers replaced shoes about once a month. The British Army Veterinary Corp. set up horse hospitals in France to treat wounded, ill, or injured horses. Blue Cross hospitals, set up by The Dumb Friends League of England, also treated horses. The blue crosses on the flags distinguished the horse hospitals from the ones with red crosses used for soldiers. Chloroform was available as an anesthetic when equine surgery was required. By the end of the war, the Blue Cross volunteers treated more than 50,000 sick and injured horses.

The U.S. counterpart to the Blue Cross was the American Red Star Animal Relief, founded in 1916. Red Star donated veterinary ambulances for use in France and at Army facilities in the U.S. They also sent supplies—bandages, surgical instruments, drugs, and other equipment.

Toward the end of the war, New Zealand gunner Bert Stokes said, "To lose a horse was worse than losing a man because men were replaceable, while horses weren't at that stage."

A strong bond formed between the soldiers and their horses. Those relationships provided some level of sanity and emotional comfort amidst the brutality of the war surrounding them.

At war's end, an officer's horse might return with his owner. But most equines never saw their homes again; it was considered too expensive to transport them back. A few were used by troops who occupied Germany post-war. Many were sold in France and Belgium to work the farms. Others were used as horse meat or simply abandoned to fend for themselves.

About 85,000 horses returned to Britain. Some remained in the army; others were sold at auction.

The Old Blacks, a team of six horses, survived the war together. The Blacks pulled the wagon carrying the body of the unknown warrior to Westminster Abbey on November 11, 1920. The burial service honored all the members of the British Armed Forces who died during the war.

Estimates of horse deaths by war:

- Civil War: one to three million
- World War I: eight million
- World War II: two to five million

50

Warrior And His General

In 1900, thirty-two-year-old Jack Seely was a captain in the British mounted forces, fighting against the Dutch during the Second Boer War in South Africa. There, he "learnt the supreme value of understanding and caring for the horse, and of treating him not as a slave, but as a brother."

During that war, Seely rode a white Arabian, Maharajah. At first, Maharajah was refused for the military because his light color would be too visible in battle. Seely solved that problem by dying the Arabian's coat brown to camouflage him.

At the conclusion of the Boer War, Seely, a friend of Winston Churchill, served as England's Secretary of State for War. In 1914, when war again broke out, the forty-six-year-old Seely returned to military duty rather than remaining in the safety of his government position. The wealthy statesman brought his personal horse, Warrior, with him.

After the Boer War, Seely had returned to England with his mount, Maharajah, and was given command of a regiment on Salisbury Plain. One day in 1902, while patrolling, a rider galloped past on the most beautiful black horse Seely had ever seen. He raced after them on Maharajah. When he caught up, Seely asked the rider if he could buy the mare.

The men returned to camp to discuss the sale. The Thoroughbred was called Cinderella. She was kind, almost human-like in intelligence, and followed her owner everywhere, much like a dog. The horse's price was set at seventy pounds. The man was surprised when Seely paid him eighty. Seely took possession of the horse immediately, loaning her former owner his regiment horse to ride home.

Maharajah wasn't as excited as his master about the purchase. He'd been Seely's constant companion and partner during the year and a half they'd served in the Boer War. Seely described the Arabian as having a "wicked look in his eye" when he saw the black mare. Despite a few friendly pats and the offer of a lump of sugar (which the horse refused), the gelding was not happy about another animal infringing on his territory. Seely tied Maharajah and Cinderella and patted both horses.

> *Cinderella never turned her head to look at Maharajah, nor did Maharajah, four feet away, pay the least attention to her. Then I made a mistake. I went forward and fondled Cinderella's head and ears, and with a pat for Maharajah, turned about and walked away.*
>
> *I had not gone ten yards when there was a scream; Maharajah had broken his headstall, and had caught Cinderella's wither firmly in his teeth!*
>
> *I dashed back to them, and they were soon separated. It was the first and last occasion on which they quarrelled, for, from that moment, they became inseparable friends. When I rode one the other followed; I have never known two horses so deeply attached to one another.*
>
> — *Warrior, the Amazing Story of a Real Warhorse, p. 31*

When Seely returned to his home on the west coast of the Isle of Wight in England with the two horses, Cinderella became a favorite of his children.

She would let my children climb up over her head, and slide down her tail, and still more remarkable, swarm up her tail and slide down over her head.

— *Warrior, p. 31*

Her devotion to Seely was so great that upon his return after extended absences, she would jump out of her pen in her haste to greet him. When Maharajah died several years later, Cinderella was inconsolable at the loss of her best friend. Her groom, Jim, suggested that a foal could provide company for her. The poor mare suffered another sorrow when her first foal died in 1906. In the spring of 1908, Cinderella had a second foal, Warrior. The sire, Straybit, was a chestnut of racing bloodlines. The colt was bay with a star on his forehead.

As the colt grew to his adult height of 15.2 hands, Jim handled his training. According to Seely, Jim had "very seldom been bucked off, but Warrior achieved that feat more often than all his other pupils put together."

Eventually, Warrior accepted a rider on his back and enjoyed his rides across the English countryside. But when Seely first rode him, Warrior bucked him off three times. Seely remembered what an Arab friend had once told him.

If you have infinite patience you can always get control of any horse, but if you decide to win the battle right away you may not succeed, and the stronger animal may beat you in the long run.

— *Warrior, p. 52*

Before mounting the fourth time, Seely had a long talk with his colt.

He looked at me, his nostrils distended, and I looked at him, trying to explain that I was a busy man, but that I loved him because I loved his mother, and would he please not buck me off anymore, and if so we might be friends together for all our lives.

— *Warrior, p. 53*

And friends the two became. Warrior and Seely survived four years of war together when many around them, both man and horse, were killed.

Seely recognized the horse's unusual courage early on, when he rode the horse into the waves at the sea. Initially, Warrior galloped away in a panic, but he learned to stand still, allowing the waves to pass around him. Seely felt the horse trembling, but it seemed Warrior was determined to stand as if he knew he had to overcome his fear.

In 1914, Seely was appointed Brigadier General of the Canadian Cavalry Brigade which consisted of Canadian and British regiments. Seely and Warrior entered the war, traveling to Southampton, then across the English Channel together, landing in Le Havre, France.

When the pair first came under fire during the Battle of Mons, Warrior responded as he had at the sea. He trembled but didn't bolt.

As we approached them another bouquet of shells fell and burst, the nearest only a few yards away. To my amazement Warrior made no attempt to run away. I could feel him tremble a little between my legs as we trotted through the gate, but he pretended to be quite unperturbed. He was trying to be brave, and succeeding in his task.

On many, many days thereafter, during the four years that were to follow, I rode Warrior in shell-fire—sometimes so heavy that he was almost the only survivor—but never once did he attempt to bolt or do any of the things which might be expected of an animal reputed to be so naturally timid as the horse. No, my stout-hearted horse not only kept his own fear under control, but by his example helped beyond measure his rider and his friend to do the same.

— *Warrior*, p. 68

As an officer's horse, Warrior had few advantages. In fact, he was a prime target, as Seely often rode near the front lines. The two experienced many battles—at Ypres, the Somme, Passchendaele, and Cambrai. Allied soldiers were inspired by the brave horse, calling him "The horse the Germans couldn't kill." General Seely later remembered, "Men would say not, 'Here comes the general,' but, 'Here's old Warrior.'" — *Warrior, p. 78*

At Ypres, the house Seely was staying in was bombed and caught on fire. Seely ran to the stable to free Warrior. Moments after the horse escaped, the stable collapsed.

Eight months later, Seely's eldest son, Frank, riding an Arabian named Akbar, joined his father's force. When Frank was killed at the Battle of Arras in 1917, Seely kept Akbar. Warrior and Akbar remained together for the rest of the war.

When Warrior turned up lame one day during the Battle of the Somme, Seely rode another horse to the front to check on the fighting. That horse was killed under him, and Seely suffered three broken ribs.

Another time, a soldier alerted Seely that something was wrong with Warrior. Seely found his horse down and thrashing about violently. Warrior had swallowed a sharp piece of metal that had been in his hay. Several other horses died from the same thing, but Warrior survived. Within a week, he was being ridden again.

On their way to Passchendaele, Warrior sank to his belly in mud. Four men were able to extricate him.

Seely and Warrior followed a tank on their way to a battle at Cambrai. At one point, Warrior was so close behind the tank, he could have reached out and touched it with his nose. As the tank crossed

a bridge, the structure collapsed, and all on it fell into the water below. Warrior and Seely avoided the collapse and escaped with no injuries.

At the Second Battle of Cambrai, Seely gave Warrior a rest and rode another horse, St. Quentin. The horse was killed and fell on Seely, who was not seriously injured.

On their way to the Battle at Moreuil Wood, Seely stabled Warrior in a room of a house, feeding the horse corn on a small table. While Seely gave orders to his men, Germans began to shell the area. One of the first shells hit the house where Warrior was stabled. The building was knocked almost completely down except for one small corner. Seely feared his horse, who had survived the war for so long, had finally met his end. But he spotted Warrior poking his head through some bricks, the ceiling joist resting on his shoulders. Men tore away at the debris until Warrior leaped out from the rubble. The horse was sore, but Seely rode him later that day.

> *His escapes were quite wonderful. Again and again he survived when death seemed certain and indeed, befell all his neighbours. It was not all hazard; sometimes it was due to his intelligence. I have seen him, even when a shell has burst within a few feet, stand still without a tremor – just turn his head and, unconcerned, look at the smoke of the burst.*
>
> *— Warrior, p. 172*

On March 30, 1918, Seely and Warrior led 1,000 cavalry horses and officers in a two-day battle against the Germans, forcing them to retreat from Moreuil Wood at the Arve River in France. Although the Germans would later retake most of that area, they suffered severe losses in the fighting. The cavalry charge at Moreuil Wood is considered a significant victory that contributed to the eventual German surrender.

In April, Seely was injured in a gas attack and returned to England. Warrior remained behind in France under the care of Colonel Patterson who replaced Seely as commander of the Canadian Cavalry. Patterson wrote letters to Seely, keeping him informed of Warrior's condition for the remainder of the war.

After the German surrender on November 11, 1918, Seely and Warrior were reunited in Valenciennes, France. The nearly starved horse was overjoyed to see his master, but was disappointed that Seely had only one biscuit for him.

Warrior returned as a war hero to the Isle of Wight, in time for Christmas 1918. Four years to the day after leading the cavalry charge at Moreuil Wood, Warrior, ridden by his groom Jim, won the

Isle of Wight Point-to-Point race. Fifteen years earlier, Warrior's father, Straybit, had won the same race.

During his retirement years, Warrior grew even closer to Seely and his family, although he was aloof with strangers. He died in 1941, a few weeks short of his thirty-third birthday. That day, Seely wrote in his diary,

I do not believe that he can be denied in heaven the soul that he held on earth.

— *Warrior, p. 168*

The PDSA (People's Dispensary for Sick Animals) is a British organization founded in 1917. The PDSA Dickin Medal, a bronze medallion, is the highest honor an animal can receive for service in military conflict.

In 2014, the Dickin Medal was awarded to Warrior. The medal was accepted for the horse by Brough Scott, grandson of Jack Seely. To date, four other horses have received the medal—Olga (1947), Upstart (1947), Regal (1947), and Reckless (2016).

51

Simpson And Murphy

When John "Jack" Kirkpatrick was twelve, his father was badly injured in a coal-mining accident. Jack began working to help provide for his family. The boy gave children donkey rides at Herd Sand Beach in England and later delivered milk with a horse-drawn wagon. Jack had little time for play, but when he did, he enjoyed spending time with his friend Billy Lowes.

After his father's death in 1909, seventeen-year-old Jack joined the British navy. The following year, he deserted his ship. For the next four years, Jack worked at various jobs in Australia, including cutting sugar cane, working in coal and gold mines, and as a coal stoker on a steamship. During his time in Australia, Jack wrote regularly to his mother and sent her money.

In 1914, at twenty-two, Jack enlisted in the Australian army. To hide his desertion from the British navy, he registered using the name John Simpson (his mother's maiden name). Perhaps he hoped as part of the Australian service he would somehow end up back home in England. Instead, he found himself at Gallipoli, working as a stretcher bearer with the 3rd Australian Field Ambulance company.

Most of the fighting in World War I was on the Western Front in or around France. But battles also occurred in Italy, at Gallipoli in the south of Turkey, and between Russia and Germany.

In 1915, England's Winston Churchill urged Allied forces to attack Turkey, an ally of Germany.

The goal was to capture Constantinople, the Turkish capital. Several land and sea forces took part in the expedition. At dawn on April 25, soldiers from Australia and New Zealand landed on the west coast of the Gallipoli Peninsula in an area that would later be named Anzac Cove.[1]

The Allies soon realized they had made a terrible mistake.

The narrow beach at Anzac Cove rose to tall, hostile cliffs. Turkish troops positioned at the top of the steep hills killed many

of the soldiers as they left the boats. The Anzacs fought bravely but could never defeat the Turkish army. John "Jack" Simpson Kirkpatrick was one of the courageous soldiers who arrived with the first Anzac group.

Carrying a stretcher required two to six men. Due to the high numbers of soldiers wounded or killed crossing the beach at Anzac Cove, stretchers and the men to carry them were in short supply. When his partners were killed that first day, Simpson carried the injured to safety on his back. On the second day of the battle, he began using a donkey to carry wounded soldiers to the hospital tent. During his weeks at Gallipoli, Simpson may have used more than one donkey. Some say the main donkey's name was Duffy. Others insist it was Murphy.

Simpson sang and whistled as he and Murphy traversed the steep hills, braving gunfire to rescue as many wounded soldiers as possible. A nearby Indian artillery unit called him "Bahadur" the "Bravest of the Brave." They made a halter for Murphy and stretched a Red Cross armband around the donkey's muzzle.

Simpson's commander, Colonel John Monash, wrote of the pair's efforts.

Private Simpson and his little beast earned the admiration of everyone at the upper end of the valley. They worked all day and night throughout the whole period since the landing, and the help rendered to the wounded was invaluable.

Simpson knew no fear and moved unconcernedly amid shrapnel and rifle fire, steadily carrying out his self-imposed task day by day, and he frequently earned the applause of the personnel for his many fearless rescues of wounded men from areas subject to rifle and shrapnel fire.

One day, Simpson rescued a badly wounded soldier. The man lapsed in and out of consciousness as the little donkey carried him to safety. Neither man recognized the other. It wasn't until he was later discharged, that Billy Lowes learned the man with the donkey who rescued him was Jack Kirkpatrick, his childhood playmate.

On Jack's last morning at Gallipoli, he stopped at the food tent where he was informed that breakfast

240

wasn't yet ready. He said, "Never mind. Get me a good dinner when I get back."

But Simpson never made it back.

On May 19, 1915, Simpson made his last trip with Murphy. On their way to rescue more soldiers, he was killed by Turkish machine gun fire.

At the burial service, George Green stated,

> *If ever there was a man who deserved the Victoria Cross it was Simpson. I often remember now the scene I saw frequently in Shrapnel Gully, of that cheerful soul calmly walking down the gully with a Red Cross armlet tied round the donkey's head. That gully was under direct fire from the enemy almost all the time.*

Simpson left a similar impression on another soldier Albert Facey.

> *I saw some brave things at Gallipoli. One thing that made a big impression on us was the actions of a man we called 'The Man with a Donkey.' He was a stretcher-bearer and he used to carry the wounded men down to the clearing station on the beach. This man, Simpson his name was, was exposed to enemy fire constantly all the days I was there, and when I left Shrapnel Gully he was still going strong. I considered, and so did my mates, that he should be given the Victoria Cross.*

Some reports indicate Simpson and Murphy saved the lives of 300 men at Gallipoli. After his death, Simpson's friend Dick Henderson used Murphy to continue the rescue work.

After nearly eleven months of fighting, with tremendous loss of life on both sides, the Allies abandoned the Gallipoli campaign. It's believed Murphy survived and was evacuated with the troops in December 1916 to the Greek island of Mudros. The soldiers placed a collar on him that read, "Murphy VC.* Please look after him."

The plan was to turn Murphy over to the Australian government, but the Anzac soldiers lost track of him that night. Murphy may have been taken by an Indian force that used pack mules to help with the evacuation.

Although recommended for the Victoria Cross by his commander John Monash, then again recommended in 1915 by men in his unit, and a third time in 1967, Simpson never received a military award. Those making the decision believed the Victoria Cross shouldn't be given to a stretcher-bearer for simply doing his job.

In 1916, a silent film about Simpson and Murphy was created. An Anzac Commemorative Medal engraved with the image of the two was later given to all Gallipoli veterans. They were also featured on a series of postage stamps in 1965. A commemorative statue of Simpson and Murphy is located outside the Australian War Memorial in Canberra.

In 1997, the Royal Society for the Prevention of Cruelty to Animals (RSPCA) awarded their Purple Cross to Murphy. The honor was said to extend to "all the donkeys used by John Simpson Kirkpatrick, for the exceptional work they performed on behalf of humans while under continual fire at Gallipoli during World War I."

1. ANZAC stands for Australian and New Zealand Army Corps. In Australia, Anzac Day on April 25, is celebrated as a national holiday, a memorial to those who served and died in war.

*VC = Victoria Cross

* It's unclear whether the two photos are of Simpson or his friend Dick Henderson.

52

Notable WWI Animals

Horses were the animals used most often in World War I, but the following animals are a few of those also connected in some manner to the war.

Winnipeg

In 1914, a trapper brought an orphaned black bear cub to the train station at White River, Ontario, Canada. Harry Colebourn, of the Fort Garry Horse Regiment and the Canadian Army Veterinary Corps, was in charge of the horses on a train that stopped at the White River station. Harry saw the bear cub and purchased it from the trapper for $20.

Although from England, Harry had been living in Winnipeg, Canada, so he named the cub Winnipeg.

Winnipeg became a favorite of the soldiers in Harry's regiment and traveled with them to England. The cub liked to sleep under Harry's cot.

When Harry was promoted to Captain, he learned he would soon be transferred to France to care for the cavalry horses. A war zone was no place for a four-month-old bear cub, so Colebourn arranged for Winnie to stay at the London Zoo until he returned.

Winnie was so trustworthy that children who visited the zoo could ride on her back. She became a favorite of many visitors,

including a Mr. Milne and his son Christopher Robin. Christopher had a stuffed bear which he had called Edward Bear, but after seeing Winnie at the zoo, he changed his toy bear's name to "Winnie-the-Pooh." Winnie inspired A.A. Milne to write stories about his son, a lovable bear, and Christopher's other stuffed animals.

The war lasted much longer than Harry Colebourn anticipated. At its end, he realized Winnie's home was at the zoo. She lived there until her death at twenty.

Cher Ami

In October, 1918, Major Charles Whittlesey and 194 of his men were trapped in a small depression on the side of a hill, surrounded by Germans. Whittlesey sent requests for help by two pigeons, but the Germans shot both birds.

Mistaking them for the enemy, Allied forces in the area also began firing on them. In desperation, Whittlesey sent out a third pigeon, Cher Ami. She carried the following note rolled into a canister attached to her left leg.

> *We are along the road parallel to 276.4. Our own artillery is dropping a barrage directly on us. For heavens sake stop it.*

When the Germans saw Cher Ami flying out of the brush, they shot her down, as well. But amazingly, the pigeon began to fly again. Cher Ami flew twenty-five miles back to headquarters, and helped to save the lives of the 194 men.

Army medics worked to save the bird's life. She was blinded in one eye, and one leg had to be amputated. When she had recovered sufficiently, Cher Ami was returned to the United States.

Lizzie

During World War I, Thomas Ward's scrap iron business provided metal for England's steel industry. After most of the horses in England were taken to serve in the war, Ward came up with a creative way to compensate for the lack of available horsepower. He leased Lizzie, an elephant from the Sedgwick Menagerie.

Each day, Lizzie plodded along the streets of Sheffield, England, pulling a cart with widened shafts specially adapted for her. She transported machinery and collected and delivered scrap metal to the steel foundries.

A local newspaper wrote about Lizzie in February 1916.

> *The weight of the load was equal to that usually allotted to three horses. Some passing horses were startled by this unexpected 'dilution' of their labour, and sniffed and shied as the elephant passed.*

The Sheffield residents loved Lizzie. Many brought her treats, such as apples or potatoes. She was known to slip her trunk through a kitchen window to help herself to a freshly baked pie and once even ate a schoolboy's hat.

The elephant wore leather boots to protect her feet from the debris that littered the ground at the scrap metal yard. After the war, Lizzie returned to her circus.

Sergeant Stubby

While at Yale University for military training, twenty-five-year-old Private J. Robert Conroy found a puppy wandering around. The pup was of mixed breed, likely part bull terrier. Conroy brought the pup to his camp where the canine became a favorite of the other soldiers. The men named him Stubby because of his short tail. The soldiers taught him tricks, such as saluting with his paw.

When Conroy's division was ordered to France, he hid Stubby in a coal bin on board until they were out at sea. The commanding officer was not pleased when he discovered the stowaway, but Stubby saluted the officer and won him over, too.

They arrived at the front line on February 5, 1918. Stubby became accustomed to the noise of gunshots and explosions. The dog was hospitalized once for inhaling poisonous gas. After recovering, Stubby was especially sensitive to that odor.

Early one morning, when the soldiers were all asleep, they were again attacked with gas. Stubby smelled it and barked until he'd awakened everyone. The men were able to escape before inhaling too much of the poison.

Stubby also served the men in other ways. His acute canine hearing allowed him to warn the men of incoming shells, since he could hear them well before the men could.

He chased away the rats in the trenches. He helped locate wounded soldiers and knew the difference between the German and English languages. This ability allowed him to locate a German spy. He attacked the man and held him in place until soldiers captured him.

Stubby was present at seventeen battles. He was wounded by shrapnel, but after surgery, he fully recovered.

At the war's end, the dog was still not permitted on a ship. Conroy again smuggled him on board for the trip home. In America, the dog received a hero's welcome and was awarded a dozen medals.

Stubby met three presidents: Woodrow Wilson, Calvin Coolidge, and Warren G. Harding. He was the first dog to be given a rank in the U.S. Army.

In 1926, Stubby passed away. His stuffed body was put on display, along with his medals, at the Smithsonian Museum in Washington. In 2018, he was the star of an animated film, *Sgt. Stubby: An American Hero.*

Rags

Rags was another dog who assisted U.S. Army soldiers in France. In 1918, the final year of the war, Private James Donovan found the scruffy stray roaming around Paris searching for food.

Donavan's job was to string communication wires between different military units and to repair damaged lines. Donovan trained Rags to carry messages attached to his collar so they could communicate even when lines were damaged. By getting messages through in heated battles, the dog helped save the lives of Allied soldiers.

In fighting on October 9, 1918, Rags and Donovan were injured. The dog's right front paw, right ear, and right eye were wounded by shrapnel. Donovan was seriously wounded and gassed. Both were carried away from the battlefield on the same stretcher. The dog lost his eye but otherwise healed quickly.

As Donovan's condition worsened, Rags remained with his friend at several field hospitals in France. The dog was smuggled by ship and train to accompany Donovan who was transported to the Fort Sheridan Army Hospital in Chicago, Illinois. When Private Donovan died in early 1919, Rags didn't eat for a week, grieving the loss of the man who had rescued him from the streets of Paris.

He continued living at the Army base, later eating at carefully selected mess halls. Rags was "adopted" by Major Raymond W. Hardenbergh and was the subject of several New York Times articles as well as a book by Jack Rohan, *Rags: The Story Of A Dog Who Went To War*. He became quite the celebrity and toured Army bases.

The dog passed away in 1936 at the age of twenty and was buried with military honors.

53

Wartime Horse Rescues

The Home of Rest in England provided retirement homes for some of the horses who returned from the war. Three of their most famous were San Toy, Roger, and Old Sam.

San Toy (1890-1922) was a survivor of the Boer War and World War I. It's said he never missed a day's duty in either war. San Toy was twenty-eight at the end of World War I. He retired at the Home of Rest where he lived another four years.

Roger (1907-1934), a 15.2 hand chestnut gelding, served as a German officer's horse until he was found wandering riderless during the Battle of the Somme (1916 France). Captured by a British officer, Roger served as his horse for the next two years. Although he now fought on the opposite side of the war, it was all the same to Roger. The horse survived and was brought to England at war's end. The British officer paid for Roger to retire at the Home of Rest.

Old Sam (1907-1930s) was eleven at the end of World War I. He spent the next nineteen years hauling firewood his owner sold on the streets. As the horse aged, his owner didn't have enough money to care for Old Sam properly, so he sent him to the Home of Rest for a well-deserved retirement.

Thousands of miles away, Dorothy Brooke had joined her husband, Geoffrey Brooke, in Egypt. In 1930, Geoffrey served as the commander of the British Cavalry Brigade in Cairo. There, Dorothy was

surprised to find an old horse that had served in World War I. She called the emaciated chestnut, Old Bill.

I shall never forget the shock he gave me. I stood staring at him. Heaven knows the other horses were bad enough but somehow he was different. Obviously he had been a good horse, once. He had been happy and well fed as other horses had never been. He had been born in England; had known our green fields, had been groomed and cared for. He had moreover served in Palestine and had suffered hardships in that Campaign as few horses have endured in modern times. And then we had sold him into this.

Dorothy wrote a letter that was published in a British newspaper, the Morning Post (now the Daily Telegraph) exposing the plight of the old warhorses.

There have been several references lately in the columns of The Morning Post as to the possibility of raising a memorial to horses killed in the War. May I make a suggestion?

Out here, in Egypt, there are still many hundreds of old Army Horses sold of necessity at the cessation of the War. They are all over twenty years of age by now, and to say that the majority of them have fallen on hard times is to express it very mildly. …

These old horses were, many of them, born and bred in the green fields of England—how many years since they have seen a field, heard a stream of water, or a kind word in English?

Many are blind—all are skeletons.

A fund is being raised to buy up these old horses. As most of them are the sole means of a precarious livelihood to their owners, adequate compensation must, of necessity, be given in each case. …

If those who truly love horses—who realise what it can mean to be very old, very hungry and thirsty, and very tired, in a country where hard, ceaseless work has to be done in great heat—will send contributions to help in giving a merciful end to our poor old war heroes, we shall be extremely grateful; and we venture to think that, in many ways, this may be as fitting (though unspectacular) part of a War Memorial as any other that could be devised.

Dorothy's letter struck a chord with the British public, and money started coming in. Five thousand former war horses were purchased, some in such horrible condition they were humanely put down. Others were provided veterinary care and lived the rest of their lives in peace.

The Brooke organization continues to work today to improve conditions for working equines all around the world.

54

Army Remount

The origin of the U.S. Army Remount Service dates back to the Civil War when it was the job of the Quartermaster Department to supply the Union Army with cavalry and artillery horses. This centralized control was in contrast to the Confederate Army where each soldier provided his own horse.

After the Civil War, the demand for horses decreased for a time. Then, in 1908, the Remount Service was established. Remount Centers or Depots, set up in twenty-three states, operated until 1948. Some of the better known ones included:

- Fort Robinson, Nebraska
- Front Royal, Virginia
- Fort Keogh, Montana
- Fort Sam Houston, Texas
- Fort Reno, Oklahoma
- Pomona Quartermaster Depot, California
- Fort Sill, Oklahoma
- Camp Plauche, Louisiana

The Remount Depots received, examined, cared for, trained, and assigned horses to mounted units as needed. Most centers were equipped to handle 4,000 to 5,000 horses. The center at Fort Robinson, Nebraska was the largest, reaching a high during World War II of 12,000 horses and mules. K-9 Corps dogs were also trained at Fort Robinson.

Remount Centers partnered with knowledgeable horsemen to establish breeding programs to improve the quality of military horses. Advertisements sought "high-class registered Thoroughbreds" to add to the Remounts. Most of the stallions in the program were Thoroughbreds, but Morgans, Arabians, and Standardbreds were also used. The stallions were placed off site, with a rancher or farmer. The Remount would then purchase foals back from those breeders.

Henry of Navarre, was one of the first Thoroughbreds to enter the Remount program. In 1894, the three-year-old Navarre won nine races in a row, including the Belmont Stakes. After spending several years in France, Henry returned to the U.S. and entered the Remount program at Front Royal, Virginia, in 1911.

Another successful racehorse to enter the program was Jack Hare Jr. In 1918, they split the Preakness race into two divisions. Jack Hare Jr. won the second division and went on to win five more races that year. The small, brown Thoroughbred, said to be built like a miniature bulldog, retired from the track in 1923. He joined the Remount Service in 1926, living at John Wiggins' Military Stock Farm in Kentucky.

A golden chestnut Thoroughbred stallion named Gunrock, born in England in 1914, was the inspiration for the University of California Davis' mascot. Gunrock's sire, English Triple Crown winner, Rock Sand, was the grandsire of Man o' War. Both Gunrock and Man o' War were owned by August Belmont, Jr. Belmont donated

Gunrock

Gunrock to the Remount Service at the U.C. Davis farm in 1921. One of the most famous Thoroughbred Remount stallions was Sir Barton, the first U.S. Triple Crown winner (1919). Sir Barton entered the military program in 1933.

The number of Arabian stallions in the Remount increased in 1943 with the acquisition of the Kellogg Arabian Ranch. W. K. Kellogg and his brother John Harvey are remembered for their development of breakfast cereals. W. K. built the Kellogg Ranch in Pomona, California in 1925, purchasing many of his horses from the famous Crabbet Arabian Stud in England.

Hoping to preserve the legacy of his farm and horses, Kellogg donated the 750-acre ranch and eighty-seven of his horses to the University of California in 1932. The school's College of Agriculture operated the farm.

In 1943, to support the United States in World War II, Kellogg convinced the University to turn the ranch over to the Army Remount Service. It was known as the Pomona Quartermaster Depot with Colonel F. W. Koester as its commanding officer.

In 1919, six hundred and fifty officers and enlisted men of Auxiliary Remount Depot No. 326 at Camp Cody in New Mexico, posed for a photo in the shape of a horse's head. (following page)

Michigan photographer Almeron Newman took the image. "The Devil" a saddle horse ridden by Major Frank G. Brewer, the Army remount commander, is presumed to be the model for the photo. It's unclear whether Brewer's horse survived the war and was alive at the time of the picture or whether the portrait is a memorial to him. Paddocks of horses at the remount center are visible in the photo's background.

As late as 1945, between 450 and 500 stallions remained in the Remount Service, and over 11,000 civilian-owned mares produced 7,000 foals. But World War II proved horses were no longer an efficient means of warfare, and the days of the Remount Service were numbered. In 1948, Congress transferred the program to the Department of Agriculture. The entire program was canceled the following year, with the remaining stock and equipment sold at public auction.

55

Exterminator

On May 30, 1915, a tall, chestnut colt was born in Kentucky. Although his registered name was Exterminator, the foal's bony, homely looks earned him the nickname "Old Bones." J. Cal Milam purchased him as a yearling for $1,500. Wealthy racehorse owners usually hire trainers to work with their colts, but Mr. Milam trained his own horses. He imagined Exterminator would grow up to destroy his competitors on the track. At that same sale, another yearling, Sun Briar, sold for $5,000 to the stable owned by Willis Kilmer.

Exterminator grew—taller than most racehorses. He was 16.3 hands by age two.[1] Although he was gentle and good-natured, the colt was considered awkward and coarse.

While the United States was entering World War I in 1917, the two-year-old Exterminator was beginning his racing career. That June, in Kentucky, he won his first race. After that, Exterminator raced in Canada, where he won again. A minor injury brought his first season to an abrupt end, and Mr. Milam sent the horse to his farm to rest and recover. Milam thought the break from racing would give Exterminator a chance to catch up with his growth. His two wins qualified the horse for a nomination to the following year's Kentucky Derby.

As Exterminator's three-year-old season approached, trainer Henry McDaniel saw the colt work out. McDaniel's boss, Willis Kilmer, owned Sun Briar, who had earned over $60,000 in his two-year-old season and was favored to win the Derby.

But Sun Briar wasn't training well. It wasn't clear whether he was just being temperamental or there was a physical problem. McDaniel thought pairing Sun Briar with another horse would push him to run faster. Kilmer authorized the trainer to spend $700 for a workout companion for his prized horse.

McDaniel liked what he saw in Exterminator—and not just as an exercise partner. He knew Milam would never take $700 for the horse. Actually, J. Cal Milam wasn't interested in

selling Exterminator at all. Because his first season had been cut short, Milam hadn't had a chance to see what the big horse was capable of. But McDaniel was determined to have Exterminator. He and Milam negotiated back and forth. Finally, an agreement was reached. McDaniel paid nine thousand dollars and two Thoroughbred fillies for Exterminator.

Mr. Kilmer was not pleased when he learned how much his trainer had spent. He was even more unhappy when he saw Exterminator. He considered the horse ugly and referred to him as a billy goat. Kilmer eventually calmed down and went along with McDaniel's plan—anything that might give Sun Briar an edge was worth it. This would be Kilmer's first entry in the prestigious Derby, and he had high hopes of winning it.

Exterminator began training with Sun Briar immediately. McDaniel believed the big horse understood what he was being used for. Sometimes, Exterminator pushed Sun Briar, and at other times, he let the moody colt comfortably maintain his lead. As he watched the daily workouts, McDaniel sensed if his rider were to let Exterminator go, the colt could blow right past Sun Briar.

As the Derby approached, Sun Briar didn't improve. The colt had ringbone, excessive growth of bone in the pastern area above his hoof. McDaniel advised Kilmer that racing the colt might result in a career-ending injury. Although devastated by the news, Kilmer scratched Sun Briar two days before the Derby.

Then, McDaniel made a surprising suggestion—enter Exterminator in Sun Briar's place. Kilmer refused. He didn't want the billy-goat horse wearing his stable's colors (green, brown, and orange). He was certain Exterminator would finish dead last, and that would be too embarrassing.

Matt Winn, president of Churchill Downs, had seen Exterminator run, and believed the horse was Derby quality. Kilmer valued Winn's opinion more highly than that of his trainer. Winn convinced him to enter Exterminator in the race. This turn of events was a surprise to Sun Briar's jockey Willie Knapp. He'd expected to ride the race favorite, but now he was assigned the big, ungainly horse most people had never heard of. With Sun Briar out of the race, Escoba and War Cloud were the new favorites.

Some questioned whether it was appropriate to hold the Kentucky Derby in the middle of a world war. To make the event more acceptable, ten percent of the proceeds from that year's race were donated to the Red Cross.

It rained the morning of the race, May 11, 1918, making the track soupy. Exterminator hadn't raced in nine months, but he didn't seem bothered by the mud. He ran near the back of the pack for most of the race. But, much to everyone's

surprise—especially Willis Kilmer's—Exterminator came from behind to win, beating Escoba by a length. War Cloud finished fourth. Willie Knapp called it "the Storybook Derby."

The only ones not surprised by Exterminator's performance were his trainer, Henry McDaniel, his groom, Mike Terry—and perhaps Exterminator himself. Although the horse would go through many trainers and jockeys over the years, Terry remained Exterminator's caretaker and exercise rider throughout the horse's lifetime.

Spectators grew to love the big horse. He was a favorite with the track starters. In the days before mechanical starting gates, many high-strung horses refused to wait patiently at the starting line for the race to begin. But Exterminator never gave the starters any trouble. Sometimes, he even helped out by pinning his ears and putting an unruly horse in his place.

Most Kentucky Derby winners retire by the age of five, but Exterminator raced until he was nine. And the big horse got better with time, often beating horses less than half his age. Over his seven-year career, he ran ninety-nine races, with a record of fifty wins, seventeen seconds, and seventeen thirds. His career earnings totaled more than $250,000.

Jockey Willie Knapp claimed,

> *When he was at his best, Exterminator could have beaten Man o' War or Citation or Kelso or any other horse that ever lived.*

Kilmer attempted to set up a match between Exterminator and Man O' War, who was two years younger, but due to disagreements over the race length, the two never met.

In 1924, when Exterminator was nine, he injured a leg in a race in Canada, and Kilmer retired the horse. Although he raced longer than most Thoroughbreds, Exterminator wasn't ready to retire. Normally mild-mannered, he became cranky and difficult to handle. His groom, Mike Terry, came up with the idea of finding a pony companion to keep the horse occupied.

Exterminator adored his little pony friend, Peanuts, and refused to go anywhere without him. The pony was small enough to walk under the tall horse's belly. Although they played together and slept in the same stall, Exterminator was careful never to hurt him.

When Mr. Kilmer died in 1940, his will stated that the farm and all the horses were to be sold, except for Sun Briar, Exterminator, and Peanuts. Those three were moved to a smaller farm in Binghamton, New York where Mike Terry continued to care for them.

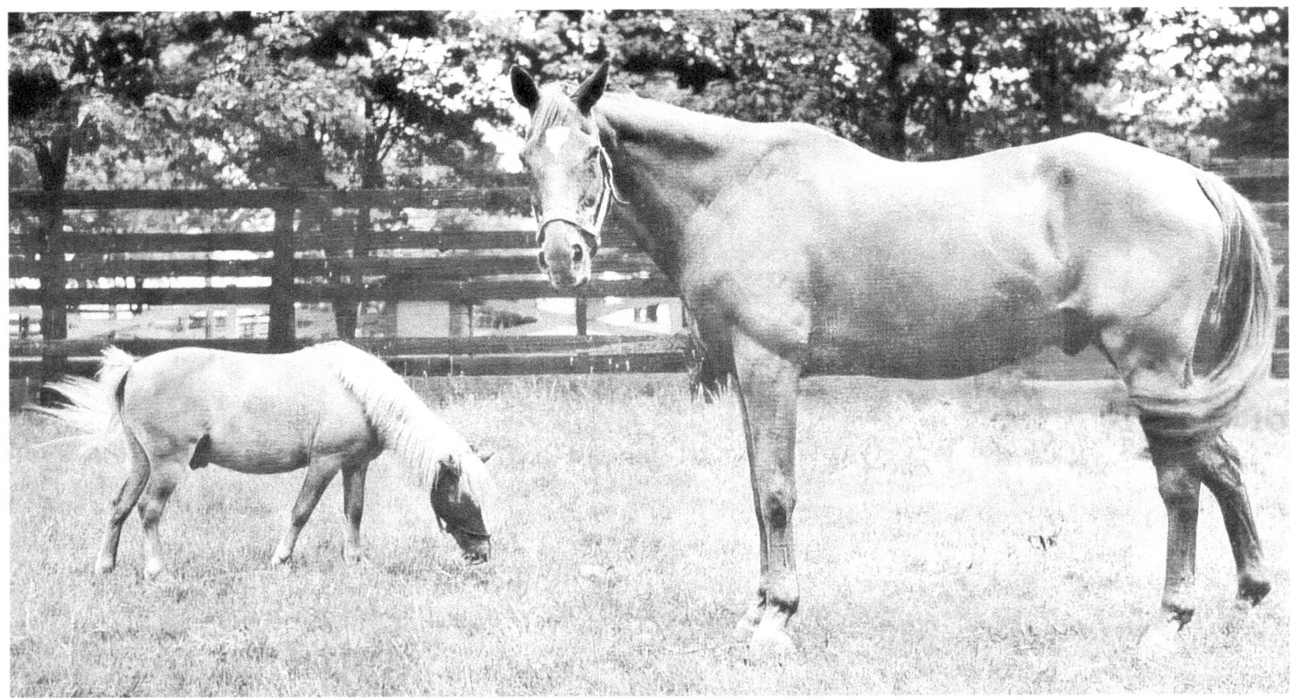

Each year, on May 30, Mrs. Kilmer and Mike held a birthday party for Exterminator. Hundreds of children and adults attended the events. Exterminator's cake was made from oats, corn, bran, and apples, with carrots serving as candles—one for each year of his age. Exterminator always shared his special cake with Peanuts.

Mike led the children around on the big horse's back. While walking, he told them someday they could tell their grandchildren they had ridden the great Exterminator.

Exterminator lived to be thirty, roughly equivalent to ninety in human years. He outlived the original Peanuts. In fact, two additional ponies were purchased to be his companions, and each was given the name Peanuts.

---

1. some sources have Exterminator's height at 16.3 hands, others say 17 hands

56

Grand Canyon Mules

No non-Natives will visit there." That was the conclusion of Lt. Joseph Ives in 1857, after leading a government expedition that explored the Colorado River area. Ives reported that the region had no value because of the river rapids and its treacherous terrain.

But his discouraging report failed to keep gold and silver prospectors away. One, believed to be the first non-Native resident of the Grand Canyon, was "Captain" John Hance. Hance made improvements to a Native American trail, later known as the Old Hance Trail. When his mining efforts proved futile, Hance set up tents around his cabin and opened the first tourist camp in the Grand Canyon in the late 1800s.

Many who visited the Canyon believed meeting Hance was almost as memorable as seeing the Canyon itself. Hance regaled his visitors with tall tales, describing how he had dug the Canyon out himself and that he'd jumped across it, from rim to rim, on his horse, Darby. (He named all his horses Darby, so it would be easy to remember them.)

God made the Canyon, John Hance the trails. Without the other, neither would be complete.

— Bucky O'Neill, early Grand Canyon resident

In 1853, at the age of seventeen, Fred Harvey left England for the United States. He got his start by working in the restaurant business in New York City. By the 1870s, Harvey had his own string of restaurants along the railroad stations in the west, providing high-quality food, served promptly at reasonable prices. When the Grand Canyon became a favorite destination for Santa Fe Rail travelers, the Harvey Company expanded its operation into that area.

As the Canyon area became more profitable, the Fred Harvey Company took over Hance's operation. Hance remained in the Canyon, working as a greeter and guide for Fred Harvey. When President Theodore Roosevelt visited the Grand Canyon in 1903, John Hance was his guide.

In 1905, the Santa Fe Railroad financed the first hotel in the Canyon, the El Tovar, on the South Rim which

was managed by the Fred Harvey Company. Additional buildings created around that time were the Hopi House, Bright Angel Lodge, and Phantom Ranch at the bottom of the Canyon. The Grand Canyon became a national park in 1919, increasing its popularity as a vacation stop.

John Hance led tourists on mule rides as early as 1887, but in the early 1900s, the Fred Harvey Company became the dominant mule-riding operation. When the Phantom Ranch opened in 1922, it was a popular destination for the longest of those rides, providing an overnight stay before the return to the rim the following morning.

Mules traveling back and forth to the Phantom Ranch use the 440-foot-long Kaibab Bridge, or Black Suspension Bridge, completed in 1928. The bridge's steel cables and wooden deck planking stretch across the Colorado River.

In 1903, brothers Ellsworth and Emery Kolb set up a photo studio at the top of the South Rim. The Kolbs snapped photos of the mule riders, starting down the Bright Angel Trail.

Since there wasn't enough water at the rim to develop the film, they packed everything onto burros and traveled down to the springs at Indian Gardens to develop the images. Then, they returned to the rim to sell the souvenir photos to the tourists at the completion of their ride. Emery Kolb worked as a photographer at the canyon until 1976.

The Harvey Company was the sole operator of South Rim mule rides until 1968 when Xanterra, who operates the rides today, purchased the company.

The steady, reliable burros, long favored by prospectors, weren't large enough to carry tourists down the steep canyon trails. The hybrid mule with his donkey father and horse mother possessed just the right

258

qualities for the job. The mule inherited the self-preservation instincts and sure-footedness of the burro along with the larger size and strength of the horse. Mules tended to be calm, not easily spooked, and were better able to tolerate the extreme summer heat than a horse.

We know little about the thousands of mules who have carried tourists through the Canyon. Ron Clayton, a modern-day head wrangler, credited a mule, Pancho, with "hauling more little kids and old grandmothers in and out of the Grand Canyon than any other mule in history."

A few of the others in Clayton's string of 150 mules were Lazy Larry, Mordecai, Pistol, Rob Roy, Mister Ed, Mercedes, Blackjack, Jethro, Clementine, Henrietta, Willow, and Roscoe.

The mules knew exactly where to stand when called into the barn for dinner. They ran in and quickly sorted out whose bucket was whose. Clayton knew the name of each mule and its unique personality. This knowledge helped him match riders to mules that best suited them.

Another wrangler's favorite was a mule named Rosie. She was a great mule, but the hardest thing for Rosie to get used to was hikers wearing large backpacks. The wrangler thought Rosie must have seen the strange combination as a "mule-eating space creature."

In his pre-ride speeches, Ron Clayton stressed the importance of riders keeping a "tight and compact group" with two to five feet between the mules. If a longer gap developed, the mule at the back, at some point, would run to catch up, and speed could be perilous on the steep, narrow trails.

Clayton warned prospective riders that some mules liked to walk close to the edge. He jokingly claimed the animals were trained that way so riders would have the best view of the Canyon. Mule riders sometimes looked down and saw nothing past their foot in the stirrup but air for hundreds of feet.

The wranglers had a saying, "No leaning, no screaming." Leaning could cause the saddle to tip sideways. And of course, screaming might startle the otherwise calm mules.

During the long rides, frequent stops allow the mules to rest. These breaks might occur right on the trail. When stopped, the mules turn with their hindquarters against the rock wall and their heads looking out over the cliff. The mule might stand with his front feet on the edge of the trail with a thousand-foot drop just past the end of his nose.

Reese Brothers, from Gallatin, Tennessee, has supplied mules to the Grand Canyon for over thirty years. The manager at the Grand Canyon Mule Barn purchases mules twice a year—about ten mules in the spring and another ten in the fall. The best mules for the Canyon are big and stout; weighing 1,000 to 1,200 pounds. They're typically five to eight years old, have a good attitude, are gentle, strong, and in good condition. Some are used as pack mules to haul supplies back and forth from Phantom Ranch while the others become riding mules.

Most of the five million annual tourists to the Grand Canyon visit the South Rim. It's more accessible from a variety of locations, has more accommodations, and provides the classic Grand Canyon views down to the Colorado River. Slightly higher in elevation, the North Rim is more remote with fewer accommodations. The South Rim is open year-round, while the North Rim is open from mid-May through mid-October.

Both rims offer mule rides, however the overnight ride to Phantom Ranch is only available at the South Rim. North Rim mule rides are operated by Canyon Trail Rides. Mule ride operators claim in the more than one hundred years of rides, they've never lost a visitor.

Over the Edge, a book on Grand Canyon deaths, states there have been 700 deaths there since 1869. The book cites one death of a person riding a mule, however, he was an employee not a tourist. Rather than involving mules, most of the fatalities at the Grand Canyon are due to falls, drowning, or health conditions such as heat stroke, heart attack, dehydration, or hypothermia.

On June 17, 1951, three Fred Harvey guides rode two mules as they shuttled the daily string of saddled trail mules from the barn to the rim where guests awaited. When the trio neared the head of the Bright Angel Trail, the mule that was being ridden double was crowded out to the edge and lost his footing. The two riders and the mule fell fifty feet. One of the riders and the mule sustained minor injuries. Unfortunately, the other rider, guide Lee Smith, was killed in the accident.

Two more recent incidents involved mules at the Grand Canyon.

- May 10, 1998 - Sheryl Flack, 48, from Glendale, California fell 500 feet to her death on the Bright Angel Trail after the mule ride stopped for lunch. Flack was not on a mule at the time but had gone to peer over a steep cliff.

- May 5, 2009 - Park rangers responded to a mule accident on the Bright Angel Trail involving a sixty-six-year-old woman from California. The Dispatch Center received a radio call from a wrangler reporting a mule had lost its footing, fell, and rolled over its rider. The accident occurred two and a half miles below the rim. The woman was rescued by helicopter and flown to Flagstaff Medical Center. According to an online comment, the woman broke multiple bones but was not killed.

57

Sir Barton

The first Triple Crown winner, in 1919, received no fanfare—because there was no such thing as a Triple Crown at that time. The chestnut Thoroughbred, Sir Barton, won the Kentucky Derby on May 10. Just four days later, on May 14, he won the Preakness. Then, he came from behind to win the third Triple Crown race, the Belmont Stakes on June 7. Only two other horses dared to challenge Sir Barton in the Belmont. Sir Barton won another race on May 24, prior to the Belmont.

It wasn't until 1930 that this series of three races began to be referred to as the Triple Crown. That year, Gallant Fox became the second horse to accomplish the feat. The New York Times stated that the jockey

> *gave all the credit to his mount which by winning the Preakness, Kentucky Derby, and Belmont, had equaled the feat of Sir Barton. These two horses are the only ones to win the "triple crown."*

In 1935, journalist Charles Hatton, of the Daily Racing Form, also used that title when a son of Gallant Fox, Omaha, became the third winner. After Omaha's victories, "Triple Crown" was widely used.

The Triple Crown trophy, a silver, three-sided vase, was created in 1950 and first awarded, retroactively, to 1948 winner, Citation. In later years, all previous winners were awarded trophies, including those first three, plus War Admiral (1937), Whirlaway (1941), Count Fleet (1943), and Assault (1946).

Although those winners came in quick succession, after Assault, it was twenty-seven years before the next Triple Crown winner, Secretariat, in 1973. But Sir Barton retains the honor of being the first.

Sir Barton also has the distinction of being the only Triple Crown winner to run the Belmont Stakes in a clockwise direction (to the right). Man o' War, not a Triple Crown winner, also ran the Belmont clockwise when he won the race in 1920. The following year, 1921, the Belmont switched to a counter-clockwise direction like other American races. (Some horse races in Europe still run clockwise.)

Sir Barton was a disagreeable horse who showed little promise as a two-year-old. After four disappointing races in 1918, his owner, John E. Madden, believed Sir Barton would be a failure and decided to sell him.

J.K.L. Ross paid $10,000 for Sir Barton, and the horse began training with H. Guy Bedwell. Part of Sir Barton's problem was the thin-walled hooves he'd inherited from his sire, Star Shoot. The horse lost a shoe in at least one race. It would have been understandably difficult for him to run at his best with tender hooves. The uncomfortable hooves also contributed to Sir Barton's temperamental disposition. He was a biter and kicker who tolerated only his grooms. Jim Ross, son of Sir Barton's owner, described the horse as "downright evil."

Trainer Bedwell addressed the foot problem by adding piano felt between Sir Barton's hooves and his shoes to absorb some of the impact when he ran.

Sir Barton also had an aversion to training. The horse saw no need to exert himself unless he was in a race. To motivate him to perform, Bedwell simulated a race atmosphere, running other horses against him in training sessions.

The colt raced twice for his new owner in 1918, finishing second in his last race that year. When a stablemate kicked him on his left hind leg, he developed blood poisoning and his racing season came to an early end.

The following year, 1919, was owned by Sir Barton. He swept the Triple Crown races, with the Kentucky Derby as his first-ever win. But his fame didn't last long, as 1920 belonged to Man o' War.

As a four-year-old, Sir Barton faced the three-year-old Man o' War in a match race at Kenilworth Park in Canada on October 12, 1920. Exterminator had been invited to the race as well, but owner Willis Kilmer declined when the other owners wouldn't agree to a longer distance—Exterminator's specialty.

Sir Barton carried 126 pounds while Man o' War had a slight advantage, carrying 120. The two raced before a record crowd of 30,000, but it wasn't much of a contest. Man o' War won by seven lengths.

Sir Barton ran three more times but never won again. He was retired the following year. In three seasons, he raced thirty-one times, winning thirteen, finishing second six times, and third five times. His career earnings were $116,857. Sir Barton's racing career is noteworthy because he often, or perhaps always, ran with some degree of soreness. It's interesting to speculate what he might have accomplished if he had been fully sound.

In retirement, Sir Barton wasn't a spectacular racing sire. His most successful offspring was the filly, Easter Stockings, winner of the 1928 Kentucky Oaks.

In 1933, at seventeen, Sir Barton was drafted into the military. They sent the stallion to the U.S. Army Remount Service at Front Royal, Virginia. Later, he transferred to Fort Robinson in Nebraska.

After Sir Barton's stint at the Remount, Wyoming rancher, Dr. Joseph Hylton bought him. At the ranch, Sir Barton sired foals from Hylton's Quarter Horse mares.

TODAY
AND
THURSDAY

USUAL PRICES

===DOUBLE FEATURE PROGRAM===

Two Features That You Will Surely Enjoy

THE RACE OF THE AGE

At an enormous expense we have secured the exclusive showing of the only actual pictures of the world's greatest race held at Windsor, Ontario—

MAN O' WAR

America's Champion Horse

VS.

SIR BARTON

Great Britain's Pride

Sir Barton died of colic on October 30, 1937, at twenty-one. Initially buried on Hylton's ranch, his remains were later moved to Washington Park in Douglas, Wyoming, near a life-size statue of the first Triple Crown winner.

58

Man o' War

New Jersey banned gambling and horse racing in 1898, resulting in the closure of racetracks across the state. New York followed suit in 1908 when Governor Charles Hughes signed the Hart-Agnew bill into Law, making betting on horse racing illegal. The law imposed fines and possible prison terms for violators.

In 1867, August Belmont, Jr. inherited Nursery Stud, his father's 1,100-acre Thoroughbred farm in New York. Belmont also owned a farm with the same name, near Lexington, Kentucky. Belmont Jr. opposed the New York law. By 1911, every horse track in New York had closed. The race named after Belmont's family, the Belmont Stakes, was suspended in 1911 and 1912.

Thoroughbred owners sent their horses out of state or overseas to race. Many of the owners, trainers, jockeys, and stable hands relocated to states more friendly to racing. Some even left the country, moving to England or France.

The financial impact of the track closures went beyond horse people. Tourism in cities like Saratoga Springs, New York dropped drastically since the people came primarily to see horse racing at the Saratoga course. Restaurants and hotels were hit hard by the drop in tourism, and real estate values plummeted.

In 1913, a New York court ruled that oral betting was legal. Racing resumed, but because of the two-year disruption and the start of World War I, public interest was low. Several tracks never reopened.

On April 6, 1917, the United States declared war on Germany. A week earlier (March 29, 1917), a chestnut colt was born at August Belmont's Nursery Stud in Kentucky. The colt's sire was Fair Play and his dam was Mahubah. That colt not only restored the public's enthusiasm for racing, he became, according to many, the best racehorse of all time.

Even greater than Belmont's love for horse racing was his love for his country. At sixty-four, he volunteered for the military, serving as a major in the U.S. Army Air Service in Spain and France. Belmont's wife,

Eleanor, named the chestnut foal, whose only markings were a star and narrow stripe, My Man o' War, in honor of her husband. The "My" was later dropped. Most of the stable help simply called him Red or Big Red.

In the spring of 1918, Belmont was out of the country. Not knowing how long the war might go on, he decided to sell his crop of twelve yearlings. That was a decision he must have regretted, especially since the war ended in November of that year.

At the Saratoga yearling sale, trainer Louis Feustel saw something he liked in the tall, rangy Man o' War. He urged Samuel Riddle of the Glen Riddle Farm to purchase him. Riddle bought the colt for $5,000.

Man o' War, at first, resisted the saddle and bridle.

He fought like a tiger. He screamed with rage and fought us so hard that it took several days before he could be handled with safety.

— Samuel Riddle

His handlers recognized the horse's intelligence and realized they couldn't force him.

I guess like every other trainer in the world, I had sense enough to know I had hold of the tail of a tiger and, while I could steer him some, I had to do a lot of swinging with him, I had to grow with him and try to out-guess him … figure things out with him and let him believe he'd done it for himself. You can't handle a temperamental horse or human being any other way.

— Louis Feustel

Feustel developed the horse with patient training techniques which soon paid off. Man o' War won his first race by six lengths at the Belmont course on June 6, 1919, against six other two-year-olds.

Man o' War continued racing, winning five more races before the Sanford Memorial at Saratoga on August 13, 1919. His companion during his racing days was a retired hunter gelding named Major Treat. His groom was Frank Loftus, no relation to the jockey Johnny Loftus.

Starting gates for horse races were invented by Clay Puett and first used in Canada in 1939. By the end of 1940, they were in use by all major American race tracks. But during Man o' War's racing days, there were no gates. The horses lined up at the start, behind a tape stretched across the track. As can be imagined, it was difficult to make multiple, fidgety horses stand still, waiting for a starting signal. Such was the case at the Sanford Memorial on August 13, 1919.

Reports state that the start was bungled by a substitute starter, Charles H. Pettingill, who was in his late seventies. After several false starts by Man o' War, jockey Johnny Loftus was repositioning the horse when Pettingill released the starting tape. Even with starting near the back of the pack and being blocked by a group of horses, forcing the jockey to swing wide to the outside, Man o' War came within a half-length of winning. He passed the winner just beyond the finish line.

The horse who beat him was named Upset, and it definitely was. That was the only race Man o' War ever lost. Over his career, he faced Upset five times, winning the other four races. Big Red finished his two-year-old season with nine victories in ten races.

In an odd twist, the Jockey Club refused to renew the licenses for Loftus and Upset's rider, Willie Knapp. Neither jockey ever raced again. Both became trainers. When Loftus' license wasn't renewed, Clarence Kummer took over as Man o' War's jockey. Kummer rode Big Red during the 1920 season, except when he was injured. Jockeys Earl Sande and Andy Schuttinger rode in Kummer's place in two races.

At the age of three, Man o' War stood 16.2 hands and weighed 1,125 pounds with a seventy-two-inch girth. The colt had a huge appetite. He possessed the longest stride of any Thoroughbred, measuring twenty-eight feet at a full gallop. The average Thoroughbred stride is twenty feet.

Although he was born and raised in Kentucky and lived most of his life there, Man o' War never raced in the state. The Kentucky Derby was the big race for three-year-olds, but Samuel Riddle believed the distance was too much to ask of his colt that early in the spring, especially when Man o' War would have carried 126 pounds.

Instead, Big Red's first race of 1920 was the Preakness Stakes on May 18. His victory in the Preakness was the beginning of an incredible season in which he won eleven races in eleven starts. And he didn't simply win; his closest competitor was a length and a half behind the big red horse. His largest margin of victory was an incredible one hundred lengths (Belmont Park, September 4, 1920).

On October 12, 1920, Man o' War outran the 1919 Triple Crown winner, Sir Barton, by seven lengths. That match race was Big Red's final outing. Man o' War had carried as much as 138 pounds that year. Riddle decided to retire him after the race against Sir Barton to avoid injuries from carrying so much weight.

Man o' War finished his career with twenty victories in twenty-one starts. $249,465 in earnings made him the record money winner at that time. He was 1920's Horse of the Year and a national hero.

Samuel Riddle turned down $1 million for the horse saying, "Lots of men might have a million dollars, but only one man can have Man o' War."

Man o' War retired to Riddle's Faraway Farm near Lexington, Kentucky. Elizabeth Daingerfield was the farm manager, an uncommon position for a woman at that time. In 1930, Daingerfield retired, and Harrie Scott became the farm manager.

Big Red was a successful sire, producing numerous stakes winners, the most famous of which was his son, War Admiral, the 1937 Triple Crown winner. Another son, Clyde Van Dusen, won the Kentucky Derby in 1929. Man o' War was the grandsire of

Seabiscuit (whose sire was Hard Tack). Battleship, a Man o' War son, was the first American horse to win the British Grand National steeple chase.

Over the years, it's estimated several million visitors thronged to the farm to get a glimpse of Man o' War. The visitors came not only to see the horse but also to hear stories told by his groom, Will Harbut, about Big Red and his achievements.

Born in 1885, Harbut had a reputation as a skilled horseman. Some even called him a horse whisperer. Harbut worked for a variety of horsemen over the years, including Harrie Scott. When Scott took the job as manager of Faraway Farm in 1930, Will went with him.

Man o' War had already been at the farm for ten years when Harbut became his groom. The two spent the next sixteen years together—from the fall of 1930 until the spring of 1946. Although Will had never seen Man o' War race, he knew he was in charge of a living legend.

Harbut refused to wake Man o' War if people arrived when the horse was sleeping. When he did accept visitors, Will told them something along these lines.

> *Here he is. This is Big Red. He's the greatest horse you ever saw because he's the greatest horse there is. He beat them all, except in that one race where he didn't have a chance. They retired him because there wasn't anything left to run against him that had a chance. When he looked them in the eye, they just folded up. Oh, yes, there's other good horses—there's great horses. But this here is the best one. There ain't but one Man o' War.*

> *— The Lexington Herald, November 4, 1947*

On May 1, 1946, Will suffered a stroke that impaired his vision and left him partially paralyzed. He was no longer able to care for Big Red. Harbut died on October 3, 1947. His obituary listed among his survivors his wife, six sons, three daughters, and Man o' War.

Man o' War died of a heart attack, at the age of thirty, on November 1, 1947, passing away a month after his faithful groom. The horse's funeral was broadcast nationally over the radio. Man o' War was initially buried at Faraway Farm. In the mid-1970s, his remains were moved to a spot of honor near the entrance to the Kentucky Horse Park near Herbert Haseltine's Man o' War statue.

Was Man o' War the greatest racehorse of all time? His owner, Samuel Riddle, believed the horse had never been pushed to the full extent of his ability. A whip was only used on him once, in the 1920 Dwyer Stakes, against a horse named John P. Grier.

We do not know to this day how fast Man o' War was, as we were afraid to let him out; knowing his intense speed, we feared he might harm himself.

— Man O' War, Page Cooper, p. 146

In 1999, Blood-Horse magazine selected a panel of seven people from the world of horse racing. Each compiled a list of who they considered the top 100 Thoroughbred racehorses of the twentieth century. Those lists were then merged. The first twenty horses from the resulting master list are shown below.

1. Man o' War
2. Secretariat
3. Citation
4. Kelso
5. Count Fleet
6. Dr. Fager
7. Native Dancer
8. Forego
9. Seattle Slew
10. Spectacular Bid
11. Tom Fool
12. Affirmed
13. War Admiral
14. Buckpasser
15. Colin
16. Damascus
17. Round Table
18. Cigar
19. Bold Ruler
20. Swaps

He was as near to a living flame as horses ever get, and horses get closer to this than anything else. It was not merely that he smashed his opposition, sometimes by a hundred lengths, or that he set world records, or that he cared not a tinker's curse for weight or distance or track or horses. It was that even when he was standing motionless in his stall, with his ears pricked forward and his eyes focused on something slightly above the horizon which mere people never see, energy still poured from him. He could get in no position which suggested actual repose, and his very stillness was that of a coiled spring, of the crouched tiger.

— This Was Racing, Joe Palmer, p. 77

59

Automobile vs. Horse

The transition from horse-drawn carriages to motorized vehicles was a gradual one, beginning with canal boats, steam power, and the early railroads. Electric vehicles of the 1830s were self-propelled, but their range was limited. Batteries that could be recharged wouldn't come along until 1859.

William Morrison, a chemist from Iowa, built an early, electric vehicle. In 1890, he applied for a patent on his four-horsepower carriage that featured front-wheel drive and a top speed of fifteen miles per hour. Its twenty-four batteries required recharging every fifty miles.

The Anderson Electric Car Company in Detroit, Michigan produced 13,000 Detroit Electric cars from 1907 to 1939. The Anderson cars had top speeds of twenty miles per hour and traveled eighty miles between charges. These cars were especially popular during World War I when gas was scarce and expensive.

Most horses were frightened when they had to share the road with "horseless carriages." In 1899, Seventh Day Adventist inventor and author, Uriah Smith,[1] patented a stylish, at least for horse lovers, vehicle body. He apparently believed horses would view his Horsey Horseless automobiles as fellow equines and wouldn't be afraid. His patent application includes:

> The leading feature of the design resides in a vehicle-body provided at its front end with a forwardly-projecting figure of a horse's head, the neck portion of the figure being curved on lines merging into the outline of the contiguous portion of the body.
>
> The figure of the horse's head is arranged in a life-like attitude and projects a material distance in advance of the dash.

Some accounts indicate the hollow horse head could serve as a fuel tank, however that isn't mentioned in the patent.

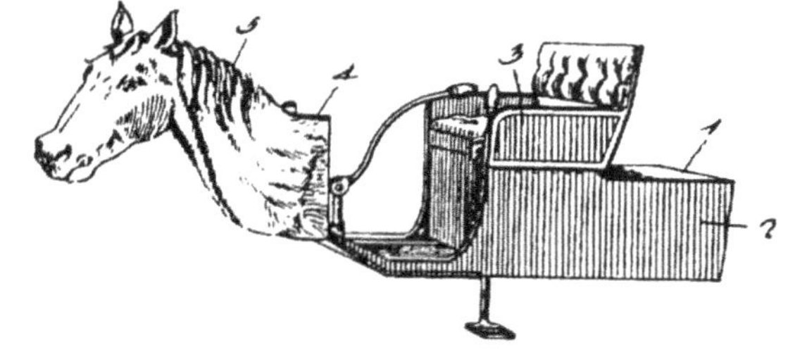

Karl Benz is generally credited with creating the first gas-powered automobile, patenting his three-wheeled Motorwagen in Germany, in 1886.

In America, the name Henry Ford is synonymous with early car development. Ford attended school only through the eighth grade. At sixteen, he left his family's Michigan farm to work as a machinist in Detroit. He later worked with Thomas Edison, toying with the idea of electric cars. But Ford is known for developing gas-powered vehicles.

In 1896, Ford built an early version, known as the Quadricycle. Over the years, he refined and improved his design, forming the Ford Motor Company in 1903.

What ignited the automobile industry was Ford's use of assembly line production. A single Model T had previously taken over twelve hours to build. By 1914, using an assembly line, one could be built in ninety-three minutes.

Mass production reduced the cost of the cars, making them affordable to more people. From 1908 to 1927, more than fifteen million Model T Fords were produced. Ford followed that with the Model A, built from 1927 to 1932.

The precise year cars surpassed horses is difficult to pinpoint, as it varied from one geographic area to the next, but it generally happened during the 1920s. Estimates are that by 1929, there were twenty-three million cars in the U.S. while the number of horses had dropped below twenty million.

Number of horses and mules in the United States[2]

1910:	24,042,882	1940:	13,931,531
1920:	25,199,552	1950:	7,604,000
1930:	18,885,856	1960:	3,089,000

Although the shift away from horses solved The Great Manure Crisis, some would argue it resulted in pollution that was even worse. The decline in horse usage had a significant economic impact in many areas. Businesses and occupations related to horse care and transportation were greatly diminished or eliminated. These included blacksmiths, veterinarians, horse breeders, grooms, trainers, drivers, livery stables, tack and carriage makers, delivery and cab services, and the farmers who produced food and bedding for the animals.

Replacing farm horses with machinery might have been a contributing factor in the Great Depression. Farmers borrowed money to purchase the new equipment. The resulting overproduction, made possible by the machinery, caused crop prices and, therefore, farmers' incomes to drop when many had gone into debt for the first time.

Motorized vehicles improved the speed of transportation in some areas, but not in congested cities.

> *Should we go back to the horse and buggy days?*
>
> *Don't laugh. Actual tests in some of the very large cities on this continent show that the average speed at which traffic moves through congested areas is less than it was during the horse and buggy days.*
>
> *When you think of the effort and money put into traffic planning and control, parking schemes, new bridges, widened streets—it's mighty discouraging.*
>
> — *The Vancouver Sun, January 12, 1956*

As of 2022, there are an estimated one and a half billion cars in the world. Was a crisis averted by the transition from horses to cars? Or was one set of problems exchanged for another? Could a workable solution have been found for the removal of manure, a natural waste product?

Is automobile pollution potentially more serious? That premise is part of the modern push for electric vehicles. But electric vehicles introduce their own set of problems.

Some even believe steam-powered engines will make a comeback. Modern technology makes steam a more workable power source, and steam engines would have less environmental impact than the batteries used for electric vehicles.

While cars and trucks do have their advantages, horses do as well. A horse can travel in remote areas where a motorized vehicle could never venture. Also they are not only energy efficient but capable of reproducing themselves.

Horses are not only self-feeding, self-controlling, self-maintaining and self-reproducing, but they are far more economical in the energy they are able to develop from a given weight of fuel material, than any other existing form of motor.

— Robert Thurston, U.S. steam engine expert, 1894

---

1. Uriah Smith (1832-1903) had two inventions that were more successful than the Horsey Horseless—an artificial leg with a flexible knee and ankle joint (1863) and a folding school desk (1875).

At twelve, Smith's leg became badly infected and had to be amputated above the knee. The operation was performed in twenty minutes on the Smith's kitchen table without the use of an anesthetic. The artificial leg he received was so cumbersome, he later invented a new, lighter version.

artificial leg—patents.google.com/patent/US39361

school desk—patents.google.com/patent/USRE8446

horsey horseless—patents.google.com/patent/USD30551S

2. Americanequestrian.com

Silent Cal's Hobby Horse

The Secret Service was created in 1865 as part of the Treasury Department. In 1894, they provided part-time protection for President Grover Cleveland. But after President William McKinley was shot in 1901, Congress requested Secret Service protection for U.S. presidents.

By the time Calvin Coolidge arrived in the White House (1923–1929), he had full-time protection. That was a good thing, but his Secret Service agents frowned on Coolidge's horseback rides.

An old college classmate, Dwight Morrow, provided a solution in the form of a mechanical horse powered by electricity. Thunderbolt was delivered to the White House, and the electric equine met the approval of both the president and his security detail.

Thunderbolt's inventor was John Harvey Kellogg of Battle Creek, Michigan, now better remembered for his cornflakes cereal. The Kellogg brothers marketed the horses with the dubious claim that they would improve one's fitness. Coolidge's horse was similar to one found in the exercise room on the ill-fated Titanic.

Coolidge stabled Thunderbolt in the presidential dressing room. It's said he rode the steed three times a day for exercise and enjoyment. Coolidge opponents, always on the lookout for a way to belittle the quiet, frugal president, turned the mechanical horse into a means of ridicule. A Kentucky Congressman wrote a satirical poem about "Silent Cal" and his "hobby horse."

THE "HOBBY HORSE"

The Prince of Wales, astride a steed,
Is a picture of world renown.
When the horse bestirs, as is its need,
The Crown Prince hits the ground.

Silent Cal is a more cautious chap
Than the young Prince, brave and good.
He profited by the Princely mishap,
And bought a horse of wood.
Electric currents fill its veins,

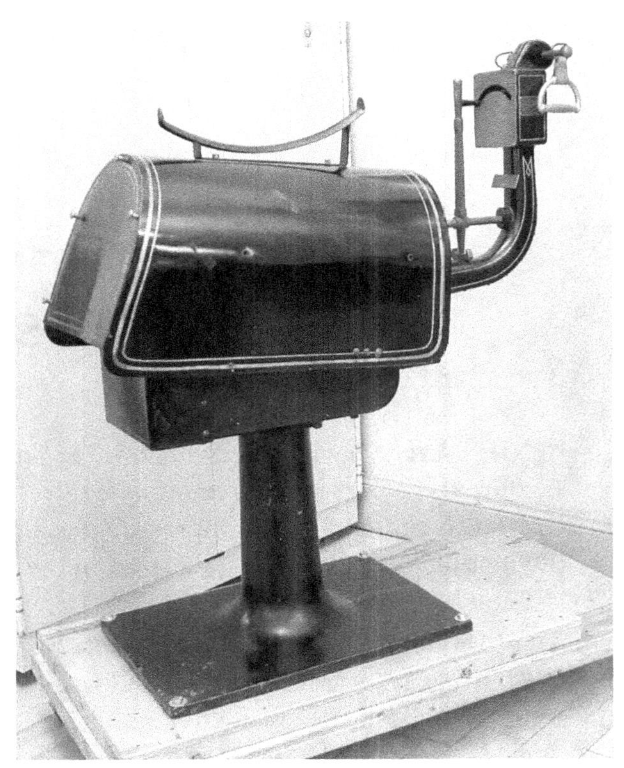

Today we find the President has become more economical in his means of transportation. We are informed he now is riding a wooden horse. I shall not be surprised if soon it will be heralded to the people that the President is riding this wooden horse for the purpose of cutting down the oats bill at the White House. And I have an idea that when in the future any program for the benefit of the livestock producers is proposed the farmers will be advised to produce wooden horses.

— The Kansas City Times, February 13, 1925

Elizabeth Jaffray began working as White House head housekeeper in 1909. She was the first female chief servant in White House history and served under four presidents—Taft, Wilson, Harding, and Coolidge. Jaffray used horses for transportation longer than anyone else at the White House. She was chauffeured in a brougham for daily shopping excursions into the mid 1920s.

Jaffray was disgusted by Calvin Coolidge's interference in her work, his tips to her on how to economize, and his frugal spending on White House entertaining. She considered him a cheapskate.

Coolidge and his wife, Grace, were no more fond of Jaffray than she was of them. Jaffray left the White House in 1926 during Coolidge's presidency.

61

Diving Horses

Although he had studied dentistry, William Frank Carver's remarkable shooting skills earned him a role in Buffalo Bill's Wild West in 1883. The two strong-willed men found it impossible to work together and soon parted ways. After leaving the Wild West, Doc Carver started his own show. In 1894, he added an unusual attraction—diving horses.

According to Carver, the inspiration for the diving act came when, riding horseback, a bridge gave way under him in Nebraska, causing him and his mount to fall into the Platte River. Known for his imaginative recollection of past events—or outright fabrication of them—it's not clear whether this actually happened.

The Great Carver Show was a family event. His son, Al, helped train and care for the horses. Al also supervised the construction of a tall ramp and diving platform. At the first shows, the horses jumped riderless. Later, Carver's daughter, Lorena, became the first rider.

New horses and riders trained on a twelve-foot platform, but performance dives averaged thirty to forty feet in height. The human diver, almost always a young woman, climbed the tower first and waited at the top for her horse to arrive. The horse traveled unaccompanied up the steep, wooden ramp, the height of a four-story building.

As the horse reached the platform, the rider vaulted onto his back and held on to leather straps on either side of his neck. Some horses leaped immediately, so it was important to grab the straps quickly. A wide, wooden board, mounted vertically below the platform, served as a brace for the horse to kick off from as he dove. Each horse jumped differently, producing a slightly different dive the rider needed to adjust for.

Over the years, Carver determined the optimal depth for the diving pool was eleven feet. After the momentum of the dive was broken by the water, the horse had to touch the bottom quickly to maintain his balance and keep himself from flipping over underwater. When his hooves touched, the horse gave a strong push toward the surface. It was crucial for the rider to keep her head to the side of the horse's neck. If not, the sudden jerk of the horse's head and neck upward could break her nose, jaw, or cheekbones.

Diving horse performances were tremendously popular and soon were the only attraction at Carver's traveling show.

When Lorena was injured in a dive, Doc Carver advertised for her replacement.

Seeking attractive young woman who can swim and dive; likes horses; desires to travel.

Twenty-year-old Sonora Webster responded to the ad and was hired in 1924. She began training from the twelve-foot platform on Klatawah, a 1,250 pound sorrel gelding. He was the oldest, but the liveliest of Carver's horses. The eighty-four-year-old Carver was a gruff man with little praise for his new diver, but Sonora refused to quit.

After twenty-one dives off the low platform, Sonora figured she was ready to begin practicing at the full-height. To her surprise, Doc Carver decided Sonora's first dive from the top would be the following week—in front of an audience.

On the day of the performance, Sonora made her way through the crowds and climbed the tall tower, waiting at the top for Klatawah. When Al Carver released the horse, his hooves clomped up the steep, wooden ramp. Sonora felt the tower vibrate. As soon as the gelding reached the top, she vaulted onto his back, frantically grabbing for the harness handles.

But Klatawah didn't jump. He stood, surveying the audience and pawing at the edge of the platform. In the early days of the show, when he dove without a rider, Klatawah was taught to stand there and paw. That hesitation created a sense of excitement and anticipation for the audience. Now that the horses had riders, Doc Carver wanted to eliminate the pawing, but Klatawah liked it and was reluctant to give it up.

Klatawah's pause gave Sonora a few moments to change her mind. She could have dismounted and abandoned the dive. A sudden change of heart at this point would be understandable, but she sat on the big horse's back and waited.

Finally, Klatawah leaped, and Sonora soared through the air. The water flew up at her, but their entry was so smooth, she barely felt it. The horse surfaced with Sonora still aboard. She was so excited that when she dismounted, Sonora forgot to bow as Carver had instructed her to do.

But Doc Carver wasn't upset. He sensed he'd found a diving girl who was going to stick with the show. He'd been gruff with her before, but after Sonora's first public performance, he treated her as a daughter.

In addition to Klatawah, Sonora rode the other Carver diving horses. Each had its own personality. Judas was white with small spots on his ears and body. He was more unpredictable than Klatawah. When Judas began twisting his body in mid-air during dives, Carver decided the horse was too dangerous to use any longer. He resolved to sell him, but could never bring himself to do it. Judas remained with the show as an expensive pet.

The third horse, Snow, was a pure-white mare who loved to eat. She became so overweight, she could no longer dive. Snow was also retired.

During her second season, Sonora rode two other horses: Lightning and John the Baptist. Lightning, a dapple-gray mare, was the largest, weighing about 1,500 pounds. Sonora liked the way Lightning whinnied and nickered to people. It seemed as if she was trying to talk to them. But the big mare was terrified of thunderstorms.

John was light brown and a little smaller at 1,400 pounds. Sonora considered him the smoothest diver. When not diving, he was mischievous. One day, John grabbed a broom in his teeth and chased the other horses around the field with it.

There were surprisingly few accidents for such a dangerous activity, but two stood out. The first happened in June 1927. Al and Lorena Carver had split off with Lightning and John, for a performance in California. Their contract required the horses to dive into the ocean rather than a pool. Lightning made a beautiful first dive, but the mare became confused in the water. Rather than heading for shore, she swam in the opposite direction. No one could reach the horse in time to save her.

Doc Carver, eighty-seven and in poor health, was heartbroken at the loss of his favorite horse. He died a few months later. The Carver show continued with Al assuming his father's responsibilities.

With the loss of Lightning, and Judas and Snow in retirement, the only horses for the act were Klatawah and John. Al needed another horse, so he traded Judas for a buckskin named Apollo. Since diving is not something a horse naturally does, there was no way to tell whether Apollo would work out until Al began training him.

Al had a busy schedule booked for the summer and needed the buckskin to learn quickly. But it quickly became obvious Apollo had no desire to become a diving horse. Rather than diving head first, he jumped feet first, performing the horse equivalent of a belly flop.

In addition to Al's horse problems, Lorena decided not to ride anymore. Instead, she worked as the show's manager. Sonora invited her younger sister, Arnette, just fifteen, to join the show as a diver. Arnette arrived in the middle of May, and Sonora put her through a rushed training program.

Al finally gave up on Apollo and scoured the countryside in a panic, trying to find a replacement. One day, he saw a beautiful pinto, standing in a field. Al asked the owner how much he wanted for the horse. The man refused to sell him, claiming the animal was an outlaw. But Al persisted and ended up coming home with the horse, Red Lips.

The next day, Al tried Red on the low platform. The horse jumped as if he'd been diving his whole life. When they were comfortable with his ability to dive alone, the next test was whether the "outlaw" horse would accept a rider. Red passed that test as well, allowing Sonora to ride him off the low dive repeatedly.

At their second show of the 1928 season, in Canada, Red dove for his first time at the full height. While they were in the air, Sonora came off his back, but she maintained a grip on the harness. When they hit the water, she came totally loose from the horse, but was able to swim back to him.

That summer, Red had some good dives and some bad ones, but he performed amazingly well for a horse with so little training and diving experience. Arnette didn't fare as well. Her diving skills were sorely lacking. At the end of the season, Sonora sent her sister home to return to school, with no plans to have her return.

Initially, there had been no romantic attraction on Sonora's part toward Al Carver, but the opposite may not have been true. After working with Al for four years, Sonora came to appreciate his admirable qualities, and that fall, the two were married.

The following year, 1929, the Carver act received a season-long contract at the Atlantic City Steel Pier in New Jersey. For the first time, they would remain in one place all summer. The first two seasons at the Pier were successful beyond their imagination.

Not since losing their horse, Lightning, had anything catastrophic happened. That changed on July 14, 1931. During that evening's performance, Red took off from the platform in a nose dive, sailing straight down, rather than at an angle. Fearing that leaning too far forward would flip the horse over—and on top of her—Sonora held herself back, trying to help the gelding maintain his balance. Rather than hitting the water with the top of her head as usual, Sonora landed face first, with her eyes wide open.

Other than her eyes stinging, she seemed fine. But back in her changing room, Sonora's vision grew cloudy. Al wanted to take her to the hospital. She refused. Sonora dove again that night and continued to perform for two more days.

When her vision didn't improve, Al contacted a former diver, Marie, to replace Sonora. He took his wife to see a doctor and learned that the bad dive on Red had resulted in detached retinas. The condition was worsened by Sonora's decision to continue diving. The doctor operated, and Sonora was required to lie as still as possible in the hospital with her eyes bandaged.

The doctors had done all they could, and Sonora realized she would never see again. She was twenty-seven years old. Alone, in the darkness one night at the hospital, she felt a powerful presence of God surrounding her.

As I lay there in the hospital, the silence around me seemed to deepen and become amplified. In the heart of this silence, seemingly at its very core, there was a feeling of presence. How else shall I describe it? There are no words. I can only say that I knew as emphatically as we know very few things in life that I was in the presence of

God seemed to tell her she would see again. But rather than physical sight, it would be through a greater mental vision. Sonora prayed for courage to accept her blindness and that she wouldn't become a burden to those around her. Even before leaving the hospital, she began to rely on her other senses, particularly hearing, to compensate for her loss of sight.

After just one week, the diver, Marie, abruptly quit. Sonora's sister, Arnette, was working another job at the Pier. She begged Sonora to let her dive again. Since their only other option was to shut down the show, Sonora and Al agreed to give Arnette another chance. Arnette's diving improved, and with her help, the Carvers kept the show open.

At the end of the season, Al and Sonora returned to their home in Philadelphia for the winter. The next spring, Al began preparing for their move back to Atlantic City. Sonora grew restless. She had an overwhelming need to feel useful. But what options could there possibly be in the Carver Show for a blind person?

Her thoughts continually returned to diving. Was it necessary to see in order to dive? After turning this over in her mind for several days, Sonora discussed it with Al. Knowing his wife well, Al wasn't surprised by her idea, but he insisted they talk to her doctor first.

The doctor didn't seem surprised either. He granted his permission—if Sonora wore a specially fitted helmet. As she waited several weeks for the custom helmet to be constructed, Sonora's biggest concern was whether she could mount the moving horse at the top of the platform before he jumped. As it turned out, she never had a chance to practice.

The show's diver was suddenly called away, and with just an hour's notice, Sonora was asked to make her first dive since losing her sight. She ascended the ramp as she'd done so many times before. But this time, Sonora counted her steps as she climbed.

At the top, she mounted the railing and waited for the sound of Red Lips coming after her. His hooves clattered up the wooden ramp, the sound growing louder as he came closer. Reaching out, she felt a soft, furry ear tip. Sonora ran her hand down the horse's neck until it reached the leather handhold. She grabbed it and leaped onto Red's back.

The gelding pranced a little, then jumped. Sonora clung to the straps and experienced the familiar sensation of flying, followed by the smooth splash at

The first version of the helmet had a plastic shield across her eyes. The horse is not Red Lips, who had a lot of white. Probably Klatawah.

the bottom. When Red climbed out of the pool, Sonora was on his back, and Al was there to greet her.

> *The audience seemed to be applauding as they had never applauded before. They could not have known and yet seemed to know that something special had happened. Al handed me Red Lips' sugar and I put it between my lips. For some time before I lost my sight we had been training him to take it from me in this fashion so that it appeared he was kissing me. Red leaned over and took it, and the audience clapped harder. This time it went on and on until it became an ovation.*
>
> *A Girl and Five Brave Horses, p. 196*

That was the first of eleven years of dives Sonora performed while blind. For many of those years, no one in their audiences knew she had lost her sight. Sonora's sister, Arnette, continued diving until 1935 when she left the show to raise a family. Due to World War II, the Carver Show closed in 1942. Red Lips was left in Houston with a friend of the Carvers and died in 1954.

Over the years, the diving horses who performed for the Carvers included: Dimah, Lightning, Emir, Gamal, Gordonel, John the Baptist, Judas, Junior, Klatawah, Lorga, Powderface, Snow, Red Lips, Shiloh, and Silver King.

The movie, *Wild Hearts Can't be Broken*, was based on the life of Sonora Webster and the diving horses, however Sonora didn't think much of it.

> *The only thing true in it was that I rode diving horses, I went blind and I continued to ride for another eleven years.*

Sonora Webster Carver didn't agree with people who called her brave for diving.

> *Actually, true courage is what it takes to make yourself do something you're afraid to do. I was not afraid of riding the horses; on the contrary, I loved it and would not have given it up willingly.*

Animal rights activists insisted the Carvers mistreated or abused the horses in order to make them jump. No evidence of that was ever found. Sonora's sister, Arnette Webster French, stated.

> *What impressed me was how Dr. Carver cared for the horses. Wherever we went, the S.P.C.A. was always snooping around, trying to find if we were doing anything that was cruel to animals. They never found anything because those horses lived the life of Riley. In all the years of the act, there was never a horse that was injured.*

Although the Carver family promoted the diving act as safe, Lorena Carver claimed to have broken at least one bone almost every year. There was also the drowning death of Lightning, and Sonora's blindness. But saddest of all, was the death in the show's early years of a young, male diver. On February 17, 1907, the diving act performed at the Electric Park in San Antonio, Texas before a crowd of two thousand. Miss Lawrence, the regular diver, was ill. Eighteen-year-old Oscar Smith, who performed in other Carver acts, had dived before and volunteered to take Miss Lawrence's place.

Powderface made a graceful dive and quickly surfaced but without his rider. Rescuers didn't reach the young man in time. Bruising on his face indicated Smith had been struck by the horse's head while underwater. Several newspapers reported the death, printing a photo of the young man on Powderface as they dove, but Oscar Smith was rarely mentioned in connection with the Carvers again.

Lady Wonder

Lady Wonder could add, subtract, spell, tell time, and answer questions as well as the best of the "educated" horses, such as Clever Hans. However, some claimed Lady Wonder's abilities extended further—into the psychic realm of extrasensory perception or ESP.

It all began with the filly's birth on February 9, 1924, in Richmond, Virginia. Clarence Fonda purchased the two-week-old filly for his wife, Claudia. Lady was the name they chose for the brown, maybe chestnut, filly with three white stockings and a wide blaze, the granddaughter of a Thoroughbred racehorse.

It's unclear why they purchased such a young foal; perhaps something had happened to the filly's mother. Claudia bottle fed Lady and kept her away from other horses. A strong bond developed between the woman and Lady.

The first clue Claudia had that there was something special about the filly came early on. Sometimes when she was merely thinking about having the horse come to her, Lady would appear at her side as if the horse could read Claudia's mind.

When Lady was two, Claudia began teaching the horse to recognize letters. She set wooden children's blocks out on a table for the horse to nudge. Within a few months, Lady had mastered the entire alphabet and could recognize numbers. From there, the horse progressed to spelling words and solving math problems.

Later, Clarence created a unique horse typewriter for Lady to use instead of the blocks. The device had keys the horse pressed which lifted tin cards containing the corresponding letter or number.

Things began to get a little spooky when the mare spontaneously spelled out E-N-G-I-N-E one day, a few moments before a tractor drove by. Claudia discovered that when she misplaced an item, the horse could type out its location.

By 1928, "Wonder" was added to the mare's name, and Lady Wonder began making predictions about the world. Over her lifetime, some 150,000 visitors came from all over the country to test Lady's psychic abilities. Claudia thought she might as well make some money at this and started charging visitors $.50 to $1.00 each. That gave them the ability to ask the horse three questions.

Although she didn't have 100% accuracy, some world events Lady Wonder predicted correctly were:

- Gene Tunney as the winner over Jack Dempsey in a 1927 boxing match

- The winner of the World Series fourteen out of seventeen times

- Lady Wonder picked Franklin Roosevelt to win the presidency before he was even nominated.

- Lady predicted the United States would enter World War II a year before it happened.

- She picked winning horses in races or numbers in lotteries. After a time, Mrs. Fonda stopped allowing questions that involved gambling.

- Lady told Associated Press reporter Paul Duke his name, birthplace, and the amount of his salary with 100% accuracy.

The horse's fame spread across the country. When two cases of missing children proved unsolvable, the "psychic" horse was consulted.

In 1951, four-year-old Danny Matson went missing in Quincy, Massachusetts. After extensive searches turned up nothing, the police, figuring they had nothing to lose, consulted Lady Wonder.

When asked, "Where can Danny Matson of West Quincy, Massachusetts be found?" Lady typed out "pittsfield water wheel."

But there was no Pittsfield Water Wheel in the area where the boy had gone missing. One night, as the police chief lay in bed pondering the case, it occurred to him that Lady might have gotten her letters confused. Maybe she intended something closer to "Pit Field Wilde Water."

There was a water-filled quarry nearby called the Field and Wilde Water Pit. It had already been searched, but based on Lady's answer, it was drained and searched again. On December 5, 1952, the body of little Danny Matson was found there.

On October 11, 1955, three-year-old Ronnie Weitkamp disappeared in Bloomington, Indiana. Frank Edwards, news director for a local television station, was asked to periodically broadcast Ronnie's picture in the hope that someone would recognize him.

By October 22, the boy had not been found, and the police were running out of leads. Frank Edwards' wife remembered the story of Lady Wonder's help in finding Danny Matson. Frank convinced friends in Washington, D.C. to drive to Claudia Fonda's home in Virginia to ask the now thirty-year-old horse about the Weitkamp boy.

Once Edwards' friends convinced Claudia of the importance of their mission, she led them to the barn. The interview with Lady went as follows.

> *Question: "Do you know why we are here?"*
>
> *Lady: "B-O-Y"*
>
> *Question: "Do you know the boy's name?"*
>
> *Lady: "R-O-N-E"*
>
> *Question: "Is he dead or alive?"*
>
> *Lady: "D-E-A-D"*
>
> *Question: "Was he kidnapped?"*
>
> *Lady: "N-O"*
>
> *Question: "Will he be found?"*
>
> *Lady: "Y-E-S"*
>
> *Question: "Where?"*
>
> *Lady: "H-O-L-E"*
>
> *Question: "Is he more than a quarter of a mile from where he was last seen?"*
>
> *Lady: "Y-E-S"*
>
> *Question: "More than a mile?"*
>
> *Lady: "N-O"*
>
> *Question: "What is near him?"*
>
> *Lady: "E-L-M"*
>
> *Question: "What kind of soil?"*
>
> *Lady: "S-A-N-D"*
>
> *Question: "When will he be found?"*
>
> *Lady: "D-E-C"*

The answers weren't what Frank Edwards had hoped for. He wondered whether he should keep the information to himself, but finally broadcast the conversation with Lady Wonder on October 24. Many ridiculed the story. But on December 4, Ronnie's body was found in thick brush, in a sandy gully, a little over a mile from where he was last seen. An elm tree stood thirty feet away. The boy had not been kidnapped but died of exposure.

In between those two cases, Lady Wonder stated that a nine-year-old boy, Gary Hayman, who had gone missing in Rhode Island, was alive in Kansas. A skull found in Rhode Island the following year is believed by some to be Gary's. Others question that. It's unclear whether Lady Wonder was wrong about that case.

As with the other horses who were claimed to have unusual levels of intelligence, Lady Wonder was tested extensively—with contradictory results. One researcher, Dr. Gayle, said of the mare's achievements.

> *I am perfectly willing to admit that I have no idea how she arrives at the correct answers to our questions. There is no conscious trickery here, I am convinced. But I am not converted to the mind-reading theory. What's the solution of the puzzle? I don't know!*
>
> — *Richmond Times-Dispatch, July 18, 1927*

The highest profile, controlled test of Lady's purported abilities was carried out by the parapsychologist, Professor Joseph Banks Rhine, of Duke University. Rhine arrived at the farm with his team in 1927 and spent a week putting Lady through hundreds of different tests. He concluded Lady was not being signaled consciously or unconsciously, and that she was "responsive to telepathy and possessed a degree of psychic power."

Although Rhine believed the horse had psychic abilities, not everyone was convinced. Magicians Milbourne Christopher and John Scarne both believed Claudia Fonda used mental tricks and subtle cues to signal the answers to her horse. Throughout her lifetime, Claudia denied any trickery.

Ivey Stone, the Fonda's neighbor, believed Claudia was the one with psychic abilities. "I think she passed it through the horse. That's what I think."

Lady Wonder died from a heart attack on March 19, 1957, at the ripe old age of thirty-three. She was buried at the Pet Memorial Park in Henrico County, Virginia. Claudia Fonda mourned the loss of her faithful friend and died two years later.

References and Credits

Chapter 1 Cowboys and Longhorns

We Pointed Them North, E.C. Abbott, Farrar & Rinehart, 1939, Illustration by Nick Eggenhofer

A Bride on the Old Chisholm Trail, in 1886, Mary Taylor Bunton, Naylor Publishing, 1939

The Life and Adventures of Nat Love, by Nat Love, Wayside Press, 1907

nationalcowboymuseum.org

legendsofamerica.com/we-charlesgoodnight

legendsofamerica.com/we-cattlekings

legendsofamerica.com/we-chisholmtraily

upload.wikimedia.org/wikipedia/commons/c/c4/cowboy1902.jpg

upload.wikimedia.org/wikipedia/commons/d/d1/HerdQuit.jpg

Chapter 2 Speedy President

nps.gov/articles/000/was-general-grant-arrested-for-speeding-in-washington-d-c.htm

whitehousehistory.org/the-executive-stables

whitehousehistory.org/presidents-on-horseback

upload.wikimedia.org/wikipedia/commons/c/c5/Evening_Star_Sun_Sep_27_1908.jpg

Chapter 3 Blind Tom

Information provided by Patricia LaBounty, Curator Union Pacific Railroad Museum, Council Bluffs, IA 51503, 402.501.3841

Statement of Thomas O'Donnell: (O'Donnell was a track laborer on the original construction of the Union Pacific. He died on May 25, 1935, aged 89 years)

uprrmuseum.org

cprr.org

news.stanford.edu/2019/04/09/giving-voice-to-chinese-railroad-workers

upload.wikimedia.org/wikipedia/commons/f/f6/Transcontinental_railroad_route.png

upload.wikimedia.org/wikipedia/commons/c/cb/UP_steam_loco.jpg

Chapter 4 Fire Horses

equineheritagemuseum.com/horse-and-wheels/fire-horses

popularmechanics.com/technology/gear/reviews/g1442/a-brief-history-of-firefighting

blogs.microsoft.com/today-in-tech/day-horse-lost-job

wildfiretoday.com/2016/09/05/horse-drawn-fire-engines

loc.gov/resource/ggbain.15067

loc.gov/resource/cph.3b44441

loc.gov/resource/cph.3a41607/

upload.wikimedia.org/wikipedia/commons/5/5f/1900_horse_drawn_fire_engine_on_linden_street.jpg

Chapter 5 Wonder Horses

messybeast.com/history/horses.htm

clements.umich.edu/linus-horse

Chapter 6 Ten-Foot Cops

amny.com/news/nypd-mounted-unit-meet-the-horses-that-patrol-nyc-s-streets-1.12327370

theglobeandmail.com/news/national/man-charged-in-death-of-prized-police-horse/article965500

brigadiersmemory.blogspot.com

wtvq.com/2019/01/08/yoder-police-horse-back-patrol

en.wikipedia.org/wiki/list_of_mounted_police_units#united_states_of_america

commons.wikimedia.org/wiki/category:police_horses

loc.gov/resource/pan.6a24922

loc.gov/item/2016799371

loc.gov/resource/det.4a18587

Chapter 7 The Great Epizootic

ncbi.nlm.nih.gov/pmc/articles/pmc2272691

journals.uchicago.edu/eprint/the_great_epizootic

gothamcenter.org/blog/the-great-epizootic-of-1872

chron.com/news/article/a-virus-crippled-u-s-cities-150-years-ago-it-17780056.php

Chapter 8 Williamsburg Warnings

In the Shadow of the Dam: The Aftermath of the Mill River Flood of 1874, Elizabeth M. Sharpe, Free Press, 2007

archive.org/details/sim_harpers-weekly_1874-06-06_18_910

credo.library.umass.edu/view/full/muph019-b001-i003

commons.wikimedia.org/wiki/File:Collins_Graves_as_he_rode_through_the_streets_of_Williamsburg,_Skinnerville,_and_Haydenville,_by_F._J._Moore.jpg

Chapter 9 Aristides

kentuckyderby.com
derbymuseum.org
factinate.com/things/42-little-known-facts-horse-racing
history.com/news/the-man-behind-the-kentucky-derby
upload.wikimedia.org/wikipedia/commons/3/33/oliver_lewis.png

Chapter 10 Sleepy Tom

harnessmuseum.com/content/sleepy-tom
harnessmuseum.com/content/little-brown-jug
daytondailynews.com/news/local/bellbrook-horse-had-tough-life-remarkable-record/ccfrvbgpnuwkhuhwxtviko/
sugarcreekoh.us/202/Sleepy-Thomas
upload.wikimedia.org/wikipedia/commons/4/40/The_pacing_wonder_Sleepy_Tom%2C_the_Blind_Horse-_with_Phillips%2C_his_driver_coaxing_him_to_"go_in_and_win"_sired_by_Tom_Rolfe%2C_son_of_Old_Pocohantus_LCCN2001700552.jpg
littlebrownjug.com

Chapter 11 Comanche

lbha.org
thevintagenews.com/2017/12/18/horse-named-comanche/
scholarsarchive.byu.edu/cgi/viewcontent.cgi?article=2881&context=facpub
upload.wikimedia.org/wikipedia/commons/3/33/comanche_fort_riley.jpg
upload.wikimedia.org/wikipedia/commons/8/84/comanche%2c_captain_keough%27s_horse.jpg
digital.denverlibrary.org/digital/collection/p15330coll22/id/69460
upload.wikimedia.org/wikipedia/commons/6/6e/comancheecuster-grabilllr.jpg

Chapter 12 Black Beauty

gutenberg.org/ebooks/271
librivox.org/black-beauty-dramatic-reading-by-anna-sewell
homeschoolspark.com/courses/black-beauty-interactive

Chapter 13 Animal Welfare

collection.nam.ac.uk/detail.php?acc=1994-06-217-8
bluecross.org.uk/sites/default/files/downloads/109890.pdf
oll.libertyfund.org/pages/1641-massachusetts-body-of-liberties
books.google.ca/books/about/Our_dumb_animals.html?id=EEcsAAAAYAAJ&redir_esc=y
bekindexhibit.org
facesofchildabuse.org/etta-angell-wheeler.html

Chapter 14 Equine Movie Star

stanforddaily.com/2023/04/03/how-the-first-moving-picture-originated-from-a-stanford-controversy
smarthistory.org/eadweard-muybridge-the-horse-in-motion
en.wikipedia.org/wiki/sallie_gardner_at_a_gallop
en.wikipedia.org/wiki/sallie_gardner_at_a_gallop#/media/file:the_horse_in_motion_high_res.jpg
tile.loc.gov/storage-services/service/pnp/ppmsca/05900/05952v.jpg

Chapter 15 Tom Bass

The Missouri Connection: Profiles Of The Famous and Infamous, by Appel, Phyllis, Graystone Enterprises, 2010
digital.shsmo.org/digital/collection/mhr/id/25386
horseconnection.com/whisper-wind-tom-bass-story-part-1
horseconnection.com/whisper-on-the-wind-the-tom-bass-story-december-2008

Chapter 16 Buffalo Bill

centerofthewest.org/our-museums/buffalo-bill
en.wikipedia.org/wiki/buffalo_bill
pbs.org/wgbh/americanexperience/features/oakley-show
npgallery.nps.gov/nrhp/getasset/nrhp/73001939_photos
en.wikipedia.org/wiki/buffalo_bill#/media/file:life-of-buffalo-bill-poster-1912.jpg
upload.wikimedia.org/wikipedia/commons/f/f8/buffalo_bill_cody_ca1875.jpg
upload.wikimedia.org/wikipedia/commons/3/35/cody-buffalo-bill-loc.jpg
commons.wikimedia.org/wiki/File:Rosa_Bonheur_-_Portrait_de_Col._William_F._Cody.jpg

Chapter 17 Twenty Mule Teams

mulemuseum.org/freighting-in-the-sierra.html
mtexpress.com/wood_river_journal/special_sections/mule-hitch-jerk-line-mechanics/article_e6644946-6fcd-11e6-a327-43c170c96ea6.html
nps.gov/deva/learn/historyculture/twenty-mule-teams.htm
gutenberg.org/ebooks/12236
upload.wikimedia.org/wikipedia/commons/b/b6/twenty_mule_team_wagon_harmony_borax_works_sw.jpg
upload.wikimedia.org/wikipedia/commons/e/ea/twenty-mule_team_hauling_borax_out_of_death_valley_to_the_railroad%2c_ca.1900_%28chs-1618%29.jpg
eu.wikipedia.org/wiki/Borax#/media/Fitxategi:Twenty_mule_team_wagon_Harmony_Borax_Works_sw.jpg
postcard painting by Ed Thistlethwaite (1900-1958)
loc.gov/resource/cph.3a21510
loc.gov/item/2013631223

Chapter 18 Riding For Ladies

gutenberg.org/files/44026/44026-h/44026-h.htm
katetattersall.com/victorian-riding-habits-horse-clothes
en.wikipedia.org/wiki/sidesaddle
upload.wikimedia.org/wikipedia/commons/c/c4/stace-esther_m.jpg
equi-libris.com/wp-content/uploads/2021/12/HistoryRecords_am-1.pdf
loc.gov/resource/npcc.00789

Chapter 19 Bucking Horses

prorodeo.com/prorodeo/rodeo/rodeo101/saddle-bronc-riding
thefencepost.com/news/midnight-the-worlds-greatest-bucking-horse
wyohistory.org/encyclopedia/wyomings-long-lived-bucking-horse
en.wikipedia.org/wiki/bronc_riding
en.wikipedia.org/wiki/bucking_horse
calgarystampede.com/heritage/history/the-early-years
buckinghorsebreeders.com
wiseabouttexas.com/cowboy-christmas-rodeo-in-texas/

Chapter 20 Beautiful Jim Key

teva.contentdm.oclc.org/digital/collection/jimkey
beautifuljimkey.com
en.wikipedia.org/wiki/beautiful_jim_key

Chapter 21 Clever Hans

hestasaga.com/en/2021/02/05/part-2-the-wonder-horse-clever-hans
horsejournals.com/popular/history-heritage/clever-hans
en.wikipedia.org/wiki/clever_hans
timesmachine.nytimes.com/timesmachine/1904/09/04/101396572.pdf
en.wikipedia.org/wiki/clever_hans#/media/file:osten_und_hans.jpg
commons.wikimedia.org/wiki/file:hans_lernt_krumm_und_gerade.jpg
upload.wikimedia.org/wikipedia/commons/1/1f/hans_an_der_schreibmaschine.jpg
upload.wikimedia.org/wikipedia/commons/3/3d/hans_lernt_addieren.jpg
upload.wikimedia.org/wikipedia/commons/e/e3/clever-hans.jpg

Chapter 22 Talking Horses of Elberfeld

archive.spectator.co.uk/article/12th-april-1913/16/the-horses-of-elberfeld
upload-wikimedia-org.translate.goog/wikipedia/commons/2/24/krall_zarif_muhamed.jpg
upload-wikimedia-org.translate.goog/wikipedia/commons/8/81/zarif_1910.jpg
upload-wikimedia-org.translate.goog/wikipedia/commons/7/74/krall_muhamed_1910.jpg
upload-wikimedia-org.translate.goog/wikipedia/commons/b/b0/zarif_muhamed_hans_elberfeld.jpg

Chapter 23 Captain

gutenberg.org/files/48844/48844-h/48844-h.htm
lrgaf.org/training/captain.htm

Chapter 24 The Great Cowboy Race

thelongridersguild.com/chadron.htm
docsmidwaycookhouse.com/cowboy-endurance-race-from-chadron-nebraska-to-the-columbian-exposition/
dawescountyhistoricalmuseum.org
en.wikipedia.org/wiki/World%27s_Columbian_Exposition#/media/File:Looking_West_From_Peristyle,_Court_of_Honor_and_Grand_Basin,_1893.jpg

Chapter 25 The Great Horse Manure Crisis

atlasobscura.com/articles/the-first-global-urban-planning-conference-was-mostly-about-manure
en.wikipedia.org/wiki/great_horse_manure_crisis_of_1894
bytesdaily.com.au/2011/07/great-horse-manure-crisis-of-1894.html
loc.gov/resource/fsa.8a09517
upload.wikimedia.org/wikipedia/commons/a/a3/the-crossingsweeper.jpg

Chapter 26 Horse vs. Bike

veloaficionado.com/blog/cyclist-versus-horse-duel
americasbestracing.net/lifestyle/2017-the-centuries-old-horses-vs-bicycles-showdown
annielondonderry.com
en.wikipedia.org/wiki/history_of_the_bicycle#/media/file:bicycling-ca1887-bigwheelers.jpg
en.wikipedia.org/wiki/history_of_the_bicycle#/media/file:draisine_or_laufmaschine,_around_1820._archetype_of_the_bicycle._pic_01.jpg
upload.wikimedia.org/wikipedia/commons/4/48/whippet_safety_bicycle.jpg

Chapter 27 Rural Free Delivery

en.wikipedia.org/wiki/rural_free_delivery
sil.si.edu/ondisplay/parcelpost/cf/view.cfm
loc.gov/item/2016865324/
upload.wikimedia.org/wikipedia/commons/d/de/rural_free_delivery_carrier_in_greenfield%2c_indiana.jpg
upload.wikimedia.org/wikipedia/commons/6/60/photograph_of_rural_free_delivery_wagon_with_horse_in_osseo%2c_minnesota_%284011437780%29.jpg

upload.wikimedia.org/wikipedia/commons/2/2f/The_Moment_of_the_Pull.jpg
upload.wikimedia.org/wikipedia/commons/b/b4/Railway_Post_Office_Clerk_in_Mail_Car.jpg

Chapter 28 Equine Moving Company

babel.hathitrust.org/cgi/pt?id=mdp.39015027759342
upload.wikimedia.org/wikipedia/commons/4/4e/downtown_katonah%2c_ny.jpg
upload.wikimedia.org/wikipedia/commons/1/19/movingkatonah.jpg

Chapter 29 Rough Walkers

gutenberg.org/ebooks/13000
upload.wikimedia.org/wikipedia/commons/7/7d/col_roosevelt_rough_rider.jpg
upload.wikimedia.org/wikipedia/commons/1/19/rough_riders_arrive_at_tampa.jpg
nationalguard.mil/resources/image-gallery/historical-paintings/heritage-series/the-rough-riders/fileid/319469

Chapter 30 Rodney

Sound of the Guns by Fairfax Downey, David McKay Company, 1955
archive.org/details/soundofguns0000fair
tradocfcoeccafcoepfwprod.blob.core.usgovcloudapi.net/fires-bulletin-archive/1933/sep_oct_1933/sep_oct_1933_full_edition.pdf
ushorsemanship.com/rodney-a-veteran-artillery-horse-merry-christmas
loc.gov/resource/hec.03778
loc.gov/resource/hec.02459
loc.gov/resource/hec.06411
upload.wikimedia.org/wikipedia/commons/e/ec/cwcaisson.jpg
en.wikipedia.org/wiki/limbers_and_caissons#/media/file:cwlimbertop.jpg
upload.wikimedia.org/wikipedia/commons/5/5e/harold_septimus_power_-_bringing_up_the_guns.jpg
upload.wikimedia.org/wikipedia/commons/5/53/SMA_Dunway_Burial_at_Arlington_National_Cemetery_2008.jpg

Chapter 31 Lifeboat Horses

The Overland Launch, C. Walter Hodges, Penguin Books, 1969
rnli.org
lifeboatmagazinearchive.rnli.org
louisalifeboat.weebly.com

Chapter 32 Horse Fountains

en.wikipedia.org/wiki/national_humane_alliance_fountains
dbpedia.org/page/national_humane_alliance_fountains
commons.wikimedia.org/wiki/file:cherry_hill_fountain,_central_park_cls_0093.jpg
en.wikipedia.org/wiki/national_humane_alliance_fontains#/media/file:national_humane_alliance_fountain_-_derby,_ct.jpg
upload.wikimedia.org/wikipedia/commons/e/e5/nhr_april1917_p.76.jpg

Chapter 33 The First Cowgirl

Thesis by Iris Koch, Northwestern State Teachers College History Department, Alva, Oklahoma, 1940
okhistory.org/crossroads/issue10/page.php?no=1
flinthillsspecial.com/2020/12/04/lucille-mulhall-and-the-mulhall-wild-west-show
atlasobscura.com/articles/the-ballad-of-lucille-mulhall-americas-original-cowgirl

Chapter 34 Horses, Dogs, Diphtheria

en.wikipedia.org/wiki/jim_(horse)
americanhistory.si.edu/blog/2013/08/how-horses-helped-cure-diphtheria.html
nlm.nih.gov/exhibition/fromdnatobeer/exhibition-interactive/illustrations/diphtheria-alternative.html
en.wikipedia.org/wiki/jim_(horse)#/media/file:jimhorse.png
wikimedia.org/wikipedia/commons/8/82/Leonhard_Seppala_with_dogs.jpg
upload.wikimedia.org/wikipedia/commons/4/4f/Gunnar_Kaasen_with_Balto.jpg

Chapter 35 Black Jockeys

Black Winning Jockeys in the Kentucky Derby, James Robert and Monica Renea Saunders, McFarland and Company, 2003
For Gold and Glory; The Story of Thoroughbred Racing in America, Charles B. Parmer
smithsonianmag.com/history/the-kentucky-derbys-forgotten-jockeys-128781428
kentuckyderby.com
derbymuseum.org
ppaath.org

Chapter 36 Wink

Wink: The Incredible Life and Epic Journey of Jimmy Winkfield, Ed Hotaling, McGraw-Hill, 2004

Chapter 37 The Midnight Ride To The Presidency

adirondack.net/history/midnight-ride
thehistorybandits.com/2015/11/22/the-midnight-rough-rider-theodore-roosevelts-ascendance-down-mount-marcy
gutenberg.org/ebooks/3335
upload.wikimedia.org/wikipedia/commons/5/52/TR_Inaugurationsketch.jpg

Chapter 38 The Roosevelts Are Horse People

whitehousehistory.org/theodore-roosevelt-familys-horses
nps.gov/thrb/learn/historyculture/roosevelt-horses.htm
presidentialpetmuseum.com/whitehousepets-2
gutenberg.org/ebooks/6467

Chapter 39 Horses And Bears

americanheritage.com/dont-spare-horses

Chapter 40 Billings' Banquet

nysun.com/on-the-town/banquet-on-horseback/11409
en.wikipedia.org/wiki/c._k._g._billings
atlasobscura.com/articles/dinner-horseback-horse-king
en.wikipedia.org/wiki/c._k._g._billings#/media/file:billingsparty.jpg
upload.wikimedia.org/wikipedia/commons/c/c7/lou_dillon%2c_horse.jpg
upload.wikimedia.org/wikipedia/commons/2/2f/Louis_Sherry_1901.jpg

Chapter 41 Horse Correspondence School

pleasanthillhistorycenter.com/people/jesse
en.wikipedia.org/wiki/jesse_beery
jessebeery.com
ia600306.us.archive.org/33/items/storyofkatequeen00beer/storyofkatequeen00beer.pdf
archive.org/details/practicalsystemo00beer

Chapter 42 Polar Ponies

The Worst Journey In The World Antarctic 1910-1913, Apsley Cherry-Garrard, Constable and Company Limited, 1922
shackletonmuseum.com
lrgaf.org/articles/snowshoes.pdf
vintagewinter.com/blogs/blog/1339782-did-the-1912-captain-scott-south-pole-expedition-fail-because-they-didnt-use-thier-horse-snowshoes
upload.wikimedia.org/wikipedia/commons/8/8a/Tethered_ponies.jpg
en.wikipedia.org/wiki/Yakutian_horse#/media/File:A_Yakutian_horse_(9762345674).jpg

Chapter 43 The Abernathy Brothers

The Ride of the Abernathy Boys, Miles Abernathy, Doubleday 1911
Bud & Me, Alta Abernathy, Dove Creek Press, 1998
budandme.com
tillmanokhistory.org/pages/remarkable_abernathys.html
brushauto.net/abernathy-kids

Chapter 44 Stable Wrecker

William Howard Taft : the life and times : a biography in two volumes, by Pringle, Henry F., American Political Biography Press , 1939
Taft and Roosevelt: The Intimate Letters of Archie Butt, Military Aide, Archibald W. Butt, Doubleday, 1930
ghostsofdc.org/2012/07/09/white-house-stables
d1y822qhq55g6.cloudfront.net/default/william-howard-taft-horse-sterrett.jpg
upload.wikimedia.org/wikipedia/commons/6/6a/strong_horse.jpg

Chapter 45 Two-Gun Nan

history.nebraska.gov/nan-j-aspinwall-western-entertainer
equineink.com/2019/05/21/cow-girl-up-two-gun-nan-aspinwall-and-her-amazing-cross-county-trip
allbreedpedigree.com/lady+ellen7

Chapter 46 The Girl from Wyoming

sanfranciscostory.com/the-girl-from-wyoming
thelongridersguild.com/library/claire/claire.htm

Chapter 47 Suffrage Riders

Why They Marched: Untold Stories of the Women Who Fought for the Right to Vote, Susan Ware, Belknap Press, 2019
upload.wikimedia.org/wikipedia/commons/e/ed/inez_milholland_1913.jpg

Chapter 48 The Overland Westerners

Saddled, Bridled, Ready to Ride, C. A. Osier, Frontier Magazine
data.kitsapsun.com/projects/1961/08/28/the-longest-ride
nationalcowboymuseum.org/explore/overland-westerners
thelongridersguild.com/overland.htm

Chapter 49 The Great War

The Fourth Horseman: One Man's Secret Campaign to Fight the Great War in America, Robert Koenig, Public Affairs Publisher, 2006
Sound of the Guns, Fairfax Downey, David McKay Company, 1955
susannaforrest.blog/2012/03/31/women-horses-and-world-war-one

commons.wikimedia.org/wiki/File:Paris_--_horses_taken_for_war_(LOC).jpg
commons.wikimedia.org/wiki/File:Horse,_First_World_War,_uniform,_men,_trench_Fortepan_11812.jpg
commons.wikimedia.org/wiki/File:A_World_War_I_veterinarian_treating_a_horse%27s_teeth,_Louvencourt,_France_(21625740102).jpg
picryl.com/media/artwork-soldiers-load-a-pack-mule-artist-emil-rizek-finland-1943-catalog-number-c3bbb1
commons.wikimedia.org/wiki/File:The_Ladies%27_Army_Remount_Dep%27t,_Russley_Park,_Wiltshire,_1918_Art.IWMART3094.jpg

Chapter 50 Warrior And His General

Warrior, the Amazing Story of a Real Warhorse, General Jack Seely, MPG Books Group, 2011—First published 1934 as My Horse Warrior
archive.org/details/warrioramazingst0000unse
warriorwarhorse.com
warriorwarhorse.com/warrior-photo-gallery.asp

Chapter 51 Simpson And Murphy

en.wikipedia.org/wiki/john_simpson_kirkpatrick
en.wikipedia.org/wiki/gallipoli_campaign
awm.gov.au/articles/blog/cold-case-what-has-become-murphy-donkey
en.wikipedia.org/wiki/Gallipoli_campaign#/media/File:Landing_at_Gallipoli_(13901951593).jpg

Chapter 52 Notable WWI Animals

en.wikipedia.org/wiki/Harry_Colebourn
si.edu/object/cher-ami%3Anmah_425415
sheffield.ac.uk/nfca/researchandarticles/lizzieelephant
en.wikipedia.org/wiki/Sergeant_Stubby
en.wikipedia.org/wiki/winnipeg_(bear)#/media/file:harry_colebourne_and_winnie.jpg
en.wikipedia.org/wiki/Rags_(dog)#/media/File:Rags_the_Dog_with_Sergeant_George_E._Hickman.jpg

Chapter 53 Wartime Horse Rescues

horsetrust.org.uk/our-story-1918/
thebrooke.org/about-us/our-history
thebrooke.org/about-brooke/history-brooke/dorothy-brookes-letter-morning-post
commons.wikimedia.org/wiki/File:Horse_and_stretcher_transport,_World_War_I_Wellcome_L0023336.jpg

Chapter 54 Army Remount

worldwar1centennial.org/index.php/brookeusa-training-for-war/4548-brooke-usa-the-remount-service.html
centennial.ucdavis.edu/timeline/history/namesakes/gun-rock.html

wikiwand.com/en/united_states_army_remount_service#media/file:fort_robinson_barn.jpg
en.wikipedia.org/wiki/united_states_army_remount_service#/media/file:the_american_soldier,_1908.jpg

Chapter 55 Exterminator

en.wikipedia.org/wiki/exterminator_(horse)
americasbestracing.net/the-sport/2022-exterminator-the-legend-old-bones
racingmuseum.org/hall-of-fame/horse/exterminator-ky

Chapter 56 Grand Canyon Mules

Over The Edge: Death In The Grand Canyon, Michael P. Ghiglieri and Thomas M. Myers, Puma Press, 2001
horseandman.com/interviews/ron-clayton-and-the-mules-of-the-grand-canyon-rare-interview
grandcanyonlodges.com/connect/the-history-of-mules-at-the-grand-canyon
xanterra.com/stories/great-grand-canyon-tours
canyonrides.com
commons.wikimedia.org/wiki/File:Hance_and_His_Burros._(9675670822).jpg
commons.wikimedia.org/wiki/File:Last_Switchback_%2850538615127%29.jpg
commons.wikimedia.org/wiki/File:Mule_train.jpg
commons.wikimedia.org/wiki/File:Grandcanyon-mules.jpg

Chapter 57 Sir Barton

thesirbartonproject.com
bloodhorse.com/horse-racing/articles/226501/backtrack-the-story-of-sir-barton

Chapter 58 Man o' War

Man O' War, Page Cooper, Westholme Publishing, 2004
Thoroughbred Champions: Top 100 Racehorses of the 20th Century. Blood Horse Publications. October 25, 2000, ISBN 9781581500240
thevaulthorseracing.wordpress.com/2011/08/23/a-living-flame-will-harbut-and-man-owar
equusmagazine.com/horse-world/man-o-war-facts
upload.wikimedia.org/wikipedia/commons/3/30/upset_%281917%29.png
en.wikipedia.org/wiki/Man_o%27_War#/media/File:Manowar1920.jpg
upload.wikimedia.org/wikipedia/commons/1/1e/Man_o%27_War_with_trainer_Joseph_Bryan_Martin.jpeg
upload.wikimedia.org/wikipedia/commons/6/6c/Man_o%27_War_in_the_Sanford.jpg

Chapter 59 Automobile vs. Horse

americanequestrian.com/pdf/US-Equine-Demographics.
pdf
accessmagazine.org/spring-2007/horse-power-horse-
power
google.com/books/edition/The_Animal_as_a_Machine_
and_a_Prime_Moto/f9YnAAAAMAAJ
tile.loc.gov/storage-services/service/pnp/fsa/
8b17000/8b17300/8b17317v.jpg
upload.wikimedia.org/wikipedia/commons/1/14/Horse_
drawn_US_Mail_car.jpg

Chapter 60 Silent Cal's Hobby Horse

paulickreport.com/news/people/american-president-
white-house-hobby-horse
washingtonpost.com/news/animalia/wp/2018/04/03/the-
brief-history-of-a-widely-mocked-electric-horse-in-the-
white-house
whitehousehistory.org/working-horses-at-the-white-
house

Chapter 61 Diving Horses

A Girl and Five Brave Horses, Sonora Carver, Doubleday,
1961
en.wikipedia.org/wiki/Sonora_Webster_Carver
equineink.com/2008/12/16/dont-try-this-at-home-the-
diving-horses-of-atlantic-city

Chapter 62 Lady Wonder

mentalfloss.com/article/81063/story-lady-wonder-psy-
chic-horse
en.wikipedia.org/wiki/Lady_Wonder
richmond.com/lady-wonder-1952/article_5173938f-
40d5-50d8-9d81-75a4a02a848c.html
strangeco.blogspot.com/2016/05/lady-wonder-horse.html
en.wikipedia.org/wiki/File:Lady_Wonder_sign.png
en.wikipedia.org/wiki/File:Lady_Wonder_with_Mrs_
Fonda.png

SONRISE STABLE

Wholesome and horsey with strong Christian themes, the Sonrise Stable series is unique among modern children's literature.

Read the books alone or use the Companion Guides for additional activities to supplement the series.

sonrisestable.com

Through their bond with humans,
horses shaped our past in ways no machine ever could.
Their contribution has been all but forgotten—
until Horsestory!

In **Volume I,** follow horses from the time they arrive with early explorers to the Americas to post Civil War.

24
Pit Ponies at Work

12
Pack Horse Librarians

The series continues with **Volume III,** picking up in the 1920s to modern times.

sonrisestable.com/horsestory

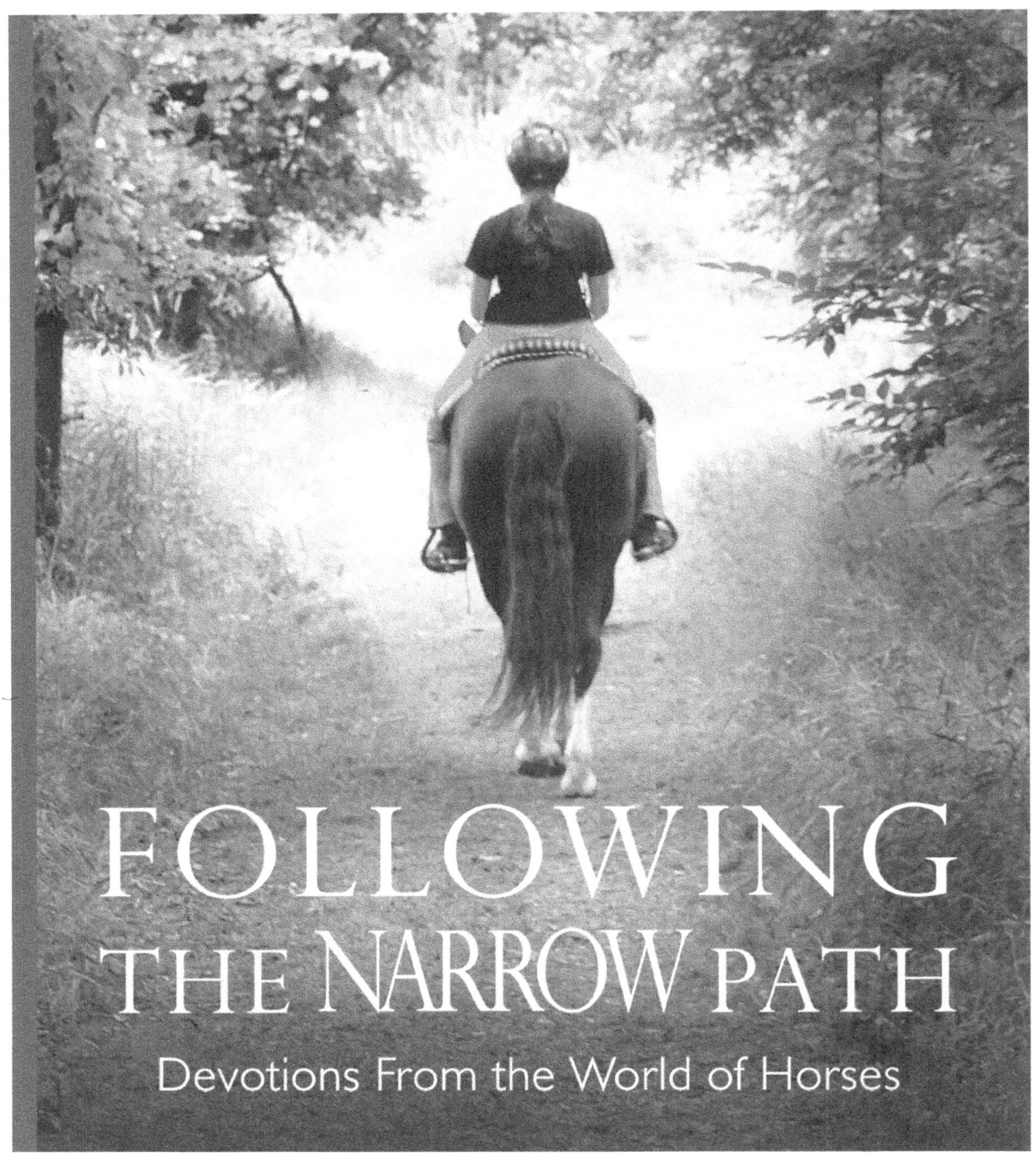

Horses, one of God's most magnificent creations, offer many insights into the nature of our Creator as well as our relationship to Him. This full-color, Christian devotional features a variety of stories, drawn from the author's experiences with her horses and Sassy, a lovable but cantankerous mule. Other famous, and not-so-famous, horses help illustrate Scriptural principles.

Available at sonrisestable.com